Top the
TOEFL

Unlocking the Secrets
of Ivy League Students

Also Published by World Scientific Publishing Co.

Forthcoming

Top the IELTS: Opening the Gates to Top QS-Ranked Universities
  by Kaiwen Leong & Elaine Leong

TOEFL

Unlocking the Secrets
of Ivy League Students

Dr. Kaiwen Leong

Nanyang Technological University, Singapore

Elaine Leong

Citibank Malaysia, Malaysia

WS Education

NEW JERSEY · LONDON · SINGAPORE · BEIJING · SHANGHAI · HONG KONG · TAIPEI · CHENNAI · TOKYO

Published by

WS Education, an imprint of
World Scientific Publishing Co. Pte. Ltd.
5 Toh Tuck Link, Singapore 596224
USA office: 27 Warren Street, Suite 401-402, Hackensack, NJ 07601
UK office: 57 Shelton Street, Covent Garden, London WC2H 9HE

Library of Congress Cataloging-in-Publication Data
Leong, Kaiwen, 1981–   author.
   Top the TOEFL : unlocking the secrets of Ivy League students / Kaiwen Leong (NTU, Singapore) ;
Elaine Leong (Citibank Malaysia, Malaysia).
      pages cm
   ISBN 978-9814663465 (alk. paper) -- ISBN 978-9814663472 (paperback)
   1. Test of English as a Foreign language--Evaluation. 2. English language--Study and teaching--
Foreign speakers. 3. English language--Ability testing. I. Leong, Elaine L. author. II. Title.
   PE1128.L4535 2015
   428.0076--dc23
                                                                2015011372

British Library Cataloguing-in-Publication Data
A catalogue record for this book is available from the British Library.

In-house Editor: Qi Xiao

Typeset by Stallion Press
Email: enquiries@stallionpress.com

Printed in Singapore

Contents

About the Authors

Kaiwen Leong

Dr. Kaiwen Leong graduated from Boston and Princeton Universities with degrees in Economics and Mathematics. He has a Bachelor of Arts (Economics and Mathematics), a Master of Arts (Economics) and a Master of Arts (Mathematics) from Boston University. From Princeton University, he obtained yet another Master of Arts (Economics) as well as a PhD in Economics. Dr. Leong is also a member of several of the most prestigious American academic societies, including Phi Beta Kappa.

However, beneath Dr. Leong's string of shining successes was a journey of immense challenge. Dr. Leong was kicked out of Junior College four times.

When Dr. Leong began studies at Boston University, he faced yet another challenge. He could not speak nor write English well. But within a short period of time, Dr. Leong developed strategies of his own to go from a failing high school dropout who could hardly write an English essay to an Ivy League PhD holder in Economics. Some of these experiences are documented in his bestselling biography *Singapore's Lost Son*, which includes improving listening skills, academic writing and speaking. His efforts culminated in being successfully published in academic journals spanning from economics to mathematics and physics.

At Princeton University, Dr. Leong applied the techniques that he had used to overcome life challenges to impart knowledge to his students. In 2010 and 2011, he was awarded the Princeton University Towbes Prize for "Outstanding Teaching."

Today, Dr. Leong is an Assistant Professor of Economics at Nanyang Technological University and an Associate Faculty Member at the Singapore Institute of Management. He is also the co-author of numerous bestselling books, including *Singapore's Lost Son* (Marshall Cavendish Business), *The Ultimate Banker* (Aktive Learning), *The Big Money Books Series* (Marshall Cavendish International) and *Intermediate Economic Theory* (McGraw Hill Education).

Elaine Leong

Elaine Leong graduated *magna cum laude* from Princeton University with a Bachelor's degree in Politics and a Certificate in Creative Writing. She entered

Princeton as a Shelby Davis International Scholar, and was once again conferred a similar honor as Princeton's "Exemplary Davis Scholar." Prior to Princeton, she attended the United World College in Wales.

Elaine has an extensive range of writing experience. She is a three-time recipient of Princeton's award for outstanding work in creative writing. Her creative writing thesis was supervised by literary critic, author, and Pulitzer Prize finalist Edmund White. She has given public readings of her work at Princeton University's Lewis Center for the Arts. She also served as a Fellow at Princeton's Writing Center, where she helped fellow Princeton students improve essays and writing skills. She has published six books with Marshall Cavendish International.

Top the TOEFL

You want to go abroad. You want to study at the world's top universities. But before you can do that, one test stands in your way: the TOEFL.

This book is designed to systematically tackle problems that most students face. The practice questions are broken down such that students take on questions on a scale of increasing difficulty. Further, students are taught a range of strategies that can be applied during the examination itself.

Each section follows the format below to ensure that students can grasp the content easily:

i. **Simple Steps** — The steps that students need to take for each strategy is boiled down into **Simple Steps**. When reviewing the material, students only need to look at the **Simple Steps** to refresh their memory. This will also serve as "handholds" for students who have trouble reading lengthy English text.

ii. **Elaboration with Examples** — The strategy is then explained in greater detail, and most importantly with examples to illustrate each point. Based on experience teaching hundreds of students English as a second language, a common technique that helps students learn much better is to show concrete examples. More importantly, we show both the correct and incorrect application of the strategies so that students can clearly understand what is "right" and what is "wrong."

iii. **TOEFL Trainer** — Lastly, to make sure that students truly understand the material that they have just read, each chapter concludes with progressive exercises. Like a personal trainer at the gym, the **TOEFL Trainer** gradually increases the exercises' level of difficulty by dividing them according to **Simple Steps** so that students will know where they stand and where they need to improve. If the student is able to complete all the exercises, this will also provide them with a boost of confidence that they need for the TOEFL.

The organization of the book is as follows:

Topping the Reading Section
1. Reading Fast and Reading Well
2. Unlocking Vocabulary

Topping the Reading Section

Reading Fast and Reading Well

The TOEFL exam is not just about whether you can read or whether you can read well. With the time restriction imposed on every student, it is ultimately a test of whether you can read well *and* fast at the same time.

The average student who sits for the TOEFL already finds English a huge challenge. Thinking in English is as troublesome as wading through a pool of thick mud. Every movement takes much longer than it should, and complicated words just confuse you to no end. When the clock is ticking down like a time bomb, what do you do?

We're here to tell you *precisely* what to do. And it begins with the following *Simple Steps*.

Simple Steps

1. Underline the keywords within the question.
2. Generate relevant mental shortcuts using the keywords.
3. Use the mental shortcuts as handholds to identify the accurate answer.

Definitions:
- **Keywords**: Important words.
- **Mental shortcuts**: Methods that can help you think faster and better.

Elaboration with Examples

1. *Underline the keywords within the question*

What precisely are the keywords that you should look out for? Here's a list:

Type	Example
Question words	Who, what, why, when, which, how etc.
Proper nouns	President Obama, the Forbidden City, Cannes Film Festival
Unusual words	Words that you do not normally see often, such as diving, nuclear, paragliding
Negation words	Except, unless, not, refused, false, incorrect, wrong etc.
Numbers	Figures such as 1989, 10,008

Let's put this step into practice.

Sample passage (brief):

The Diary of Dang Thuy Tram

The diary of Dang Thuy Tram as published begins in April 1968 and ends in June 1970. At the beginning of the diary, she was 25 years old and the chief physician of a field hospital in the Quang Ngai Province, which was in the mountains of central Vietnam. Her entries are focused around her daily life in times of war, particularly of tending to the wounded and sick, and her thoughts on the war itself. In the earlier part of the diary, she also writes about her frustration at not being accepted into the Communist Party. She was only accepted in September 1968, at a point at which joy was no longer as sweet as it would have been were she accepted immediately. As she puts it, "for a child exhausted by hunger for her mother's milk, the milk no longer tastes so sweet". Interspersed between her writings on the Vietnam War are also reflections on her own personal life.

What is most valuable about this diary is the insight it provides the reader, specifically insight from the point of view of a Vietnamese at the battlefront of the Vietnam War. The Vietnamese perspective provided by Dang often clashes with the conventional American perspective at that time, allowing the reader to recognize and reconcile the complexity of the war. Subsequently, by piecing the two views together, the reader can begin to understand why the Vietnam War went on for so long (until 1975) despite American military and technological superiority that should have made it an easy job.

Sample question:
According to paragraph 1, all of the following statements are true of Dang Thuy Tram, <u>EXCEPT</u>:
a) Dang Thuy Tram was always a member of the <u>Communist Party</u>.
b) Dang Thuy Tram's writing focused on what happened during the <u>war</u>.
c) Dang Thuy Tram was in the <u>medical field</u>.
d) Dang Thuy Tram was <u>not always happy</u>.

2. *Generate relevant mental shortcuts using the keywords*

Next, use the keywords to create mental shortcuts for yourself. Why are mental shortcuts important? Well, the average student knows that the TOEFL tests your basic understanding of English. But you have to ask yourself what "basic understanding" actually entails.

Basic understanding doesn't just involve identifying keywords within the question. More importantly, it tests whether you are able to draw links between the question and the passage. This involves thinking of synonyms, antonyms or items closely related to the original keyword.

"Mental shortcuts" is our term for training you to do precisely that. It trains you to do a quick analysis of the keyword to generate important conclusions that can help you evade mistakes. It also involves coming up with relevant keywords that can help you find the answer in the passage as quickly as possible.

Part	Keyword	Type	Mental Shortcut
Question	Except	Negation	The opposite of "true" is false, hence remember that you have to identify the *false* statement
(a)	Communist Party	Proper Noun	Communism
(b)	War	Unusual word	Guns, blood, soldiers, weapons, battle, bullets etc.
(c)	Medical field	Unusual word	Doctor, physician, nurse, medicine, wounds, heal
(d)	Not always happy	Negation	Sad, depressed, frustrated, disappointed, not joyful, not elated

3. *Use the mental shortcuts as handholds to identify the accurate answer*

After you have a list of mental shortcuts, you can use them to easily identify whether each statement is true or false.

The Diary of Dang Thuy Tram

The diary of Dang Thuy Tram as published begins in April 1968 and ends in June 1970. At the beginning of the diary, she was 25 years old and the chief

physician of a field **hospital** in the Quang Ngai Province, which was in the mountains of central Vietnam. Her entries are focused around her daily life in times of **war**, particularly of tending to the **wounded** and **sick**, and her thoughts on the **war** itself. In the earlier part of the diary, she also writes about her **frustration** at not being accepted into the **Communist Party**. She was only accepted in September 1968, at a point at which joy was no longer as sweet as it would have been were she accepted immediately. As she puts it, "for a child exhausted by hunger for her mother's milk, the milk no longer tastes so sweet". Interspersed between her writings on the Vietnam War are also reflections on her own personal life.

What is most valuable about this diary is the insight it provides the reader, specifically insight from the point of view of a Vietnamese at the battlefront of the Vietnam War. The Vietnamese perspective provided by Dang often clashes with the conventional American perspective at that time, allowing the reader to recognize and reconcile the complexity of the war. Subsequently, by piecing the two views together, the reader can begin to understand why the Vietnam War went on for so long (until 1975) despite American military and technological superiority that should have made it an easy job.

Answer	Keyword	Mental Shortcut in Passage	Relevant Portion in Passage
(a)	Communist Party	Communist Party	"In the earlier part of the diary, she also writes about her frustration at not being accepted into the **Communist Party**. She was only accepted in September 1968…"
(b)	War	War	"Her entries are focused around her daily life in times of **war**, particularly of tending to the wounded and sick, and her thoughts on the **war** itself."
(c)	Medical field	Physician, wounded, sick	"At the beginning of the diary, she was 25 years old and the chief **physician** of a field **hospital** in the Quang Ngai Province…"
(d)	Not always happy	Frustration	"In the earlier part of the diary, she also writes about her **frustration** at not being accepted into the Communist Party."

Sample question:

According to paragraph 1, all of the following statements are true of Dang Thuy Tram, <u>EXCEPT</u>:

a) Dang Thuy Tram was always a member of the <u>Communist Party</u>.
b) Dang Thuy Tram's writing focused on what happened during the <u>war</u>.
c) Dang Thuy Tram was in the <u>medical field.</u>
d) Dang Thuy Tram was <u>not always happy.</u>

The answer is (a) as the relevant portion of the passage clearly states that Dang Thuy Tram was only accepted into the Communist Party in September 1968.

As you can see, by using mental shortcuts, you can isolate relevant portions of the passage very quickly.

By doing so, you can then efficiently decide whether the statements are true or false. In short, you have:

- Trained your mind to think quickly and to constantly generate links between one word and another.

- Broken down a 259 word passage into 100 words, meaning you only needed to thoroughly read **39%** of the passage.

- Arrived at the correct answer.

Furthermore, this method is not just limited to true/false statement type questions. You can use it for any question that tests your basic understanding of a passage. Let's take a look at another question based on an extended version of the same passage:

Sample passage (extended):

The Diary of Dang Thuy Tram

The diary of Dang Thuy Tram as published begins in April 1968 and ends in June 1970. At the beginning of the diary, she was 25 years old and the chief physician of a field hospital in the Quang Ngai Province, which was in the mountains of central Vietnam. Her entries are focused around her daily life in times of war, particularly of tending to the wounded and sick, and her thoughts on the war itself. In the earlier part of the diary, she also writes about her frustration at not being accepted into the Communist Party. She was only accepted in September 1968, at a point at which joy was no longer as sweet as it would have been were she accepted immediately. As she puts it, "for a child exhausted by hunger for her mother's milk, the milk no longer tastes so sweet". Interspersed between her writings on the Vietnam War are also reflections on her own personal life.

What is most valuable about this diary is the insight it provides the reader, specifically insight from the point of view of a Vietnamese at the battlefront of the Vietnam War. The Vietnamese perspective provided by Dang often clashes with the conventional American perspective at that time, allowing the reader to recognize and reconcile the complexity of the war. Subsequently, by piecing the two views together, the reader can begin to understand why the Vietnam War went on for so long (until 1975) despite American military and technological superiority that should have made it an easy job.

By using this approach, the start of the Vietnam War itself is brought into question. For the Americans, it may have begun in 1964, after the Tonkin Gulf Resolution authorized the President to use force. At the earliest, it begun in 1950, when US military advisors first entered Vietnam. For the Vietnamese however, as shown by Dang, "the South has been at war for twenty-five years," making the start of the war 1945, right after World War II. At other points, Dang even calls it a "thousand-year vendetta," very possibly referencing how Vietnam has been ruled by others before US invasion, not just by the French but also the Chinese. When the Vietnamese struggle is understood as a twenty-five, possibly even thousand-year effort, one can begin to comprehend their determination to gain independence.

On the American side, the general belief at the time was that the war was one to contain communism, as Eisenhower's Domino Effect Theory called for. Yet, it is important to note that nowhere in the book did Dang explicitly call the war a war against democracy. She did not express any hatred nor recognized any split between the North and the South, but neither did she appear to recognize the rule of South Vietnam leader, Diem. Conversely, she continually questioned, "When can the South have Peace, Freedom, and Independence?". Evidently, she viewed Diem as a puppet of the US. Thus, it is apparent that while the Americans were fighting to stop the spread of communism in **Southeast Asia** (in lieu of communist uprisings in Malaya at the time), the Vietnamese were strongly focused on a war for independence, against the Americans who were seen as imperialists.

Underline the keywords within the question.

Sample question:

According to paragraph 4, how do we know that Vietnam was <u>not the only place</u> the Americans were fighting in to stop the spread of communism?
a) Dang did not explicitly call the war a <u>war against democracy</u>.
b) Dang did not recognize the rule of <u>South Vietnam</u> leader, Diem.
c) Americans were fighting to stop the spread of communism in <u>Southeast Asia</u>.
d) Americans were seen as <u>imperialists</u>.

Generate relevant mental shortcuts using the keywords.

Here, you may notice that it's a little difficult to generate mental shortcuts for very specialized words such as "Diem," which is a person's name. In such cases, it is alright to use the original keywords as your mental shortcuts.

Why? If the word is so special, it is highly unlikely that the passage will be able to substitute it for something else. Thus, it's probable that the word appears as it does in the passage.

Part	Keyword	Type	Mental Shortcut
Question	Not the only place	Negation	Look for portions in the passage that relate to **places** other than Vietnam
(a)	War against democracy	Unusual word	Battle, communism, fight, freedom
(b)	South Vietnam; Diem	Proper noun	South Vietnam, Diem
(c)	Southeast Asia	Proper noun	Southeast Asia
(d)	Imperialists	Unusual word	Imperialists

Use the mental shortcuts as handholds to identify the accurate answer.

You can go on to use the mental shortcuts to identify relevant portions in the passage, but you will soon realize that you don't have to.

By identifying the mental shortcuts in Step 2, you have already arrived at three important conclusions:

- The answer must directly or indirectly mention **places** because the question specifically looks for a place other than Vietnam.

- The only two answer options that mention **places** are (b) and (c).

- Further, the place must be somewhere that is *not* specifically Vietnam. Since (b) refers to South Vietnam, the answer is (c).

To be safe, double check:

Answer	Keyword	Mental Shortcut in Passage	Relevant Portion in Passage
(c)	Southeast Asia	Southeast Asia	"Thus, it is apparent that while the Americans were fighting to stop the spread of communism in **Southeast Asia** (in lieu of communist uprisings in **Malaya** at the time), the Vietnamese were strongly focused on a war for independence, against the Americans who were seen as imperialists."

TOEFL Trainer

Step I: *Underline keywords within the question*

Test your ability to underline the most important keywords within each question. Time yourself such that you are able to do so within 2 minutes:

1. According to paragraph 2, how do we know that the National Park Service is a large organization in terms of manpower?
   a) It oversees 401 units, of which 59 are officially national parks.
   b) It is a federal agency of the United States.
   c) It employs over 20,000 employees.
   d) It is governed by the National Park Service Organic Act.

2. According to the passage, what new discovery has the National Aeronautics and Space Administration (NASA) made?
   a) New planets
   b) Neil Armstrong's footprints on the moon
   c) Possible traces of water on Mars
   d) A blackhole

3. According to paragraph 4, the following are true regarding the Fields Medal in Mathematics, EXCEPT:
    a) It can only be awarded to mathematicians who are below 40 years of age.
    b) The prize does not come with any monetary award.
    c) An Iranian professor became the first woman to receive the award in 2014.
    d) The Fields Medal is also known as the Nobel Prize of Mathematics.

4. Who wrote the lyrics of the song, *Old Nassau*?
    a) Franz Liszt
    b) Karl Langlotz
    c) Harlan Page Peck
    d) John Notman

5. Which of the following was the most dominant industry of the Industrial Revolution?
    a) Automobile
    b) Railways
    c) Farming
    d) Textiles

6. Why is a high quality diet an important factor in animal migration?
    a) May increase an individual's exposure to a variety of diseases
    b) Prevents nematode infections
    c) Needs to fuel the energetic demands of migration
    d) Reduce disease transmission

Answers:

1. According to paragraph 2, how do we know that the National Park Service is a <u>large</u> organization in terms of <u>manpower</u>?
    a) It oversees <u>401</u> units, of which <u>59</u> are officially national parks.
    b) It is a <u>federal agency</u> of the <u>United States</u>.
    c) It employs over <u>20,000</u> employees.
    d) It is governed by the <u>National Park Service Organic Act</u>.

2. According to the passage, what <u>new discovery</u> has the National Aeronautics and Space Administration (NASA) made?
   a) New planets
   b) <u>Neil Armstrong's</u> footprints on the moon
   c) Possible traces of water on <u>Mars</u>
   d) A <u>blackhole</u>

3. According to paragraph 4, the following are true regarding the Fields Medal in Mathematics, <u>EXCEPT</u>:
   a) It can only be awarded to mathematicians who are below <u>40</u> years of age.
   b) The prize does not come with any <u>monetary</u> award.
   c) An <u>Iranian</u> professor became the first woman to receive the award in <u>2014</u>.
   d) The Fields Medal is also known as the <u>Nobel Prize of Mathematics.</u>

4. Who wrote the <u>lyrics</u> of the song, *Old Nassau*?
   a) <u>Franz Liszt</u>
   b) <u>Karl Langlotz</u>
   c) <u>Harlan Page Peck</u>
   d) <u>John Notman</u>

5. Which of the following was the <u>most dominant industry</u> of the Industrial Revolution?
   a) <u>Automobile</u>
   b) <u>Railways</u>
   c) <u>Farming</u>
   d) <u>Textiles</u>

7. Why is a <u>high quality diet</u> an <u>important factor</u> in <u>animal migration</u>?
   a) May <u>increase</u> an <u>individual's exposure</u> to a variety of <u>diseases</u>
   b) <u>Prevents nematode infections</u>
   c) Needs to fuel the <u>energetic demands</u> of <u>migration</u>
   d) <u>Reduce disease transmission</u>

Step II: *Generate relevant mental shortcuts using the keywords*

Next, test your ability to generate mental shortcuts for each keyword, if necessary. Learning how to categorize each keyword will also train your mind to recognize such words whenever you come across them in the exam.

1. According to paragraph 2, how do we know that the National Park Service is a <u>large</u> organization in terms of <u>manpower</u>?

a) It oversees <u>401</u> units, of which <u>59</u> are officially national parks.
b) It is a <u>federal agency</u> of the <u>United States</u>.
c) It employs over <u>20,000</u> employees.
d) It is governed by the <u>National Park Service Organic Act</u>.

Part	Keyword	Type	Mental Shortcut
Question			
(a)			
(b)			
(c)			
(d)			

2. According to the passage, what <u>new discovery</u> has the National Aeronautics and Space Administration (NASA) made?
a) New planets
b) <u>Neil Armstrong's</u> footprints on the moon
c) Possible traces of water on <u>Mars</u>
d) A <u>blackhole</u>

Part	Keyword	Type	Mental Shortcut
Question			
(a)			
(b)			
(c)			
(d)			

3. According to paragraph 4, the following are true regarding the Fields Medal in Mathematics, <u>EXCEPT</u>:
a) It can only be awarded to mathematicians who are below <u>40</u> years of age.
b) The prize does not come with any <u>monetary</u> award.

c) An <u>Iranian</u> professor became the first woman to receive the award in <u>2014</u>.

d) The Fields Medal is also known as the <u>Nobel Prize of Mathematics</u>.

Part	Keyword	Type	Mental Shortcut
Question			
(a)			
(b)			
(c)			
(d)			

4. Who wrote the <u>lyrics</u> of the song, <u>*Old Nassau*</u>?
   a) <u>Franz Liszt</u>
   b) <u>Karl Langlotz</u>
   c) <u>Harlan Page Peck</u>
   d) <u>John Notman</u>

Part	Keyword	Type	Mental Shortcut
Question			
(a)			
(b)			
(c)			
(d)			

5. Which of the following was the <u>most dominant industry</u> of the Industrial Revolution?
   a) <u>Automobile</u>
   b) <u>Railways</u>
   c) <u>Farming</u>
   d) <u>Textiles</u>

Part	Keyword	Type	Mental Shortcut
Question			
(a)			
(b)			
(c)			
(d)			

6. Why is a <u>high quality diet</u> an <u>important factor</u> in <u>animal migration</u>?
   a) May <u>increase</u> an <u>individual's exposure</u> to a variety of <u>diseases</u>
   b) <u>Prevents nematode infections</u>
   c) Needs to fuel the <u>energetic demands</u> of <u>migration</u>
   d) <u>Reduce disease transmission</u>

Part	Keyword	Type	Mental Shortcut
Question			
(a)			
(b)			
(c)			
(d)			

Answers:
1. According to paragraph 2, how do we know that the National Park Service is a <u>large</u> organization in terms of <u>manpower</u>?
   a) It oversees <u>401</u> units, of which <u>59</u> are officially national parks.
   b) It is a <u>federal agency</u> of the <u>United States</u>.
   c) It employs over <u>20,000</u> employees.
   d) It is governed by the <u>National Park Service Organic Act</u>.

Part	Keyword	Type	Mental Shortcut
Question	Large; manpower	Unusual words	Relevant keywords (large): Big, huge, or a figure that represents a large number Relevant keywords (manpower): Human resources, employees, workers
(a)	401; 59	Number	As is
(b)	Federal agency; United States	Unusual words; proper noun	As is
(c)	20,000	Number	As is
(d)	National Park Service Organic Act	Proper noun	As is

2. According to the passage, what <u>new discovery</u> has the National Aeronautics and Space Administration (NASA) made?
   a) New planets
   b) <u>Neil Armstrong's</u> footprints on the moon
   c) Possible traces of water on <u>Mars</u>
   d) A <u>blackhole</u>

Part	Keyword	Type	Mental Shortcut
Question	New discovery	Unusual words	Fresh finding, revelation, detection, sighting
(a)	Planet	Unusual words	As is
(b)	Neil Armstrong	Proper noun	As is
(c)	Mars	Proper noun	As is
(d)	Blackhole	Unusual words	As is

3. According to paragraph 4, the following are true regarding the Fields Medal in Mathematics, <u>EXCEPT</u>:
   a) It can only be awarded to mathematicians who are below <u>40</u> years of age.
   b) The prize does not come with any <u>monetary</u> award.
   c) An Iranian professor became the first woman to receive the award in <u>2014</u>.
   d) The Fields Medal is also known as the <u>Nobel Prize of Mathematics</u>.

Part	Keyword	Type	Mental Shortcut
Question	Except	Negation	Look for false statements about the Fields Medal in Mathematics
(a)	40	Number	As is
(b)	Monetary	Unusual words	Financial, money, cash
(c)	Iranian; 2014	Proper noun; number	As is
(d)	Nobel Prize of Mathematics	Proper noun	As is

4. Who wrote the <u>lyrics</u> of the song, <u>*Old Nassau*</u>?
   a) <u>Franz Liszt</u>
   b) <u>Karl Langlotz</u>
   c) <u>Harlan Page Peck</u>
   d) <u>John Notman</u>

Part	Keyword	Type	Mental Shortcut
Question	Old Nassau	Proper noun	As is
(a)	Franz Liszt	Proper noun	As is
(b)	Karl Langlotz	Proper noun	As is
(c)	Harlan Page Peck	Proper noun	As is
(d)	John Notman	Proper noun	As is

5. Which of the following was the <u>most dominant industry</u> of the Industrial Revolution?
   a) <u>Automobile</u>
   b) <u>Railways</u>
   c) <u>Farming</u>
   d) <u>Textiles</u>

Part	Keyword	Type	Mental Shortcut
Question	Most dominant industry	Unusual words	Most important, most significant
(a)	Automobile	Unusual words	Cars, vehicles, engines
(b)	Railways	Unusual words	Trains
(c)	Farming	Unusual words	Agriculture, farmers, anything related to agricultural produce such as vegetables and fruits
(d)	Textiles	Unusual words	Cloth, cotton, wool, yarn

6. Why is a <u>high quality diet</u> an <u>important factor</u> in <u>animal migration</u>?
   a. May <u>increase</u> an <u>individual's exposure</u> to a variety of <u>diseases</u>
   b. <u>Prevents nematode infections</u>
   c. Needs to fuel the <u>energetic demands</u> of <u>migration</u>
   d. <u>Reduce disease transmission</u>

Part	Keyword	Type	Mental Shortcut
Question	High quality diet; important factor; animal migration	Unusual words	Rich food intake; crucial
(a)	Increase individual's exposure, diseases	Unusual words	Raise, high, boost
(b)	Prevents nematode infections	Unusual words	Avoid diseases, sickness
(c)	Energetic demands, migration	Unusual words	High demands, requirements
(d)	Reduce disease transmission	Unusual words	Prevent sicknesses

Step III: *Use the mental shortcuts as handholds to identify the accurate answer*

In Step 3 of the exercise, you will have to match the mental shortcuts to the passage. Then, identify the relevant portions of the passage to arrive at the correct answer.

1. The United States National Park Service was established in 1916 in order to facilitate more effective management of the natural beauty of America. The push for a dedicated federal agency was initiated by two individuals, Stephen Mather and Horace McFarland. They were far-sighted in the sense
5   that they could see how much historic, educational and recreational value that the country's natural beauty had to offer if they were more efficiently managed.

    Through the efforts of Mather and McFarland, President Woodrow Wilson approved the National Park Service Organic Act that gave the
10 National Park Service the responsibility of conserving scenery for the enjoyment of all as well as future generations. Stephen Mather, who had spearheaded the effort, then became the first Director of the National Park Service.

    Today, the National Park Service has grown to become a large
15 organization with 21,989 employees. Altogether, it oversees 59 national parks. The number of national parks may seem small given the size of the United States, but that is because the National Park Service applies a strict set of criteria in determining what a "national park" is.

According to paragraph 2, how do we know that the National Park Service is a large organization in terms of manpower?

a) It oversees 401 units, of which 59 are officially national parks.
b) It is a federal agency of the United States.
c) It employs over 20,000 employees.
d) It is governed by the National Park Service Organic Act.

Answer	Keyword	Mental Shortcut	Relevant Portion in Passage
Question	Large; manpower	Big, huge, or a figure that represents a large number Human resources, employees, workers	
(a)	401; 59	As is	
(b)	Federal agency; United States	As is	
(c)	20,000	As is	
(d)	National Park Service Organic Act	As is	

2. Despite the advanced technology that we possess today, there is still much that we do not know about this world, and even more we have yet to discover. It was because of the thirst for more knowledge, especially that beyond our planet, that contributed to the establishment of the National Aeronautics
5 and Space Administration in the United States. Today, this administration is more commonly known as "NASA."

NASA was officially established in 1958 to replace another agency called the National Advisory Committee for Aeronautics (NACA). NACA had a very different purpose and was in fact a reactionary measure that was taken
10 during World War I in order to promote better coordination on war-related projects, especially between industrial, academic and governmental parties.

The NASA we know today is very different from its predecessor. It has a more civilian focus, which differs from NACA's military projects. It is most well-known for its moon-exploration efforts, especially for making Neil
15 Armstrong the first person to stand on the moon in July 1969. However, NASA's projects extend far beyond just this galaxy. It has also sent robots to Mars to find out more about the planet. Most recently, for example, NASA

discovered 715 new planets. These planets appear to be more similar to Earth in terms of size and in terms of having a surface temperature that
20 could support water.

According to the passage, what <u>new discovery</u> has the National Aeronautics and Space Administration (NASA) made?
a) New planets
b) <u>Neil Armstrong's</u> footprints on the moon
c) Possible traces of water on <u>Mars</u>
d) A <u>blackhole</u>

Answer	Keyword	Mental Shortcut	Relevant Portion in Passage
Question	New discovery	Fresh finding, revelation, detection, sighting	
(a)	Planet	As is	
(b)	Neil Armstrong	As is	
(c)	Mars	As is	
(d)	Blackhole	As is	

3. International competitions are traditionally used to measure excellence on a global level. Although you may argue that the selection of who is the "best" can be, to an extent, subjective, there is no doubt that such prizes do hold weight. Take for example the Olympics and the Nobel Prize. Olympic gold
5 medalists and Nobel Prize recipients are much admired, and sometimes even revered.

However, in instances where no international competitions exist for a certain subject, organizations do create similar awards to fill the gap. One example is the field of mathematics. People often forget that the Nobel Prize
10 does not include a prize for the subject of mathematics. Instead, there is a famous mathematics award known as the Fields Medal instead, which is also called the Nobel Prize of Mathematics. Winners are elected once every four years and are eligible for a 15,000 Canadian dollar cash prize. However, unlike the Nobel Prize, there is an age limit — this prize can only be awarded
15 to those who are below 40 years of age. Funnily enough, although the award

was established in 1924, no woman won the prize until 2014 when an Iranian professor became the first female to receive the award.

According to paragraph 4, the following are true regarding the Fields Medal in Mathematics, <u>EXCEPT</u>:

a) It can only be awarded to mathematicians who are below <u>40</u> years of age.

b) The prize does not come with any <u>monetary</u> award.

c) An Iranian professor became the first woman to receive the award in <u>2014</u>.

d) The Fields Medal is also known as the <u>Nobel Prize of Mathematics</u>.

Answer	Keyword	Mental Shortcut	Relevant Portion in Passage
Question	Except	Look for false statements about the Fields Medal in Mathematics	
(a)	40	As is	
(b)	Monetary	Financial, money, cash	
(c)	Iranian; 2014	As is	
(d)	Nobel Prize of Mathematics	As is	

4. Many Ivy League colleges have a rich and colorful history, and Princeton University's Nassau Hall is a typical example. Although it currently houses administrative offices and is used for ceremonial events, there is more than meets the eye. For example, not many people know that Nassau Hall once
5 hosted the entire American government when Princeton temporarily became the capital of the United States during the American Revolutionary War.

The hall also became a central part of Princeton University's song, *Old Nassau*, when Harlan Page Peck wrote and published the lyrics in 1859. Peck had intended for the song to be sung according to the tune of *Auld Lang*
10 *Syne*. However, when this did not work out, Professor Karl Langlotz who

was a Princeton professor of music who had also studied under the famous composer Franz Liszt, rewrote the melody.

Today, Princeton University's graduation ceremonies are traditionally held in front of Nassau Hall. Each graduating class will sing *Old Nassau*
15 one final time before leaving the university as graduates.

Who wrote the <u>lyrics</u> of the song, *Old Nassau*?
a) <u>Franz Liszt</u>
b) <u>Karl Langlotz</u>
c) <u>Harlan Page Peck</u>
d) <u>John Notman</u>

Answer	Keyword	Mental Shortcut	Relevant Portion in Passage
Question	Lyrics; Old Nassau	As is	
(a)	Franz Liszt	As is	
(b)	Karl Langlotz	As is	
(c)	Harlan Page Peck	As is	
(d)	John Notman	As is	

5. The Industrial Revolution is arguably one of the most important revolutions in the history of mankind. Without the Industrial Revolution, we would still be producing most goods by hand and our standards of living would be much lower. After all, the three key changes that the Industrial Revolution
5   brought to mankind were machines, steam power and the creation of the factory system to produce goods en-masse.

Many people think of fancier inventions like cars and trains when they think of "revolution," but the whole movement actually began with a much more humble industry — textiles. Before machines were invented, people
10 had to weave cloth by hand. However, several inventions in the United Kingdom managed to speed up this process significantly. The first was John Kay's "flying shuttle," which was invented in 1733. This was followed by several other inventions, and most notably the invention of the steam

engine by Boulton and Watt, which became the main power source for
15 cotton factories.

It was only after the mechanization of the textiles industry that other industries such as automobiles and railways were able to develop further. Steam-powered railways only gained traction later in the 19th century whereas the Ford Motor Company only manufactured its first car in 1903.

Which of the following was the <u>most dominant industry</u> of the Industrial Revolution?
a) <u>Automobile</u>
b) <u>Railways</u>
c) <u>Farming</u>
d) <u>Textiles</u>

Answer	Keyword	Mental Shortcut	Relevant Portion in Passage
Question	Most dominant industry	Most important, most significant	
(a)	Automobile	Cars, vehicles, engines	
(b)	Railways	Trains	
(c)	Farming	Agriculture, farmers, anything related to agricultural produce such as vegetables and fruits	
(d)	Textiles	Cloth, cotton, wool, yarn	

6. The amazing phenomenon of animal migration has led scientists to explore how the behavior relates to resource availability and climate. Of particular interest to this study is the relationship between migration and exposure to disease. In a review by Altizer *et al.* (2011), it is suggested that migration
5   may increase an individual's exposure to a variety of diseases. On the other hand, it has also been proposed that migration can reduce the prevalence or risk of infections by moving away from an area of high transmission or by predation on the weak and ill. Many confounding factors exist such as

population density and diet. Denser populations or communities interact
10 more and so have increased contact, thus disease transmission may become
more efficient. A study of nematode infections in roe deer showed a positive
relationship between population density and parasite load. Additionally, diet
is an important factor in both migration and disease risk. A quality diet
is necessary to meet the energetic demands of migration and to maintain
15 immunocompetence. A study of winter supplemental feeding for elk
suggested that aggregation of elk increased transmission of gastrointestinal
infections but later reduced susceptibility due to better nutrition in the
winter. Altizer *et al.* (2011) also proposed the possibility that lower virulence
in disease strains and/or higher disease tolerance in migratory species may
20 evolve over time due to the stress of migration. This was supported by a
study of migratory and non-migratory monarch butterflies.

Author: Flora Wong

Why is a <u>high quality diet</u> an <u>important factor</u> in <u>animal migration</u>?
a. May <u>increase</u> an <u>individual's exposure</u> to a variety of <u>diseases</u>
b. <u>Prevents nematode infections</u>
c. Needs to fuel the <u>energetic demands</u> of <u>migration</u>
d. <u>Reduce disease transmission</u>

Answer	Keyword	Mental Shortcut	Relevant Portion in Passage
Question	High quality diet; important factor; animal migration	Rich food intake; crucial	
(a)	Increase individual's exposure, diseases	Raise, high, boost	
(b)	Prevents nematode infections	Avoid diseases, sickness	
(c)	Energetic demands, migration	High demands, requirements	

(d)	Reduce disease transmission	Prevent sicknesses	

Answers:

1. The United States National Park Service was established in 1916 in order to facilitate more effective management of the natural beauty of America. The push for a dedicated **federal agency** was initiated by two individuals, Stephen Mather and Horace McFarland. They were far-sighted in the sense
5   that they could see how much historic, educational and recreational value that the country's natural beauty had to offer if they were more efficiently managed.

    Through the efforts of Mather and McFarland, President Woodrow Wilson approved the **National Park Service Organic Act** that gave the
10 National Park Service the responsibility of conserving scenery for the enjoyment of all as well as future generations. Stephen Mather, who had spearheaded the effort, then became the first Director of the National Park Service.

    Today, the National Park Service has grown to become a **large**
15 organization with **21,989 employees**. Altogether, it oversees 59 national parks. The number of national parks may seem small given the size of the United States, but that is because the National Park Service applies a strict set of criteria in determining what a "national park" is.

According to paragraph 2, how do we know that the National Park Service is a <u>large</u> organization in terms of <u>manpower</u>?

  a.   It oversees <u>401</u> units, of which <u>59</u> are officially national parks.

  b.   It is a <u>federal agency</u> of the <u>United States</u>.

  c.   It employs over <u>20,000</u> employees.

  d.   It is governed by the <u>National Park Service Organic Act</u>.

Answer	Keyword	Mental Shortcut	Relevant Portion in Passage
(a)	401; 59	As is	"Altogether, it oversees **59** national parks."
(b)	Federal agency; United States	As is	"The push for a dedicated **federal agency** was initiated by two individuals, Stephen Mather and Horace McFarland."

(c)	20,000	As is	"Today, the National Park Service has grown to become a **large** organization with 21,989 **employees** that oversees 59 national parks."
(d)	National Park Service Organic Act	As is	"Through the efforts of Mather and McFarland, President Woodrow Wilson approved the **National Park Service Organic Act** that gave the National Park Service the responsibility of conserving scenery for the enjoyment of all as well as future generations."

The answer is (b) because it is the only option that refers to the size of the workforce.

2. Despite the advanced technology that we possess today, there is still much that we do not know about this world, and even more we have yet to discover. It was because of the thirst for more knowledge, especially that beyond our planet, that contributed to the establishment of the National Aeronautics

5 and Space Administration in the United States. Today, this administration is more commonly known as "NASA."

   NASA was officially established in 1958 to replace another agency called the National Advisory Committee for Aeronautics (NACA). NACA had a very different purpose and was in fact a reactionary measure that was taken

10 during World War I in order to promote better coordination on war-related projects, especially between industrial, academic and governmental parties.

   The NASA we know today is very different from its predecessor. It has a more civilian focus, which differs from NACA's military projects. It is most well-known for its moon-exploration efforts, especially for making **Neil**

15 **Armstrong** the first person to stand on the moon in July 1969. However, NASA's projects extend far beyond just this galaxy. It has also sent robots to **Mars** to find out more about the planet. Most recently, for example, NASA **discovered** 715 new **planets**. These planets appear to be more similar to Earth in terms of size and in terms of having a surface temperature that

20 could support water.

According to the passage, what <u>new discovery</u> has the National Aeronautics and Space Administration (NASA) made?

a) New <u>planets</u>

b) <u>Neil Armstrong's</u> footprints on the moon

c) Possible traces of water on <u>Mars</u>

d) A <u>blackhole</u>

Answer	Keyword	Mental Shortcut	Relevant Portion in Passage
(a)	Planets	As is	"Most recently, for example, NASA **discovered** 715 new **planets**."
(b)	Neil Armstrong	As is	"It is most well-known for its moon-exploration efforts, especially for making **Neil Armstrong** the first person to stand on the moon in July 1969."
(c)	Mars	As is	"It has also sent robots to **Mars** to find out more about the planet."
(d)	Blackhole	As is	None

The answer is (a) because "new discovery" matches us to the sentence that states NASA has "discoverd" 715 new planets.

3. International competitions are traditionally used to measure excellence on a global level. Although you may argue that the selection of who is the "best" can be, to an extent, subjective, there is no doubt that such prizes do hold weight.

5   Take for example the Olympics and the Nobel Prize. Olympic gold medalists and Nobel Prize recipients are much admired, and sometimes even revered.

However, in instances where no international competitions exist for a certain subject, organizations do create similar awards to fill the gap. One example is the field of mathematics. People often forget that the Nobel Prize

10 does not include a prize for the subject of mathematics. Instead, there is a famous mathematics award known as the Fields Medal instead, which is also called the **Nobel Prize of Mathematics**. Winners are elected once every four years and are eligible for a 15,000 Canadian dollar **cash** prize. However, unlike the Nobel Prize, there is an age limit — this prize can only be awarded

15 to those who are below **40** years of age. Funnily enough, although the award was established in 1924, no woman won the prize until **2014** when an **Iranian** professor became the first female to receive the award.

According to paragraph 4, the following are true regarding the Fields Medal in Mathematics, <u>EXCEPT</u>:

a) It can only be awarded to mathematicians who are below <u>40</u> years of age

b) The prize does not come with any <u>monetary</u> award

c) An <u>Iranian</u> professor became the first woman to receive the award in 2014

d) The Fields Medal is also known as the <u>Nobel Prize of Mathematics</u>

Answer	Keyword	Mental Shortcut	Relevant Portion in Passage
(a)	40	As is	"However, unlike the Nobel Prize, there is an age limit — this prize can only be awarded to those who are below **40** years of age"
(b)	Monetary	Financial, money, cash	"Winners are elected once every four years and are eligible for a 15,000 Canadian dollar **cash** prize"
(c)	Iranian; 2014	As is	"Funnily enough, although the award was established in 1924, no woman won the prize until **2014** when an **Iranian** professor became the first female to receive the award."
(d)	Nobel Prize of Mathematics	As is	"Instead, there is a famous mathematics award known as the Fields Medal instead, which is also called the **Nobel Prize of Mathematics**."

The answer is (c) because the passage states that winners are eligible for a 15,000 Canadian dollar cash prize. A cash prize is a monetary reward.

4. Many Ivy League colleges have a rich and colorful history, and Princeton University's Nassau Hall is a typical example. Although it currently houses administrative offices and is used for ceremonial events, there is more than meets the eye. For example, not many people know that Nassau Hall once
5 hosted the entire American government when Princeton temporarily became the capital of the United States during the American Revolutionary War.

The hall also became a central part of Princeton University's song, *Old Nassau,* when **Harlan Page Peck** wrote and published the lyrics in 1859. Peck had intended for the song to be sung according to the tune of *Auld*

10 *Lang Syne.* However, when this did not work out, Professor **Karl Langlotz** who was a Princeton professor of music who had also studied under the famous composer **Franz Liszt**, rewrote the melody.

Today, Princeton University's graduation ceremonies are traditionally held in front of Nassau Hall. Each graduating class will sing *Old Nassau*

15 one final time before leaving the university as graduates.

Who wrote the <u>lyrics</u> of the song, <u>*Old Nassau*</u>?
a) <u>Franz Liszt</u>
b) <u>Karl Langlotz</u>
c) <u>Harlan Page Peck</u>
d) <u>John Notman</u>

Answer	Keyword	Mental Shortcut	Relevant Portion in Passage
(a)	Franz Liszt	As is	"However, when this did not work out, Professor **Karl Langlotz** who was a Princeton professor of music who had also studied under the famous composer **Franz Liszt**, rewrote the melody"
(b)	Karl Langlotz	As is	"However, when this did not work out, Professor **Karl Langlotz** who was a Princeton professor of music who had also studied under the famous composer **Franz Liszt**, rewrote the melody"
(c)	Harlan Page	As is	"The hall also became a central part of Princeton University's song, *Old Nassau*, when **Harlan Page Peck** wrote and published the lyrics in 1859."
(d)	John Notman	As is	Not available in passage

The answer is (c) because it clearly states that Harlan Page Peck wrote the lyrics. Professor Karl Langlotz rewrote the melody whereas Franz Liszt was Langlotz's teacher.

5. The Industrial Revolution is arguably one of the most important revolutions in the history of mankind. Without the Industrial Revolution, we would still be producing most goods by hand and our standards of living would be much lower. After all, the three key changes that the Industrial Revolution

5   brought to mankind were machines, steam power and the creation of the factory system to produce goods en-masse.

Many people think of fancier inventions like **cars** and trains when they think of "revolution," but the whole movement actually began with a much more humble industry — **textiles**. Before machines were invented, people

10   had to weave cloth by hand. However, several inventions in the United Kingdom managed to speed up this process significantly. The first was John Kay's "flying shuttle," which was invented in 1733. This was followed by several other inventions, and most notably the invention of the steam engine by Boulton and Watt, which became the main power source for

15   cotton factories.

It was only after the mechanization of the **textiles** industry that other industries such as **automobiles** and **railways** were able to develop further. Steam-powered railways only gained traction later in the 19th century whereas the Ford Motor Company only manufactured its first **car** in 1903.

Which of the following was the most dominant industry of the Industrial Revolution?
a) Automobile
b) Railways
c) Farming
d) Textiles

Answer	Keyword	Mental Shortcut	Relevant Portion in Passage
(a)	Automobile	Cars, vehicles, engines	"Many people think of fancier inventions like **cars** and trains when they think of "revolution," but the whole movement actually began with a much more humble industry — textiles." OR "It was only after the mechanization of the textiles industry that other industries such as **automobiles** and

			railways were able to develop further." OR "Steam-powered railways only gained traction later in the 19th century whereas the Ford Motor Company only manufactured its first **car** in 1903."
(b)	Railways	Trains	"It was only after the mechanization of the textiles industry that other industries such as **automobiles** and **railways** were able to develop further."
(c)	Farming	Agriculture, farmers, anything related to agricultural produce such as vegetables and fruits	Not available
(d)	Textiles	Cloth, cotton, wool, yarn	"Many people think of fancier inventions like **cars** and trains when they think of "revolution," but the whole movement actually began with a much more humble industry — **textiles**." OR "It was only after the mechanization of the **textiles** industry that other industries such as **automobiles** and **railways** were able to develop further."

The answer is (d) because it states that the revolution began with the textiles industry, hence it was the most dominant (important) industry at the time.

6. The amazing phenomenon of animal migration has led scientists to explore how the behavior relates to resource availability and climate. Of particular interest to this study is the relationship between migration and exposure to disease. In a review by Altizer *et al.* (2011), it is suggested that migration

5   may increase an individual's exposure to a variety of diseases. On the other

hand, it has also been proposed that migration can reduce the prevalence or risk of infections by moving away from an area of high transmission or by predation on the weak and ill. Many confounding factors exist such as population density and diet. Denser populations or communities interact

10 more and so have increased contact, thus disease transmission may become more efficient. A study of nematode infections in roe deer showed a positive relationship between population density and parasite load. Additionally, **diet is an important factor** in both migration and disease risk. A **quality diet** is necessary to meet **the energetic demands** of migration and to maintain

15 immunocompetence. A study of winter supplemental feeding for elk suggested that aggregation of elk increased transmission of gastrointestinal infections but later reduced susceptibility due to better nutrition in the winter. Altizer *et al.* (2011) also proposed the possibility that lower virulence in disease strains and/or higher disease tolerance in migratory species may

20 evolve over time due to the stress of migration. This was supported by a study of migratory and non-migratory monarch butterflies.

Why is a high quality diet an important factor in animal migration?
a) May increase an individual's exposure to a variety of diseases
b) Prevents nematode infections
c) Needs to fuel the energetic demands of migration
d) Reduce disease transmission

Answer	Keyword	Mental Shortcut	Relevant Portion in Passage
Question	High quality diet; important factor; animal migration	Rich food intake; crucial	"Additionally, **diet** is an **important factor** in both migration and disease risk. A **quality diet** is necessary to meet **the energetic demands** of migration and to maintain immunocompetence."
(a)	Increase individual's exposure, diseases	Raise, high, boost	"In a review by Altizer *et al.* (2011), it is suggested that migration may increase an individual's exposure to a variety of diseases."

(b)	Prevents nematode infections	Avoid diseases, sickness	"A study of nematode infections in roe deer showed a positive relationship between population density and parasite load."
(c)	Energetic demands, migration	High demands, requirements	"A **quality diet** is necessary to meet **the energetic demands** of migration and to maintain immunocompetence."
(d)	Reduce disease transmission	Prevent sicknesses	"Denser populations or communities interact more and so have increased contact, thus disease transmission may become more efficient."

The answer is (c) because the relevant portion in the passage as highlighted by the keywords clearly states that a quality diet is necessary to meet the energetic demands of migration.

Unlocking Vocabulary

Simple Steps

If you know the meaning of the word or phrase in question, all is well for you. But what if you don't? Well, if you don't, then don't worry. We have devised strategies for you to employ whenever you don't know the answer. This is so that even if you have no clue, you will still stand a decent chance at securing the points nonetheless.

1. Break up the word into smaller pieces.
2. Understand the small pieces to come to an understanding of the word overall.
3. Understand the context by analyzing the words *around* the vocabulary word in question.

Use this simple framework to organize your thoughts:

Answer	Replacement	Roots	Contextualization
(a)			
(b)			
(c)			
(d)			

Elaboration with Examples

1. *Break up the word into smaller pieces*

Let's see how this works in an example.

Sample passage:

Was Eisenhower Right?

In his farewell Presidential Address, President Dwight D. Eisenhower warned Americans to "guard against the acquisition of unwarranted influence, whether sought or unsought, by the military-industrial complex." It is difficult to find scholars nowadays who would **dispute** that there is such a thing as a "military-industrial complex." Historians like Andrew Bacevich, Michael Sherry, Campbell Craig and Frank Logevall all acknowledge its existence. Other sources, like the documentary "Why We Fight," suggest that it is not just the military and the industry involved in this "complex," but that there are other actors as well, such as Congress and think tanks.

Sample question:

What does the word "dispute" in the passage mean?
a) discourage
b) disagree
c) compute
d) rebel

In order to break up the words, you can either break them up according to syllables (a unit of sound). For example, darkness consists of two syllables ("dark-ness").

Alternatively, if you recognize a word within a word, you can isolate the word on its own. For example, suppose you see the word "encourage" and you recognize the word "courage." You can then break down the word into "en" and "courage."

	Part 1	Part 2	Part 3
Dispute	Dis	Pute	—
Discourage	Dis	Courage	—
Disagree	Dis	Agree	—
Compute	Compute	—	—
Rebel	Rebel	—	—

2. *Understand the small pieces to come to an understanding of the word overall*

Try your best to understand the smaller parts of each word. Then, use this as handholds to arrive at an overall meaning of the word:

	Part 1	Part 2	Overall Meaning
Dispute	Dis: To go against	Pute: From the Latin word "putare" which means to "consider"	To have the opposite consideration on a topic
Discourage	Dis: To go against	Courage: Ability or willingness to confront challenges	To make someone feel demotivated
Disagree	Dis: To go against	Agree: To have the same opinion about something	To have an opposing view on a certain topic
Compute	Compute: Similar to the word "computer"	—	To calculate something
Rebel	Rebel: Similar to the word "rebellion"	—	From the Latin word "rebellare" which means to revolt or to go against in the form of war

3. *Understand the context by analyzing the words around the vocabulary word in question*

At this point, you have some idea of what the words mean. You may even have narrowed your choices down to perhaps two or three answers.

The last step you need to follow is to contextualize. Sometimes words can have similar meanings and you may not know which to select until you know the context.

To understand the context, make sure you know what the paragraph is about. Break it down into sentences and verify that you know what each sentence is saying.

Original Sentence	Contextualization
It is difficult to find scholars nowadays who would **dispute** that there is such a thing as a "military-industrial complex."	Not many would **dispute** the existence of a "military-industrial complex."
Historians like Andrew Bacevich, Michael Sherry, Campbell Craig and Frank Logevall all acknowledge its existence.	These historians are examples of those who agree that the complex exists.

If you read carefully, you will realize that the sentence that follows immediately gives you a clearer idea regarding the context. It reinforces the key point in the preceding sentence by stating that other historians also agree.

Extrapolate this a bit further and "acknowledging its existence" is the same as agreeing with the previous sentence. Therefore, you can deduce that "dispute" is the opposite of "agree."

Now that you have this piece of information, you can safely confirm that the answer is (b) disagree. It ticks all the boxes and most importantly fits the context.

Let's take a look at another example before you try out the *TOEFL Trainer*.

Sample passage:

The Evolution of Whales

There is still a huge controversy surrounding the evolution and ancestral origin of whales from fully **terrestrial** mammals to marine creatures circa 50 million years ago. Who were their ancestors? How did they move from land to water, and what were the factors surrounding their move? Paleontologists have proposed that mesonychids were most closely related to whales while scientists argued that hippopotamids were the true ancestors of whales. However, the discovery of two new important skeletons in 2001 has resulted in scientists claiming that artiodactyls were, in fact, the group with the closest relationship to whales.

It is necessary to begin with some vital background knowledge on whales before launching into discussion about their ancestral origin. Whales belong to the order Cetecea, a highly distinctive and specialized order of vertebrate mammals including 80 or so living animal species such as dolphins, porpoises, belugas, blue whales and humpback whales. Ceteceans came to be during the Eocene period around 50 million years ago and evolved to be fully aquatic in about 8 million years. They are further divided into two suborders, Odontoceti (toothed whales) and Mysticeti (baleen whales). Modern whales bear live young who possess hair at the beginning of life, just like most mammals, and nurse them with milk produced by the mother's body.

Author: Darell Koh

Sample question:

The word "terrestrial" in the passage is closest in meaning to:

a) terrible
b) developed
c) aquatic
d) land

Break up the word into smaller pieces.

	Part 1	**Part 2**	**Part 3**
Terrestrial	Terres	Trial	—
Terrible	Terrible	—	—
Developed	Develop	Ed	—
Aquatic	Aqua	Tic	—
Land	Land	—	—

Understand the small pieces to come to an understanding of the word overall.

	Part 1	**Part 2**	**Overall Meaning**
Terrestrial	Terres: From "terrain" or the Latin word, "terra," which means earth or land	Trial: The suffix "-al" turns the word into a descriptor	Pertaining to the earth or land
Terrible	Terrible: Extremely bad or serious	—	Extremely bad or serious
Developed	Develop: Advance	Ed: The suffix "-ed" makes the word the past tense	To have advanced (past tense)
Aquatic	Aqua: Related to water	Tic: The suffix "-tic" turns the word into a descriptor	Pertaining to water
Land	Land	—	Pertaining to land

You will notice that "terrestrial" seems most closely related to "land." However, to confirm this answer, always double check by contextualizing.

Understand the context by analyzing the words
around the vocabulary word in question.

Original Sentence	Contextualization
There is still a huge controversy surrounding the evolution and ancestral origin of whales from fully **terrestrial** mammals to marine creatures circa 50 million years ago.	This essay focuses on the debate over how whales turned from "fully terrestrial" mammals to "marine" creatures.
Who were their ancestors? How did they move from land to water, and what were the factors surrounding their move?	The essay asks how whales moved "from land to water" and what were the factors surrounding the move.

The subsequent sentence restates the key point of the first sentence, asking how whales moved "from land to water."

Match this to the original sentence and you can conclude that "fully terrestrial" means land whereas "marine" means water.

The answer is therefore (d) land.

TOEFL Trainer

Step I: *Break up the word into smaller pieces*

Learn how to break up each word into smaller chunks so that you can digest them more easily.

1. The adapted physical characteristics to give modern whales an advantage in an aquatic environment include: streamlined bodies with a highly compressed neck vertebrae, tail and fin flukes, small to non-existent hind limbs, modified flipper forelimbs, elongated anterior skull bones and nostrils
5   that form blowholes at the top of the head. It is possible that Odontoceti and Mysticeti **evolved** these new features as a response to a huge tectonic reorganization of sea currents that redistributed heat on the earth's surface

during the Oligocene period, resulting in the formation of icy, nutrient-rich seawater to concentrate along the western edges of the earth's continents.

The word "evolved" in the passage is closest in meaning to:

a) revolved
b) destroyed
c) created
d) elongated

	Part 1	Part 2	Part 3
Evolved			—
Revolved			—
Destroyed			—
Created			—
Elongated			—

2. The availability of new DNA data on the various groups from the last 12 to 13 years, however, placed hippos as having the most similar DNA to whales, resulting in two conflicts — it disproved the accuracy of the Thewissen report while weakening the claims of the Mesonychian Hypothesis at the same time.
5 Like all methods, DNA evidencing is not completely free from **drawbacks.** Situations may occur where DNA is not enough or not available for certain fossils to be sequenced. Another flaw in the Hippopotamid Hypothesis is that the gap between the oldest found records of hippopotamids and their last common ancestor with the ceteceans is approximately 40 million years,
10 a span of time too substantial not to be taken into account.

The word "drawbacks" in the passage is closest in meaning to:

a) shortcomings
b) drawbridges
c) advantages
d) benefits

	Part 1	Part 2	Part 3
Drawbacks			—
Shortcomings			—
Drawbridges			—
Advantages			—
Benefits			—

3. Next in the lineage of archaeocetes, the Basilosaurids and Dorudontids emerged in the middle Eocene around 35–45 million years ago. Mostly distributed around the eastern part of United States and in Egypt, the Basolosaurids were huge, snake-like creatures that could span 60 feet long whereas Dorudontids

5 were shaped rather like the dolphins of today. Both species possess tailflukes. However, they probably relied more on their long, strong body to **propel** themselves forward in water. Studies on the fossilized stomach contents of a particular Basilosaurus specimen showed that it ate fish, including sharks.

The word "propel" in the passage is closest in meaning to:

a) protect
b) fly
c) push
d) position

	Part 1	Part 2	Part 3
Propel			—
Protect			—
Fly			—
Push			—
Position			—

4. There is no doubt that the clarity of the chronological and morphological development of these archeocete fossil intermediates provides convincing support and weight to the Artiodactyl Hypothesis, especially when compared

to the **sparse** data provided by the defenders of the Mesonychian and
5 Hippopotamid Hypotheses. Not only are we able to perceive and predict
the patterns in the ancient whales' increasing adaptations to life in the water,
the level of correspondence between fossil morphology and stratigraphic
position is also highly plausible.

The word "sparse" in the passage is closest in meaning to:

a) special
b) scant
c) robust
d) detailed

	Part 1	Part 2	Part 3
Sparse			—
Special			—
Scant			—
Robust			—
Detailed			—

5. Firstly, there needs to be more research on the origin and evolutionary
background of artiodactyls themselves in our quest to fully understand
their relationship to whales in greater depth. More studies on the whale
fossil records from the same fossil bed or region would aid in providing a
5 broader perspective on a particular family group as well, considering how
much of the analysis is performed on just one representative specimen.
Last but not least, there should be a constant **corroboration** of evidence
between paleontologists, scientists and molecular systematists: results from
the many molecular hybridization, DNA sequencing and immunological
10 tests should be compared as often as possible to the yield of fossil records —
the ideal environment for anyone professing an interest in investigating the
Artiodactly Hypothesis to a fuller extent.

The word "corroboration" in the passage is closest in meaning to:

a) collaboration
b) corrosion

c) elaboration
d) verification

	Part 1	Part 2	Part 3
Corroboration			—
Collaboration			—
Corrosion			—
Elaboration			—
Verification			—

Answers:

1.

	Part 1	Part 2	Part 3
Evolved	Evolve	-ed	—
Revolved	Revolve	-ed	—
Destroyed	Destroy	-ed	—
Created	Create	-ed	—
Elongated	E	Long	-ated

2.

	Part 1	Part 2	Part 3
Drawbacks	Draw	-backs	—
Shortcomings	Short	-comings	—
Drawbridges	Draw	-bridges	—
Advantages	Ad	-vantages	—
Benefits	Bene	-fits	—

3.

	Part 1	Part 2	Part 3
Propel	Pro	-pel	—
Protect	Pro	-tect	—
Fly	Fly	—	—
Push	Push	—	—
Position	Po	-sit	-ion

4.

	Part 1	Part 2	Part 3
Sparse	Sparse	—	—
Special	Spec	-ial	—
Scant	Scant	—	—
Robust	Ro	-bust	—
Detailed	Detail	-ed	—

5.

	Part 1	Part 2	Part 3
Corroboration	Corrobora	-tion	—
Collaboration	Collabora	-tion	—
Corrosion	Corro	-sion	—
Elaboration	Elabora	-tion	—
Verification	Verifica	-tion	—

Step II: *Understand the small pieces to come to an understanding of the word overall*

Based on the breakdown you have completed in Step I, now try to understand each component individually to arrive at an understanding of the overall word.

1.

	Part 1	Part 2	Part 3	Overall Meaning
Evolved	Evolve	-ed	—	
Revolved	Re	volve	-ed	
Destroyed	Destroy	-ed	—	
Created	Create	-ed	—	
Elongated	E	Long	-ated	

2.

	Part 1	Part 2	Part 3	Overall Meaning
Drawbacks	Draw	-backs	—	
Shortcomings	Short	-comings	—	
Drawbridges	Draw	-bridges	—	
Advantages	Ad	-vantages	—	
Benefits	Bene	-fits	—	

3.

	Part 1	Part 2	Part 3	Overall Meaning
Propel	Pro	-pel	—	
Protect	Pro	-tect	—	
Fly	Fly	—	—	
Push	Push	—	—	
Position	Posit	-ion	—	

4.

	Part 1	Part 2	Part 3	Overall Meaning
Sparse	Sparse	—	—	
Special	Spec	-ial	—	
Scant	Scant	—	—	
Robust	Robust	—	—	
Detailed	Detail	-ed	—	

5.

	Part 1	Part 2	Part 3	Overall Meaning
Corroboration	Corrobora	-tion	—	
Collaboration	Collabora	-tion	—	
Corrosion	Corro	-sion	—	
Elaboration	Elabora	-tion	—	
Verification	Verifica	-tion	—	

Answers:

1.

	Part 1	Part 2	Part 3	Overall Meaning
Evolved	Evolve: Related to the word "evolution," meaning to develop or progress	-ed: Past tense	—	Developed or progressive
Revolved	Re: To repeat something	Volve: To turn	-ed: Past tense	To repeatedly move around something
Destroyed	Destroy: To wipe out	-ed: Past tense	—	To wipe out something
Created	Create: To make something	-ed: Past tense	—	To make something

Elongated	E: No meaning	Long: To make something longer	-ated: Paste tense	To make something longer

2.

	Part 1	Part 2	Part 3	Overall Meaning
Drawbacks	Draw: The act of pulling something out, like a drawer	-backs: To pull something away from the front	—	Something that pulls you back; a weakness or a flaw
Shortcomings	Short: Insufficient or inadequate	-comings:	—	Something about you that is insufficient or inadequate; a weakness or a flaw
Drawbridges	Draw: The act of pulling something out, like a drawer	-bridges: Structure built to cross rivers or large gaps in the ground	—	A bridge that can be pulled back up
Advantages	Ad: Positive, such as advance (to move forward)	-vantages: Linked to "advance," meaning to move forward or to be in advance of someone else	—	Something that makes you more superior than others
Benefits	Bene: Related to the word "benevolent," meaning something good	-fits: Plural, no particular meaning	—	Something that is of help or assistance to you

3.

	Part 1	Part 2	Part 3	Overall Meaning
Propel	Pro: To go forward, to be in front	-pel: From the Latin word "pellere," meaning to push	—	To push forward

Protect	Pro: To go forward, to be in front	-tect: From the Latin word "tegere," meaning to cover	—	To cover and keep someone or something from harm
Fly	Fly: To soar through the air	—	—	To soar through the air
Push	Push: To move something forward with force	—	—	To move something forward with force
Position	Posit: To be placed or situated somewhere	-ion: Suffix	—	To be placed or situated somewhere

4.

	Part 1	Part 2	Part 3	Overall Meaning
Sparse	Sparse: From the Latin word "sparsus" which means to be scattered	—	—	Few, scattered
Special	Spec: Related to "species" and "specific" meaning different from the others.	-ial: Suffix	—	Of a particular kind that stands out from the rest
Scant	Scant: Meaning few, short or brief.	—	—	Few, short or brief
Robust	Robust: From the Latin word "robustus" which means strong and hardy	—	—	Strong and hardy
Detailed	Detail: From the French word "Detailler" which means to divide into small pieces or to provide more specific information	-ed: Past tense, suffix	—	To provide very specific information

5.

	Part 1	Part 2	Part 3	Overall Meaning
Corroboration	Corrobora: From the Latin word "corroborare," meaning to strengthen or receive support	-tion: Suffix	—	To receive strong support for something
Collaboration	Collabora: Related to "collaborate" which means to cooperate on something	-tion: Suffix	—	To work on something together
Corrosion	Corro: Related to "corrode," which means to be destroyed or weakened slowly	-sion: Suffix	—	
Elaboration	Elabora: The "labor" in "elaboration" pertains to work or struggle, whereas the "e" comes from "ex-" or "out." When put together, this means to work something out.	-tion	—	To work something out in greater detail
Verification	Verifica: Related to "verify," which means to find out the truth about	-tion	—	To confirm that something is true

Step III: *Understand the context by analyzing the words around the vocabulary word in question*

Lastly, although you may already have an answer option in mind, it is always a good idea to confirm it against the context of the sentence in question.

1. The adapted physical characteristics to give modern whales an advantage in an aquatic environment include: streamlined bodies with a highly compressed neck vertebrae, tail and fin flukes, small to non-existent hind limbs, modified flipper forelimbs, elongated anterior skull bones and nostrils
5   that form blowholes at the top of the head. It is possible that Odontoceti and Mysticeti **evolved** these new features as a response to a huge tectonic reorganization of sea currents that redistributed heat on the earth's surface

during the Oligocene period, resulting in the formation of icy, nutrient-rich seawater to concentrate along the western edges of the earth's continents.

The word "evolved" in the passage is closest in meaning to:

a) revolved
b) destroyed
c) created
d) elongated

Original Sentence	Contextualization

2. The availability of new DNA data on the various groups from the last 12 to 13 years, however, placed hippos as having the most similar DNA to whales, resulting in two conflicts — it disproved the accuracy of the Thewissen report while weakening the claims of the Mesonychian Hypothesis at the same time.
5 Like all methods, DNA evidencing is not completely free from **drawbacks.** Situations may occur where DNA is not enough or not available for certain fossils to be sequenced. Another flaw in the Hippopotamid Hypothesis is that the gap between the oldest found records of hippopotamids and their last common ancestor with the ceteceans is approximately 40 million years,
10 a span of time too substantial not to be taken into account.

The word "drawbacks" in the passage is closest in meaning to:

a) shortcomings
b) drawbridges
c) advantages
d) benefits

Original Sentence	Contextualization

3. Next in the lineage of archaeocetes, the Basilosaurids and Dorudontids emerged in the middle Eocene around 35–45 million years ago. Mostly distributed around the eastern part of United States and in Egypt, the Basolosaurids were huge, snake-like creatures that could span 60 feet long
5 whereas Dorudontids were shaped rather like the dolphins of today. Both species possess tailflukes. However, they probably relied more on their long, strong body to **propel** themselves forward in water. Studies on the fossilized stomach contents of a particular Basilosaurus specimen showed that it ate fish, including sharks.

The word "propel" in the passage is closest in meaning to:

a) protect
b) fly
c) push
d) position

Original Sentence	Contextualization

4. There is no doubt that the clarity of the chronological and morphological development of these archeocete fossil intermediates provides convincing support and weight to the Artiodactyl Hypothesis, especially when compared to the **sparse** data provided by the defenders of the Mesonychian and
5 Hippopotamid Hypotheses. Not only are we able to perceive and predict the patterns in the ancient whales' increasing adaptations to life in the water, the level of correspondence between fossil morphology and stratigraphic position is also highly plausible.

The word "sparse" in the passage is closest in meaning to:

a) special
b) scant

c) robust
d) detailed

Original Sentence	Contextualization

5. Firstly, there needs to be more research on the origin and evolutionary background of artiodactyls themselves in our quest to fully understand their relationship to whales in greater depth. More studies on the whale fossil records from the same fossil bed or region would aid in providing a
5   broader perspective on a particular family group as well, considering how much of the analysis is performed on just one representative specimen. Last but not least, there should be a constant **corroboration** of evidence between paleontologists, scientists and molecular systematists: results from the many molecular hybridization, DNA sequencing and immunological
10 tests should be compared as often as possible to the yield of fossil records — the ideal environment for anyone professing an interest in investigating the Artiodactly Hypothesis to a fuller extent.

The word "corroboration" in the passage is closest in meaning to:

a) collaboration
b) corrosion
c) elaboration
d) verification

Original Sentence	Contextualization

Answers:

1.

Original Sentence	Contextualization
It is possible that Odontoceti and Mysticeti **evolved** these new features as a response to a huge tectonic reorganization of sea currents that redistributed heat on the earth's surface during the Oligocene period, resulting in the formation of icy, nutrient-rich seawater to concentrate along the western edges of the earth's continents.	The word "evolved" has to do with creating something new, as "new features" are mentioned.

The answer is (c) created, *as it has to do with creating something new.*

2.

Original Sentence	Contextualization
Like all methods, DNA evidencing is not completely free from **drawbacks**.	Every method has "drawbacks."
Situations may occur where DNA is not enough or not available for certain fossils to be sequenced.	An undesirable situation whereby there is inadequate DNA for sequencing
Another flaw in the Hippopotamid Hypothesis is that the gap between the oldest found records of hippopotamids.	A drawback is a "flaw."

The answer is (a) shortcomings, *as it also means flaws.*

3.

Original Sentence	Contextualization
However, they probably relied more their long, strong body to **propel** themselves forward in water.	Propel has to do with moving forward in water.

The answer is (c) push, *as it can replace the word propel to also mean moving forward in water.*

4.

Original Sentence	Contextualization
There is no doubt that the clarity of the chronological and morphological development of these archeocete fossil intermediates provides convincing support and weight to the Artiodactyl Hypothesis, especially when compared to the **sparse** data provided by the defenders of the Mesonychian and Hippopotamid Hypotheses.	"Sparse" data does not provide convincing support and weight.

The answer is (b) scant, *as that is the only descriptive word that negatively describes data.*

5.

Original Sentence	Contextualization
Last but not least, there should be a constant **corroboration** of evidence between paleontologists, scientists and molecular systematists: results from the many molecular hybridization, DNA sequencing and immunological tests should be compared as often as possible to the yield of fossil records…	Corroboration is something that happens between scientists to make sure they have the correct results.

The answer is (d) verification, *as scientists need to verify their data in order to obtain accurate results.*

Structure and Organization I

In the TOEFL, there is a type of question that is called the "Category Chart" question. This is essentially a test of not just whether you understand a passage, but whether you are also subsequently able to also reorganize the key points.

You will be given two categories as well as several answer choices. Your job is to match the answer choices to the categories. Some of the answer choices will not be used, and the question is worth 4 points.

Simple Steps

1. Underline keywords in the question or two categories provided.
2. Underline keywords in the answer choices provided.
3. Match keywords to passage to obtain the correct answer.

Elaboration with Examples

Sample passage:

The Russo-Japanese War of 1904–1905

The Russo-Japanese War, which lasted from 1904 to 1905, was the first great war of the twentieth century. It is also notable for being a war where the underdog, Japan, not only started the war, but also defeated Russia catastrophically and decisively.

Manchuria and Korea were the key issues of conflict between Russia and Japan. Manchuria was the keynote of Russia's Eastern policy since it possessed Port Arthur. It was the only nearly ice-free naval outlet for Russia in her vast dominion in Asia. Furthermore, the Manchurian and Great Siberian Railways connected Port Arthur in Manchuria with the army bases in Siberia and European Russia. For Japan, it was not only militarily disadvantageous if Russia controlled Manchuria. There were also economic issues at stake because Manchuria was a great market and field for emigration as well as an increasingly important supply region of raw and food products. Korea, on the other hand, was crucial to Japan's fate as a nation because it served as a protective buffer against Russia. Furthermore, Korea's location was of naval and commercial importance. However, negotiations to solve these issues eventually broke down in February 1904, followed by the outbreak of the Russo-Japanese War.

Any attempt to understand the Russo-Japanese War during 1904–1905 must begin with the peace treaty that followed Japan's decisive victory over China in the Sino-Japanese War during 1894–1895. Among the terms of the treaty were the absolute independence of Korea, the cession to Japan of the Liao-tung Peninsula, Formosa and the Pescadores. In particular, Liao-tung was crucial for Japan because it prevented China from attempting to dominate Korea and it established an effective barrier against the southern expansion of Russia.

However, in late April 1895, Russia, Germany and France "persuaded" Japan to retrocede the Liao-tung Peninsula, in what is known as the Three-Power Intervention. Japan had fifteen days to answer the Three Powers. In the meantime, the Eastern fleets of the Three Powers were made ready as if for immediate action. In addition, Russia prepared army contingents in the Amur region for quick mobilization. Unwilling to take the risk, Japan gave into the Three Powers' demands. In reaction to the Intervention, there was public rage against Prime Minister Ito Hirobumi and his weak cabinet. There were no strong anti-Russian feelings yet. But, more importantly, in the words of General Kuropatkin, Russia's Imperial War Minister, "It was the first of the acts of Russia to excite Japan's hostility." In July 1895, Japan decided upon an ambitious armament expansion program that would take up 58 percent of the country's budget.

The Sino-Japanese War was followed by the Far Eastern Crisis during 1897–1898, which sparked the anti-Russian sentiments in Japan. On November 1, 1897, two German Catholic missionaries were killed by the Chinese in Shantung. Two weeks later, Germany occupied the fort of Tsingtao as a form of reprisal. In March 1898, the occupation became legal and Germany obtained a lease of the whole of Kiaochow Bay for a period of ninety-nine years.

This triggered a chain reaction from other Powers, which constituted the Far Eastern Crisis. Russia and Britain proceeded to occupy territories in Manchuria and China as well. But Japan remained neutral throughout the crisis. Back in Japan, Foreign Minister Aoki criticized Prime Minister Ito for facing the crisis "with arms folded." Protests were also directed against Russia and Germany, but over time Russia became the prime "villain" of eastward expansion. Pressure groups such as "the society of like-minded fellows against Russia" were formed. The Far Eastern Crisis set the precedent for anti-Russian displays for the years to come.

Sample question:

Drag your answer choices to the spaces where they belong.

Answer choices:

a) The only nearly ice-free naval outlet for Russia in her vast dominion in Asia
b) A great market and field for emigration
c) Served as a protective buffer against Russia
d) Location of naval and commercial importance
e) Effective barrier against the southern expansion of Russia
f) Increasingly important supply region of raw and food products
g) The Great Siberian Railways connected Port Arthur with the army bases in Siberia and European Russia
h) Prevented China from attempting to dominate Korea

Category 1: Aspects that made Manchuria important

-
-

Category 2: Aspects that made Korea important

-
-

1. *Underline keywords in the two categories provided*

Start with identifying keywords in the two categories provided because you have to have some sense of what you're looking for.

      Category 1: <u>Aspects</u> that made <u>Manchuria important</u>
      Category 2: <u>Aspects</u> that made <u>Korea important</u>

Based on the keywords, you can get a clear idea of what you're looking for.

      In Category 1, you have to find out *important aspects of Manchuria*. In Category 2, you should do the same except this time for Korea.

2. *Underline keywords in the answer choices provided*

Next, underline keywords in the answer choices. This will make it easier for you to identify the relevant portions of the passage

a) The only nearly <u>ice-free naval outlet</u> for <u>Russia</u> in her vast dominion in Asia

b) A great market and field for <u>emigration</u>
c) Served as a <u>protective buffer against Russia</u>
d) <u>Location</u> of <u>naval</u> and <u>commercial</u> importance
e) Effective barrier against the <u>southern expansion of Russia</u>
f) Increasingly important supply region of <u>raw and food products</u>
g) The <u>Great Siberian Railways</u> connected <u>Port Arthur</u> with the army bases in Siberia and European Russia
h) <u>Prevented China</u> from attempting to dominate <u>Korea</u>

3. *Match keywords to passage to obtain the correct answer*

By doing so, you will realize that most of the answers exist within the second and third paragraph:

> Manchuria and Korea were the key issues of conflict between Russia and Japan. Manchuria was the keynote of Russia's Eastern policy since it possessed Port Arthur. It was the only nearly <u>ice-free naval outlet for Russia</u> in her vast dominion in Asia. Furthermore, <u>the Manchurian and Great Siberian Railways connected Port Arthur in Manchuria with the army bases in Siberia and European Russia.</u> For Japan, it was not only militarily disadvantageous if Russia controlled Manchuria. There were also economic issues at stake because Manchuria was a <u>great market and field for emigration</u> as well as an <u>increasingly important supply region of raw and food products</u>. Korea, on the other hand, was crucial to Japan's fate as a nation because it served as a <u>protective buffer against Russia.</u> Furthermore, Korea's location was of <u>naval and commercial importance.</u> However, negotiations to solve these issues eventually broke down in February 1904, followed by the outbreak of the Russo-Japanese War.
>
> Any attempt to understand the Russo-Japanese War during 1904–1905 must begin with the peace treaty that followed Japan's decisive victory over China in the Sino-Japanese War during 1894–1895. Among the terms of the treaty were the absolute independence of Korea, the cession to Japan of the Liao-tung Peninsula, Formosa and the Pescadores. In particular, Liao-tung was crucial for Japan because it <u>prevented China from attempting to dominate Korea</u> and it established an <u>effective barrier against the southern expansion of Russia.</u>

After identifying the relevant portions in the passage, match the keywords in order to obtain the correct answer. Refer to the following example:

Answer Choice	Relevant Portion in Passage	Category
The only nearly <u>ice-free naval outlet</u> for <u>Russia</u> in her vast dominion in Asia	**Manchuria** was the keynote of Russia's Eastern policy since it possessed Port Arthur. It was the only nearly <u>ice-free naval outlet for Russia</u> in her vast dominion in Asia.	1: Manchuria
A great market and field for <u>emigration</u>	There were also economic issues at stake because **Manchuria** was a <u>great market and field for emigration</u> as well as an <u>increasingly important supply region of raw and food products</u>.	1: Manchuria
Served as a <u>protective buffer against Russia</u>	Korea, on the other hand, was crucial to Japan's fate as a nation because it served as a <u>protective buffer against Russia.</u>	2: Korea
<u>Location</u> of <u>naval</u> and <u>commercial</u> importance	Furthermore, Korea's location was of <u>naval and commercial importance.</u>	2: Korea
Effective barrier against the <u>southern expansion of Russia</u>	In particular, **Liao-tung** was crucial for Japan because it prevented China from attempting to dominate Korea and it established an <u>effective barrier against the southern expansion of Russia.</u>	Be careful! This sentence describes Liao-tung, even though Korea is mentioned.
Increasingly important supply region of <u>raw and food products</u>	There were also economic issues at stake because **Manchuria** was a <u>great market and field for emigration</u> as well as an <u>increasingly important supply region of raw and food products.</u>	1: Manchuria
The <u>Great Siberian Railways</u> connected <u>Port Arthur</u> with the army bases in Siberia and European Russia	Furthermore, the **Manchurian** and Great Siberian Railways connected Port Arthur in Manchuria with the army bases in Siberia and European Russia.	1: Manchuria
<u>Prevented China</u> from attempting to dominate <u>Korea</u>	In particular, **Liao-tung** was crucial for Japan because it <u>prevented China from attempting to dominate Korea</u> and it established an effective barrier against the southern expansion of Russia.	Be careful! This sentence describes Liao-tung, even though Korea is mentioned.

By doing so, you have quickly and efficiently answered the question. These *Simple Steps* have:

- Cut down the words you have to read from 338 to 281 (a 17% deduction).
- Enabled you to find the accurate answer in a systematic way.

This strategy will also work in scientific passages. Let's take a closer look at an article on the blue wildebeests of Africa.

Sample passage:

Comparing disease risks between sedentary and migratory wildebeests (*Connochaaetes taurinus*) of the Serengeti-Masai Mara

This passage will explore the link between disease risk and migration in the blue wildebeests (*Connochaaetes taurinus*) of the Serengeti-Masai Mara ecosystem. Wildebeests of the Serengeti perform an annual migration north to the Masai-Mara region when the dry season sets in. They travel over an area of approximately 30,000 km^2 in search of water and quality food. At the same time, sedentary populations also exist such as those found in the Ngorongoro Crater, fenced parks or agriculturally fragmented areas. Studies have found that migration allows wildebeest populations to escape from resident predators and to respond to spatial and temporal heterogeneity in vegetation. Restricting wildebeests to a fixed range year-round may thus lead to increased density and lower fitness due to a lack of quality vegetation in the dry season. One aspect of this study is to explore whether these effects can be observed, and, if so, how disease risks may change.

Furthermore, wildebeests are vulnerable to a host of diseases, which may affect their demography as much as predation and resource availability. In this study the diseases bovine brucellosis (BB), anthrax (AN) and foot-and-mouth disease (FM) will be focused on. These are economically and socially significant due to the possibility of transmission from wildebeests to cattle or humans. The causative agents for BB, AN and FM are *Brucella abortus*, *Bacillus anthracis* and foot-and-mouth disease virus respectively. There are several strains of BB and FM, and there exists some data on their differing levels of virulence. AN on the other hand is monomorphic whereby virulence is dependent on dosage. Another aspect of this study is to investigate the possibility that BB and FM can evolve differentially due to migration.

To date there has been no study of disease risk and prevalence in the two types of wildebeest populations. As humans continue to change the landscape of the Serengeti-Masai Mara ecosystem, migration routes have become increasingly altered, migratory populations may become cut off and new sedentary populations may form. Apart from predation and resource stress, these populations may experience higher disease risks due to changes in density, nutrition and parasite virulence evolution.

Results that show a significantly higher disease prevalence in sedentary populations would suggest that the disruption of migratory routes may lead to lower fitness of wildebeests at the ecosystem level. The data may also indicate if the difference in prevalence can be explained by variations in density or nutrition. On the other hand, if the results do not show a significant difference, it could indicate that migratory behavior has no critical impact on wildebeest health. Furthermore, if there is a correlation between strain virulence and the formation of sedentary populations, one might suggest then that these populations may suffer greater decreases in fitness over time.

The wildebeest is regarded as a keystone species because of its numbers and movements in the ecosystem. Their grazing patterns facilitate resource utilization by other herbivores in the savanna, and may influence community structure and diversity. Additionally, the study of wildebeest disease risk has implications from the social and economic perspectives. Wildebeests often come in contact with cattle and humans as in the case of the Masai. If diseases can evolve to be more virulent as a result of being sedentary, the risk associated with transmission may be more severe. This not only impacts cattle production, but also affects the risk of zoonosis. This study could lead to many further studies of disease virulence in wildebeests.

As land is increasingly fragmented by anthropogenic causes, such as conversion to farmland or roads, migration in wildebeests is being impeded or altered. If the results of this study support the hypotheses, then there may be a strong argument for better land use management, one that would take into account wildebeest migratory routes.

Author: Flora Wong

Sample question:

Drag your answer choices to the spaces where they belong.

Answer choices:

a) Improve land use management by taking into account wildebeest migratory routes
b) To search for water and better quality food
c) To flee from resident predators
d) To control risks related to disease transmission from wildebeests
e) To respond to spatial and temporal heterogeneity in vegetation
f) To investigate the possibility of that BB and FM can evolve differentially due to migration
g) In response to the start of the dry season
h) To avoid negative impact on cattle production

Category 1: Factors that could explain why wildebeests migrate
•
•
•
•
Category 2: Aspects that make this study on wildebeests important
•
•
•
•

Underline keywords in the question or two categories provided.

Start with identifying keywords in the two categories provided because you have to have some sense of what you're looking for.

Category 1: <u>Factors</u> that could explain <u>why wildebeests migrate</u>
Category 2: <u>Aspects</u> that make <u>this study</u> on wildebeests <u>important</u>

Based on the keywords, you can get a clear idea of what you're looking for.
In Category 1, you have to find out *why wildebeests migrate*. In Category 2, you should understand *why this study is important*.

Underline keywords in the answer choices provided.

Next, underline keywords in the answer choices. This will make it easier for you to identify the relevant portions of the passage

a) Improve <u>land use management</u> by taking into account wildebeest migratory routes
b) To search for <u>water and better quality food</u>
c) To flee from <u>resident predators</u>
d) To control risks related to <u>disease transmission</u> from wildebeests
e) To respond to <u>spatial and temporal heterogeneity</u> in vegetation
f) To investigate the possibility of that <u>BB and FM</u> can evolve differentially due to migration
g) In response to the start of the <u>dry season</u>
h) To avoid negative impact on <u>cattle production</u>

Match keywords to passage to obtain the correct answer.

By doing so, you will realize that most of the answers exist within the start and end of the passage:

This passage will explore the link between disease risk and migration in the blue wildebeests (*Connochaaetes taurinus*) of the Serengeti-Masai Mara ecosystem. Wildebeests of the Serengeti perform an annual migration north to the Masai-Mara region when the **dry season** sets in. They travel over an area of approximately 30,000 km^2 in search of **water and quality food**. At the same time, sedentary populations also exist such as those found in the Ngorongoro Crater, fenced parks or agriculturally fragmented areas. Studies have found that migration allows wildebeest populations to escape from **resident predators** and to respond to **spatial and temporal heterogeneity** in vegetation. Restricting wildebeests to a fixed range year-round may thus lead to increased density and lower fitness due to a lack of quality vegetation in the dry season. One aspect of this study is to explore whether these effects can be observed and if so, how disease risks may change.

Furthermore, wildebeests are vulnerable to a host of diseases, which may affect their demography as much as predation and resource availability. In this study the diseases bovine brucellosis (BB), anthrax (AN) and foot-and-mouth disease (FM) will be focused on. These are economically and socially significant due to the possibility of transmission from wildebeests to cattle or humans. The causative agents for **BB**, AN and **FM** are Brucella abortus, Bacillus anthracis and foot-and-mouth disease virus respectively. There are several strains of BB and FM, and there exists some data on their differing levels of virulence. AN on the other hand is monomorphic whereby virulence is dependent on dosage. Another aspect of this study is to investigate the possibility that **BB and FM** can evolve differentially due to migration.

To date there has been no study of **disease risk** and prevalence in the two types of wildebeest populations. As humans continue to change the landscape of the Serengeti-Masai Mara ecosystem, migration routes have become increasingly altered, migratory populations may become cut off and new sedentary populations may form. Apart from predation and resource stress, these populations may experience higher disease risks due to changes in density, nutrition and parasite virulence evolution.

Results that show a significantly higher disease prevalence in sedentary populations would suggest that the disruption of migratory routes may lead to lower fitness of wildebeests at the ecosystem level. The data may also indicate if the difference in prevalence can be explained by variations in density or nutrition. On the other hand, if the results do not show a significant difference, it could indicate that migratory behavior has no critical impact on wildebeest health. Furthermore, if there is a correlation between strain virulence and the formation of sedentary populations, one might suggest then that these populations may suffer greater decreases in fitness over time.

The wildebeest is regarded as a keystone species because of its numbers and movements in the ecosystem. Their grazing patterns facilitate resource utilization by other herbivores in the savanna, and may influence community structure and diversity. Additionally, the study of wildebeest disease risk has implications from the social and economic perspectives. Wildebeests often come in contact with cattle and humans as in the case of the Masai. If **diseases** can evolve to be more virulent as a result of being sedentary, the **risk** associated with transmission may be more severe. This not only impacts **cattle production**, but also affects the risk of zoonosis. This study could lead to many further studies of disease virulence in wildebeests.

As land is increasingly fragmented by anthropogenic causes, such as conversion to farmland or roads, migration in wildebeests is being impeded or altered. If the results of this study support the hypotheses, then there may be a strong argument for better **land use management,** one that would take into account wildebeest migratory routes.

After identifying the relevant portions in the passage, match the keywords in order to obtain the correct answer. Refer to the following example:

Answer Choice	Relevant Portion in Passage	Category
Improve <u>land use management</u> by taking into account wildebeest migratory routes	If the results of this study support the hypotheses, then there may be a strong argument for better **land use management**, one that would take into account wildebeest migratory routes.	2: Why the study is important
To search for <u>water and better quality food</u>	They travel over an area of approximately 30,000km² in search of **water and quality food**.	1: Why wildebeests migrate
To flee from <u>resident predators</u>	Studies have found that migration allows wildebeest populations to escape from **resident predators**.	1: Why wildebeests migrate
To control risks related to <u>disease transmission</u> from wildebeests	To date there has been no study of **disease risk** and prevalence in the two types of wildebeest populations. AND: If **diseases** can evolve to be more virulent as a result of being sedentary, the **risk** associated with transmission may be more severe.	2: Why the study is important

To respond to <u>spatial and temporal heterogeneity</u> in vegetation	Studies have found that migration allows wildebeest populations to escape from resident predators and to respond to **spatial and temporal heterogeneity** in vegetation.	1: Why wildebeests migrate
To investigate the possibility of that <u>BB and FM</u> can evolve differentially due to migration	The causative agents for **BB**, AN and **FM** are *Brucella abortus*, *Bacillus anthracis* and foot-and-mouth disease virus respectively. AND: Another aspect of this study is to investigate the possibility of that **BB and FM** can evolve differentially due to migration.	2: Why the study is important
In response to the start of the <u>dry season</u>	Wildebeests of the Serengeti perform an annual migration north to the Masai-Mara region when the **dry season** sets in.	1: Why wildebeests migrate
To avoid negative impact on <u>cattle production</u>	This is not only impacts **cattle production**, but also affects the risk of zoonosis. This study could lead to many further studies of disease virulence in wildebeests.	2: Why the study is important

TOEFL Trainer

You will encounter a series of short passages. Use the *Simple Steps* to categorize the answer choices accurately.

Passage 1:

Breakfasts vary greatly depending on your country or culture. In the United States and the United Kingdom, people are used to having cold breakfasts that consist of cereal and cold milk. Those who want more filling meals may opt for the "English breakfast," which consists of sausage or bacon, toast, eggs,
5 baked beans and mushrooms. The United States and the United Kingdom are therefore similar in that sense, but something that is exclusive to the British is "black pudding." This "pudding" which is named after its color is actually made with pig's blood, and is seen as a local delicacy.

Halfway across the world in China and Hong Kong, breakfast is very
10 much different. Many have light congee — rice that is boiled until it is soft — with various condiments that include salted egg, spring onions, dried anchovies and so on. They may even have sticks of fried dough, which is a

traditional snack. The traditional beverage option would be soy milk, which is so ubiquitous that it is served in McDonald's and KFCs too, as part of
15 efforts to adapt to local tastes.

In countries like India and Malaysia, however, breakfasts are very much different and can include spicy cuisine. In India, you may receive a piece of flatbread or "chapatti," which is eaten together with curry or dhal. Malaysians' breakfasts are even heavier and the traditional fare consists of rice cooked
20 in coconut milk, anchovies, egg and sambal (a spicy accompaniment). Some may find the spicy flavors too strong to handle in the early hours of the morning.

Answer choices:

a) Pig's blood is a part of traditional breakfast.
b) Flatbread and dhal is the breakfast of choice.
c) Rice cooked in coconut milk is eaten early in the morning.
d) Some people do not like spicy food.
e) No anchovies are included in breakfast meals.
f) Breakfast cuisine is spicy.
g) Breakfasts are different across the world
h) Local preferences are so strong that they have influenced McDonald's to adapt accordingly.

Category 1: Breakfast in the United Kingdom
-
-

Category 2: Breakfast in China and Hong Kong
-

Category 3: Breakfast in Malaysia
-
-

Answers for passage 1:

Category 1: Breakfast in the United Kingdom
- Pig's blood is a part of traditional breakfast.
- No anchovies are included in breakfast meals.

Category 2: Breakfast in China and Hong Kong

- Local preferences are so strong that they have influenced McDonald's to adapt accordingly.

Category 3: Breakfast in Malaysia

- Rice cooked in coconut milk is eaten early in the morning.
- Breakfast cuisine is spicy.

Answer (b) is irrelevant because it relates to India, which is not a listed category. Answers (d) and (g) are general statements and cannot be categorized.

Passage 2:

Budget travelers have never been more fortunate. In the advent of low-cost airlines such as AirAsia, RyanAir and EasyJet, getting across the globe has never been more affordable. If travelers book far ahead or take advantage of promotional fares, they could be able to travel for a fraction of the price.

5 Some even receive "zero-fare" deals, which means they only need to pay for airport taxes and fees to be able to fly. This has led to a surge in tourism especially among the lower-income groups, students and spontaneous travelers.

However, there is a catch — travelers who wish to take advantage of

10 cheap fares need to be aware of several items. First, budget airlines are "no-frills" airlines, which mean they don't provide cabin food or luggage unless otherwise stated. This means that the traveler would have to fork out more money if they wished to check in luggage, book a seat or eat during the journey. This can come up to considerable sums that may place

15 the fares of budget airlines on par with regular airlines. Secondly, there are other charges such as "credit card charges." Some airlines impose an extra fee if credit cards are used. Depending on the airline, you may be able to complete the transaction for free if you use a debit card or conduct a local bank transfer, but not everyone has this option open to them. Third, "no-

20 frills" also means that you may not receive as much support as you would with a regular carrier if a disaster were to happen or your plane is delayed.

For budget travelers who are looking for something even cheaper than budget airlines, hitchhiking is an option. This involves waiting by motorways and sticking your hand out in the hope that someone will be willing to let

25 you hop onto their vehicle for a free ride. Long-distance truck drivers are

usually obliging because they would not have company otherwise on the long journey, and it doesn't cost them anything to pick someone up. Hitchhiking requires a great deal of courage, determination and patience. You have to accept that you may go for days without anyone consenting to give you a
30 ride, and that could involve nights spent in rest stops or service stations. You don't have much control in terms of schedule and itinerary. It can also be dangerous, as you can never be sure if the driver who picks you up has good intentions. However, the rewards can be great. For one, you get free travel. Additionally, if you're lucky, you may also gain new friends along
35 the journey and you'll be able to experience travel in a wholly unique way.

Answer choices:

a)   Unable to control your schedule and itinerary.
b)   Potential to have a unique adventure.
c)   Baggage fees are usually not included in the promotional fares.
d)   Low or near-zero fares make it possible for nearly everyone to travel.
e)   Travel is absolutely free.
f)   A potentially dangerous endeavor.
g)   Possible to gain new friends along the way.
h)   Relatively limited support in the event of disasters.
i)   Credit card charges are sometimes passed onto the consumer.

Category 1: Downsides of travelling with budget airlines
-
-
-

Category 2: Upsides of hitchhiking
-
-
-

Answers for passage 2:

Category 1: Downsides of travelling with budget airlines
- Baggage fees are usually not included in the promotional fares.
- Relatively limited support in the event of disasters.
- Credit card charges are sometimes passed onto the consumer.

Category 2: Upsides of hitchhiking

- Potential to have a unique adventure.
- Travel is absolutely free.
- Possible to gain new friends along the way.

Answers (a) and (h) are irrelevant because they are downsides of hitchhiking. Answer (d) is irrelevant because it is an upside of budget airlines.

Passage 3:

One of the greatest mysteries that remains today is the reason why dinosaurs went extinct. Despite the advances that have been made in both archeology and technology, scientists still have not been able to pinpoint the exact explanation. Granted, the extinction of dinosaurs occurred some 65 million

5   years ago, and it is difficult to piece the story together. But it is equally difficult to imagine how some of the most powerful creatures to roam the earth could ever been wiped out completely, which makes it an even greater mystery.

A popular hypothesis is called the "extraterrestrial impact theory." According to this theory, there must have been some impact either from

10 meteorites or volcanic lava that contributed to the dinosaurs' extinction. This is supported by the discovery of a layer of rock rich in iridium from the time that the extinction occurred. Because iridium is very rare and can only be found from certain sources such as meteorites and volcanic lava, scientists believe that there is a possible link between the two.

15   Another hypothesis is that the dinosaurs contracted a fatal and highly contagious disease. This coincides with shifting continents towards the end of the Cretaceous period, which could have allowed for diseases to spread on a more rapid scale. However, there is no clear evidence of such diseases. While we may simply lack the technology to identify these diseases based

20 on fossils, scientists have used a technique called "bone pathology" on the assumption that diseased organisms have weakened bones. Unless bone pathology has overlooked a crucial aspect, it would be difficult to subscribe to the disease hypothesis.

A third hypothesis suggests that dinosaurs died from global floods.

25 Those who support this theory point to the reasoning that dinosaur fossils could not exist if the dinosaurs were not buried rapidly by water. In addition, they point to the existence of "dinosaur graveyards." One such dinosaur

graveyard was found in Montana, United States, where an estimated 10,000 duckbill dinosaurs were buried together in a thin layer. They had apparently
30 been hit by such great force that many of the bones were disarticulated and disassociated, suggesting that a massive flood had swept them by surprise.

Answer choices:

a) The extinction of dinosaurs occurred approximately 65 million years ago.
b) Bone pathology suggests that dinosaurs did not die from diseases.
c) In Montana, a "dinosaur graveyard" was discovered with about 10,000 duckbill dinosaurs buried together.
d) There is a layer of rock with a high percentage of iridium, dating back to when dinosaurs were estimated to have gone extinct.
e) Continents shifted, especially towards the end of the Cretaceous period.
f) Many of the bones found in the dinosaur graveyards were disarticulated.
g) Iridium is a very rare element.
h) Water is needed in order to produce dinosaur fossils.
i) Meteorites and volcanic lava contain iridium.
j) Many dinosaur fossils do not suggest any weakened or deformed bones.

Category 1: Evidence supporting extraterrestrial impact theory
-
-
-

Category 2: Evidence supporting the global flood theory
-
-
-

Answers for passage 3:

Category 1: Evidence supporting the extraterrestrial impact theory
- There is a layer of rock with a high percentage of iridium, dating back to when dinosaurs were estimated to have gone extinct.
- Iridium is a very rare element.
- Meteorites and volcanic lava contain iridium.

Category 2: Evidence supporting the global flood theory
- In Montana, a "dinosaur graveyard" was discovered with about 10,000 duckbill dinosaurs buried together.
- Many of the bones found in the dinosaur graveyards were disarticulated.
- Water is needed in order to produce dinosaur fossils.

Answer (a) is a general statement and does not belong to a specific category.
Answers (b), (e) and (j) are related to the theory that dinosaurs were wiped out by diseases.

Passage 4:

Acne is a common problem that nearly everyone experiences. It manifests itself in the form of pimples that are often irritated, painful and sometimes contain pus. Depending on the severity of the acne, scarring may also follow, which can be detrimental towards the patient's self-esteem.

5   Despite the fact that acne is fairly common and easy to diagnose, its causes are not as straightforward. For most young adults and teenagers, the top reason for acne is hormonal change. Children, as can be observed, do not suffer from acne. Conversely, those who suffer from polycystic ovary syndrome tend to have problems with acne. Doctors believe that when there
10   is increased androgen or male hormones in both men and women, excess oil is created which clogs hair follicles. Bacteria thrives in these clogged pores, which turns into pimples.

While acne may seem like a harmless condition, it can leave permanent impact in the form of acne scarring. This in turn can have an emotional
15   impact on the patient, which includes social withdrawal, reduced self-esteem and lack of acceptance from peers. If serious, these can all culminate in depression. Some even end up suffering from "dysmorphophobic acne," whereby even the most minor cases of acne is enough to trigger deep psychological and social impact for the patient.

20   Those with acne are advised to avoid picking or squeezing the pimples, as this can damage the surrounding tissue and increase the possibility of a permanent scar. Instead, if extraction is truly needed, they should make an appointment with a dermatologist or a professional skincare expert. Furthermore, acne patients are also advised to maintain a low-glycemic diet
25   rich with omega-3 fats, as well as plenty of fruits and vegetables. While the link between acne and diet has not yet been established, it does not hurt to eat as healthily as possible.

Answer choices:

a) Excess oil is created by hormonal changes, which clogs hair follicles.
b) Scarring may occur as a result of acne.
c) Avoid picking or squeezing the pimples.
d) Make an appointment with a dermatologist.
e) Those suffering from acne may experience social withdrawal and lowered self-esteem.
f) Pick and squeeze pimples to remove them as soon as possible.
g) Hormonal changes are to blame for acne.
h) Even the most minor cases of acne are sufficient to cause great impact for those suffering from "dysmorphophobic acne."
i) Maintain a low-glycemic diet and consume large quantities of fruit and vegetables.

Category 1: The impact of acne
•
•
•

Category 2: How to combat acne
•
•
•
•

Answers for passage 4:

Category 1: The impact of acne
• Scarring may occur as a result of acne.
• Those suffering from acne may experience social withdrawal and lowered self-esteem.
• Even the most minor cases of acne are sufficient to cause great impact for those suffering from "dysmorphophobic acne."

Category 2: How to combat acne
• Avoid picking or squeezing the pimples.
• Make an appointment with a dermatologist.
• Maintain a low-glycemic diet and consume large quantities of fruit and vegetables.

Answers (a) and (g) relate to the causes of acne, and how acne is formed.
Answer (f) is a false statement.

Passage 5:

Each year, thousands of students worldwide apply for admission to American universities. Many aspire to gain a spot in one of the Ivy League universities, which include Harvard, Princeton, Yale, Dartmouth, Brown and Cornell. However, each year, many are disappointed, as the admissions rate is often
5 in the single digits. This means that for every 100 applicants, fewer than 10 are successful. Apart from Ivy League universities, smaller liberal arts colleges like Williams, Amherst and Swarthmore are also very popular and competitive. There are also famous universities that are commonly misperceived as being part of the Ivy League, such as the Massachusetts
10 Institute of Technology (MIT) and Stanford.

Student life at American universities and colleges varies greatly. At Princeton University, students are divided into six "residential colleges," much like the British versions of "boarding houses." Students spend at least the first two years of college life at these residential colleges, which means
15 they both live in residential college accommodation and dine at any one of the residential college dining halls. The initiative was intended to foster a greater sense of community and cohesiveness within the university. In the third year, however, students can opt to live independently, or stay in "upperclassmen" housing which would entitle them to select their own dining
20 options. This means that they no longer have to subscribe to a residential college dining hall meal plan. Many choose upperclassmen housing, as this would enable them to join one of the "Eating Clubs," which are clubs that have their own dining arrangements and social identity. Others can join a cooperative, which means they share food costs and cooking duties
25 with a small group of other students. Or, students can choose to go entirely independent and source for food on their own.

Academic life is very stringent at American universities. Students are expected to write a great deal and to learn how to produce academic papers. In many universities, freshmen (first-year students) are subject to mandatory
30 writing classes in order to prepare them for this goal. This is because writing in university is very much different from writing in high school, and many students may find it challenging to adapt. Students are also expected to take classes from a wide range of subjects, in line with the ideals of the American

liberal arts education which aims to produce well-rounded students. At
35 Princeton University, for example, each student must take at least one course
in quantitative analysis, science and a second language. They must also take
courses in literature and the social sciences. Sometimes, during the course
of trying different subjects, the student may discover that they prefer a field
that is different from the field they first applied for.

40   A generous amount of financial aid is also available for students who
are in need. This ensures that every applicant — regardless of background
and financial standing — stands a chance to attend one of the world's best
universities. With stellar standing worldwide, vibrant student life and an
intellectually stimulating environment, it is not surprising that students are
45 competing to apply for higher education in the United States.

Answer choices:

a) Students are expected to write academic papers.

b) The admissions rate for top American universities is very low.

c) Students are often required to take subjects across different fields.

d) Students live in one of six residential colleges.

e) A generous amount of financial aid is available for students who need assistance.

f) After the first two years of university life, students have the option of joining an Eating Club.

g) Many universities make it compulsory for freshmen to participate in writing classes.

h) Thousands of students apply for admission to Princeton University each year.

i) During the first two years of university life, students eat at any one of the residential college dining halls.

Category 1: Student life at Princeton University

-
-
-

Category 2: Academic life in the United States

-
-
-

Answers for passage 5:

Category 1: Student life at Princeton University
- Students live in one of six residential colleges.
- After the first two years of university life, students have the option of joining an Eating Club.
- During the first two years of university life, students eat at any one of the residential college dining halls.

Category 2: Academic life in the United States
- Students are expected to write academic papers.
- Students are often required to take subjects across different fields.
- Many universities make it compulsory for freshmen to participate in writing classes.

Answers (b) and (h) are general statements.
Answer (e) relates specifically to financial aid.

Structure and Organization II

These *Simple Steps* can also be used for the other type of organizational questions that you will encounter in the TOEFL — with a slight modification. This second type of organizational question tests whether you have understood *how* an author has presented his or her ideas. Therefore, they are slightly more complex, and are categorized under the "reading to learn" component of the TOEFL.

However, this is nothing that *Simple Steps* cannot solve.

Simple Steps

1. Categorize the question by identifying keywords.
2. Underline keywords in the answer choices provided.
3. Use keywords as handholds to analyze the answer choices while referring to the passage and select the correct answer.

Elaboration with Examples

Let's refer to an example:

Sample passage:

Virginia Woolf: "A Sketch of the Past"

"It is only by putting it into words that I make it whole; this wholeness means that it has lost its power to hurt me, it gives me, perhaps because by doing so I take away the pain, a great delight to put the severed parts together." Such is the way Virginia Woolf describes how she overcomes the "sudden shocks" of life in "A Sketch of the Past" — and that is through her language, her writing. By delving deeper into Woolf, we find her returning again and again to the subject of writing. Writing seems to offer her revelation and a sense of purpose; after writing about her "three instances of exceptional moments, Woolf remarks, "Now that for the first time I have written them down, I realize something that I have never realized before." Language also seems to be a way for her to draw conclusions about things, people or events. Of Goldie Dickinson, she admits, "It bores me to write of him, to try and describe him, partly because it is all so familiar… It is all contained and complete and already summed up."

Sample question:

In paragraph 1, the author explains why writing is important to Virginia Woolf by

a) comparing Virginia Woolf with Goldie Dickinson
b) arguing that we need to delve deeper into Virginia Woolf's writing
c) describing several examples of how writing is important to Virginia Woolf
d) identifying three exceptional moments

Let's see how we can put the *Simple Steps* into practice.

1. *Categorize the question by identifying keywords*

There are four common organization types that students must recognize:

- **Classification:** Categorizing thoughts or items
  Example: The Ancient Greeks were among the first to begin exploring and recording philosophical thought.
- **Compare/contrast:** Putting two or more items side by side and analyzing their similarities as well as differences.
  Example: President Obama's era was much different from President Clinton's, in that he led in a world that was far more "digitalized."
- **Cause/effect:** The reason for and implication of a certain action or item
  Example: The meteorite was the reason dinosaurs were wiped out from the planet.
- **Problem/solution:** A complication and the method that is used to resolve that complication.

  Example: Environmental pollution is an increasing concern not just for the United States but also for many other countries globally, and trading carbon credits has been identified as one of the ways to tackle the issue.

How do you categorize the organization types? It starts with identifying the keywords, like this:

"In paragraph 1, the author explains <u>why writing is important to Virginia Woolf</u> by"

Each keyword gives you a strong indication as to what type of structure the question is asking about. To make it simple, let us map it out for you:

Category/Type	Top Tip	Possible Keywords
Classification	This tests your most basic level of understanding. Sentences written for "classification" purposes are often information-only without any analysis or opinion.	• What is the author describing? • How can we get to the island?
Compare/contrast	Comparing and contrasting involves a scale, for example from good to bad or from dark to fair. Thus, if you see sentences like "which is best?" you are likely being asked to compare items.	• Which method is the best? • How do you compare petroleum with crude palm oil? • What is the difference between aluminum and steel?
Cause/effect	Cause and effect is most easily recognizable by the keyword "why".	• Why did the man cross the road? • Why did the United States change its foreign policy? • Why is this book so important?
Problem/solution	For this type of sentence, there must be a problem or dilemma before there can be a solution. Usually, questions that ask how something is done are problem/solution type questions.	• How did the general win the war? • What should the activist do?

If you look back to the sample question, it's clear that it is a cause/effect type question:

"In paragraph 1, the author explains <u>why writing is important to Virginia Woolf</u> by"

It is essentially asking how the author explains writing is important to Virginia Woolf. What caused the author to have this kind of thinking?

2. *Underline keywords in the answer choices provided*

For this type of question, underlining the keywords in the answer choice is especially important. The first word especially is crucial in testing your understanding of how the author has presented his or her thoughts:

a) comparing Virginia Woolf with Goldie Dickinson
b) arguing that we need to delve deeper into Virginia Woolf's writing
c) describing several examples of how writing is important to Virginia Woolf
d) identifying three exceptional moments

3. *Use keywords as handholds to analyze the answer choices while referring to the passage and select the correct answer*

Note: You won't have to explicitly list down the type of each sentence, but training your mind to think this way is a good way to practice structure and organization.

	Keyword	Type	Analysis
	Why writing is important to Virginia Woolf	Cause/effect	
(a)	comparing with Goldie Dickinson	Compare/contrast	Incorrect — unrelated to the importance of writing
(b)	arguing that we need to delve deeper	Classification	Incorrect — merely stating we need to delve deeper without any reasoning why
(c)	describing several examples	Cause/effect	Correct — examples or evidence to show why writing is important to Virginia Woolf
(d)	identifying three exceptional moments	Classification	Incorrect — merely listing three exceptional moments

The answer is (c) because it is the only answer that provides some evidence or reasoning to prove why writing is important to Virginia Woolf.

Let's look at a longer and more complicated passage:

Sample passage:

Global Justice

The simplistic view that all members of a belligerent nation should be held responsible for the nation's prosecution of the war is flawed when one considers two types of governance: democracies and dictatorships. In the former, the government does not represent every voter and in the latter, there are no elections. Even if the state represents the general view, as argued by Thomas Hobbes, war is only sanctioned as an action against the state, not all citizens, hence excusing citizens from responsibility. The interpretation of responsibility here is that if one is responsible, one can be targeted in war. An assumption is that the nations involved are engaged in open armed conflict.

Traditionally, the distinction made in war is that combatants can be targeted whereas non-combatants cannot. The definition of combatant for the purposes of this paper will be someone who has actual participation in hostile force. Non-combatants are those who are engaged only in the sort of activities that would be carried on even if the nation were not at war. The questions that these definitions raise are: What about a conscripted soldier who does not want to fight in war, but is forced to? Conversely, what about a non-combatant who supports the war wholly? Essentially, is it right to kill a combatant who is unwilling to go to war, but a non-combatant who pushes the buttons for war is considered immune? The problem lies within excusing certain people from taking responsibility while aiming to take down the state's ability to prosecute war at the same time. This can be reconciled by using proportionality of responsibility to allow the targeting of certain non-combatants who occupy crucial roles in the prosecution of war. Specifically, the targeting of certain non-combatants by drones and assassinations should be allowed. The focus is on non-combatants, as within the combatant category it is impossible to make further distinctions because all combatants pose a threat regardless of background or intent.

Sample question:

The author shows that the traditional distinction in war, which is that combatants can be targeted whereas non-combatants cannot, is flawed by

a)   describing the views of Thomas Hobbes
b)   comparing combatants with non-combatants to show that non-combatants could shoulder more responsibility than combatants
c)   arguing that all combatants pose a threat regardless of background or intent
d)   contrasting democracies with dictatorships

Categorize the question by identifying keywords.

"The author <u>shows</u> that <u>the traditional distinction</u> in war, which is that combatants can be targeted whereas non-combatants cannot, is <u>flawed</u> by"

This is a problem/solution type question. The problem is that the traditional distinction is flawed. Next, how did the author pose a solution to this problem?

Let's break it down a little further so that it's easier to digest. The traditional distinction is that:

- Combatants can be targeted in war
- Non-combatants cannot be targeted in war

If the author wants to show that this is flawed, this means he wants to prove that:

- There are some instances whereby combatants cannot be targeted in war
- Non-combatants can be targeted in war

Your job is to find the answer that best proves the author's points.

Underline keywords in the answer choices provided.

Next, underline the keywords in the answer choices provided before you launch into an in-depth analysis. This will help you grasp the important points within each answer choice.

a)   <u>describing</u> the <u>views</u> of Thomas Hobbes
b)   <u>comparing</u> combatants with non-combatants to show that <u>non-combatants could shoulder more responsibility than combatants</u>

c) arguing that all combatants pose a threat regardless of background or intent
d) contrasting democracies with dictatorships

Use keywords as handholds to analyze the answer choices while referring to the passage and select the correct answer.

Lastly, after you have highlighted all the keywords, it's time to do some analysis:

	Keyword	Type	Analysis
	The author shows that the traditional distinction in war, which is that combatants can be targeted whereas non-combatants cannot, is flawed by	Problem/solution	If the author wants to show that this is flawed, this means he wants to prove that: • There are some instances whereby combatants cannot be targeted in war • Non-combatants can be targeted in war
(a)	Describing the views of Thomas Hobbes	Classification	Thomas Hobbes' view: Even if the state represents the general view, war is only sanctioned as an action against the state, not all citizens, hence excusing citizens from responsibility. Incorrect — Thomas Hobbes' view argues that non-combatants *cannot* be targeted in war
(b)	Comparing combatants with non-combatants to show that non-combatants could shoulder more responsibility than combatants	Compare/contrast	Correct — compare/contrast is used to show that non-combatants could shoulder more responsibility than combatants and therefore *can be* targeted in war

(c)	Arguing that all combatants pose a threat regardless of background or intent	Classification	Incorrect — This does not support the author's view in any way, as it argues that combatants pose a threat, which is the "traditional distinction"
(d)	Contrasting democracies with dictatorships	Compare/contrast	Incorrect — contrasting democracies with dictatorships has no direct relation

TOEFL Trainer

Step I: *Categorize the question by identifying keywords*

1. The author explains that zero energy buildings have come to be seen as the next frontier for new construction by

   Type:

2. The author shows what an important role Lilly Reich played in Mies van der Rohe's life by

   Type:

3. The author shows that urban renewal was closely associated with the politics of a city by

   Type:

4. The author shows that international awareness of the East Timor issue continued to increase by

   Type:

5. The author shows that energy use of buildings have a significant impact on the environment by

   Type:

Answers:

1. The author explains that <u>zero energy buildings</u> have come to be seen as the <u>next frontier for new construction</u> by

   Type: Cause/effect

2. The author shows what an <u>important role Lilly Reich</u> played in Mies van der Rohe's life by

   Type: Cause/effect

3. The author shows that <u>urban renewal</u> was <u>closely associated</u> with the <u>politics of a city</u> by

   Type: Cause/effect

4. The author shows <u>that international awareness of the East Timor issue</u> continued to <u>increase</u> by

   Type: Cause/effect

5. The author shows that <u>energy use of buildings</u> have a <u>significant impact</u> on the <u>environment</u> by

   Type: Cause/effect

Step II: *Underline keywords in the answer choices provided*

1. The author explains that <u>zero energy buildings</u> have come to be seen as the <u>next frontier for new construction</u> by
   a) describing the growing burden on worldwide energy demands and the effects of climate change
   b) stating that zero energy buildings are the "gold standard"
   c) showing how devastating the impact of global warming can be
   d) comparing European countries' views with America's views

2. The author shows what an <u>important role Lilly Reich</u> played in Mies van der Rohe's life by
   a) stating that few individual designers have worked with Mies van der Rohe during the transitional stage of his career
   b) describing Mies van der Rohe as "an intensely private man by nature"
   c) highlighting that Mies van der Rohe did not fully develop any contemporary furniture successfully before or after his collaboration with Reich
   d) describing the success of Mies van der Rohe's domestic dwellings such as Tugendhat House

3. The author shows that <u>urban renewal</u> was <u>closely associated</u> with the <u>politics of a city</u> by
    a) describing how the ruler could install new monuments and statues to exult the current king's newfound power
    b) arguing that citizens may rebel against the rise of a new national power
    c) comparing the different cultures and governmental structure of early cities
    d) describing the sense of frustration expressed by Aldo Rossi

4. The author shows <u>that international awareness of the East Timor issue</u> continued to <u>increase</u> by
    a) describing the 1991 Santa Cruz massacre
    b) showing that Amos Wako did not witness the massacre
    c) highlighting that the Nobel Peace Prize was awarded to José Ramos-Horta and Bishop Carlos Ximenes Belo in recognition of the Timorese cause
    d) arguing that the Indonesian occupation of East Timor was ignored

5. The author shows that <u>energy use of buildings</u> have a <u>significant impact</u> on the <u>environment</u> by
    a) arguing that we must first understand the reasons behind the need for more energy-efficient buildings
    b) comparing fossil fuel energy use in the United States and European Union
    c) describing how much fossil fuel energy is used by commercial and residential buildings
    d) identifying that worldwide energy demands are growing

Answers:

1. The author explains that <u>zero energy buildings</u> have come to be seen as the <u>next frontier for new construction</u> by
    a) <u>describing</u> the <u>growing burden</u> on <u>worldwide energy demands</u> and the effects of <u>climate change</u>
    b) <u>stating</u> that <u>zero energy buildings</u> are the "<u>gold standard</u>"
    c) <u>showing</u> how <u>devastating</u> the impact of <u>global warming</u> can be
    d) <u>comparing European</u> countries' views with <u>America's</u> views

2. The author shows what an <u>important role Lilly Reich</u> played in Mies van der Rohe's life by
   a) <u>stating</u> that <u>few individual designers</u> have <u>worked with Mies van der Rohe</u> during the <u>transitional</u> stage of his career
   b) <u>describing</u> Mies van der Rohe as "<u>an intensely private man by nature</u>"
   c) <u>highlighting</u> that Mies van der Rohe <u>did not fully develop</u> any <u>contemporary furniture successfully</u> before or after his collaboration with <u>Reich</u>
   d) <u>describing</u> the <u>success</u> of Mies van der Rohe's <u>domestic dwellings</u> such as <u>Tugendhat House</u>

3. The author shows that <u>urban renewal</u> was <u>closely associated</u> with the <u>politics of a city</u> by
   a) <u>describing</u> how the ruler could install <u>new monuments</u> and <u>statues</u> to <u>exult</u> the current king's <u>newfound power</u>
   b) <u>arguing</u> that <u>citizens</u> may <u>rebel</u> against the rise of a <u>new national power</u>
   c) <u>comparing</u> the different <u>cultures</u> and <u>governmental structure</u> of early cities
   d) <u>describing</u> the sense of <u>frustration</u> expressed by <u>Aldo Rossi</u>

4. The author shows <u>that international awareness of the East Timor issue</u> continued to <u>increase</u> by
   a) <u>describing</u> the <u>1991 Santa Cruz massacre</u>
   b) <u>showing</u> that <u>Amos Wako</u> <u>did not witness</u> the massacre
   c) <u>highlighting</u> that the <u>Nobel Peace Prize</u> was awarded to José Ramos-Horta and Bishop Carlos Ximenes Belo in recognition of the <u>Timorese cause</u>
   d) <u>arguing</u> that the <u>Indonesian occupation of East Timor</u> was <u>ignored</u>

5. The author shows that <u>energy use of buildings</u> have a <u>significant impact</u> on the <u>environment</u> by
   a) <u>arguing</u> that we must <u>first understand the reasons</u> behind the need for <u>more energy-efficient buildings</u>
   b) <u>comparing fossil fuel energy</u> use in the <u>United States</u> and <u>European Union</u>
   c) <u>describing</u> how much <u>fossil fuel energy</u> is used by <u>commercial and residential buildings</u>
   d) <u>identifying</u> that <u>worldwide energy demands</u> are <u>growing</u>

Step III: *Use keywords as handholds while referring to the passage to analyze the answer choices and select the correct answer*

1. In most European countries and parts of America, zero energy buildings have come to be seen as the next frontier or gold standard for new construction across all sectors of the building industry. This constant push for the highest level of sustainability in buildings, for the most part, comes as a result of

5   the growing burden on worldwide energy demands and the increasingly unpredictable effects of climate change, which in turn makes zero energy buildings a very attractive solution to help mitigate the devastating impacts of global warming on our world.

Author: Darell Koh

The author explains that <u>zero energy buildings</u> have come to be seen as the <u>next frontier for new construction</u> by

a) <u>describing</u> the <u>growing burden</u> on <u>worldwide energy demands</u> and the effects of <u>climate change</u>

b) <u>stating</u> that <u>zero energy buildings</u> are the "<u>gold standard</u>"

c) <u>showing</u> how <u>devastating</u> the impact of <u>global warming</u> can be

d) <u>comparing European</u> countries' views with <u>America's</u> views

	Keyword	Type	Analysis
	<u>Zero energy buildings — the next frontier</u>		
(a)	<u>Describing growing burden</u> on <u>worldwide energy demands</u>; effects of <u>climate change</u>		
(b)	<u>Stating zero energy buildings</u> are the "<u>gold standard</u>"		
(c)	<u>Showing devastating</u> impact of <u>global warming</u>		
(d)	<u>Comparing European</u> views with <u>America's</u>		

2. Little is known about the few individual designers who have worked with Mies van der Rohe during the transitional stage of his career, which took place shortly after World War I. Even less is known about the German-born female designer Lilly Reich who received little recognition for her

5   immense contribution to the success of Mies's domestic dwellings such as

the Tugendhat House (1928–1930) despite being Mies's constant collaborator and companion from 1925 till he left for the United States in 1938.

An intensely private man by nature, Mies maintained this image of himself in public light, only letting those who had studied or worked with
10   him observe the development of his creative process. While their fourteen years of correspondence represented only a fraction of Mies's sixty-two year career, the extent of Reich's influence on Mies can be considered in the words of Albert Pfeiffer, "Mies did not fully develop any contemporary furniture successfully before or after his collaboration with Reich." It is not
15   preposterous to argue that Mies's success in exhibition and home design, generally regarded as the most experimental and fruitful time of his career, began and ultimately flourished because of his relationship with Reich.

Author: Darell Koh

The author shows what an <u>important role Lilly Reich</u> played in Mies van der Rohe's life by

a)   <u>stating</u> that <u>few individual designers</u> have <u>worked with Mies van der Rohe</u> during the <u>transitional</u> stage of his career

b)   <u>describing</u> Mies van der Rohe as "<u>an intensely private man by nature</u>"

c)   <u>highlighting</u> that Mies van der Rohe <u>did not fully develop</u> any <u>contemporary furniture successfully</u> before or after his collaboration with <u>Reich</u>

d)   <u>describing</u> the <u>success</u> of Mies van der Rohe's <u>domestic dwellings</u> such as <u>Tugendhat House</u>

	Keyword	Type	Analysis
	The <u>important role Lilly Reich</u> in Mies van der Rohe's life		
(a)	Stating <u>few individual designers</u> <u>worked with Mies van der Rohe</u> during his career's <u>transitional</u> stage		
(b)	Describing Mies van der Rohe as "<u>an intensely private man by nature</u>"		
(c)	Highlighting that Mies van der Rohe <u>did not fully develop</u> any <u>contemporary furniture successfully</u> before or after his collaboration with <u>Reich</u>		
(d)	Describing the <u>success</u> of Mies van der Rohe's <u>domestic dwellings</u> such as <u>Tugendhat House</u>		

3. Urban renewal in ancient times was closely associated with the politics of a city or nation. The dependence of ancient urban renewal on the ruler's will is often interpreted as a mechanism to prevent citizens from rebelling against the rise of a new national power. Some of the most common methods
5   of early urban renewal include the demolition of monuments and statues from the preceding ruler's reign to make way for the installation of new ones exulting the current king's newfound power.

The idea of clearing up crowded streets and overgrowth to create an open public space for ceremonial processions was also popular in early urban
10 renewal. Though these little changes may seem insignificant, they reinforce the omnipresence and power of the king when implemented throughout the whole city. This accumulation of power expressed in physical terms also indicates the growth and wealth of a city.

Despite the different cultures and governmental structure of these
15 early cities, the universal idea of ancient urban renewal suggests that of destruction, impermanence and potential displacement of history. The sense of frustration that rises from this limited and vicious template of city renewal is best expressed by Aldo Rossi who once wrote that "one is forced to look beyond (an urban monument) to the present-day actions that modify
20 it" (59) in order to understand its significance.

Author: Darell Koh

The author shows that <u>urban renewal</u> was <u>closely associated</u> with the <u>politics of a city</u> by
a) <u>describing</u> how the ruler could install <u>new monuments</u> and <u>statues</u> to <u>exult</u> the current king's <u>newfound power</u>
b) <u>arguing</u> that <u>citizens</u> may <u>rebel</u> against the rise of a <u>new national power</u>
c) <u>comparing</u> the different <u>cultures</u> and <u>governmental structure</u> of early cities
d) <u>describing</u> the sense of <u>frustration</u> expressed by <u>Aldo Rossi</u>

	Keyword	Type	Analysis
	Urban renewal <u>closely associated</u> with <u>politics of a city</u>		
(a)	<u>Describing</u> <u>new monuments</u> and <u>statues</u> to <u>exult</u> current king's <u>newfound power</u>		
(b)	<u>Arguing</u> <u>citizens</u> may <u>rebel</u> against <u>new national power</u>		
(c)	<u>Comparing</u> different <u>cultures</u> and <u>governmental structure</u> of early cities		
(d)	<u>Describing</u> <u>frustration</u> expressed by <u>Aldo Rossi</u>		

4. For many years, the Indonesian occupation of East Timor was ignored, until the 1991 Santa Cruz massacre in Dili. On November 12, 1991, several hundred mourners attended the services for a student activist, Sebastião Gomes. Over 1,000 demonstrators followed the family of mourners with
5 banners that called for independence. However, upon reaching the cemetery, the mourners and protesters were mowed down by automatic weapons operated by the Indonesian army. What made this massacre different was that a British journalist captured it on film and smuggled the footage out of East Timor and into televisions across the world. The massacre occurred
10 during a visit to Indonesia and East Timor by UN Special Rapporteur Amos Wako. However, he did not witness it. On January 8, 1992, Wako published a report concluding that torture was commonplace in East Timor and made eleven recommendations to help address the problem.

International awareness of the East Timor issue continued to increase.
15 In 1996, the Nobel Peace Prize was awarded to Sydney-based José Ramos-Horta and Dili-based Bishop Carlos Ximenes Belo in recognition of the Timorese cause. Between 1997 and 1998, there were numerous riots and public protests by activists in Indonesia.

The author shows that <u>international awareness of the East Timor issue</u> continued to <u>increase</u> by

a) <u>describing</u> the <u>1991 Santa Cruz massacre</u>
b) <u>showing</u> that <u>Amos Wako</u> <u>did not witness</u> the massacre
c) <u>highlighting</u> that the <u>Nobel Peace Prize</u> was awarded to José Ramos-Horta and Bishop Carlos Ximenes Belo in recognition of the <u>Timorese cause</u>
d) <u>arguing</u> that the <u>Indonesian occupation of East Timor</u> was <u>ignored</u>

	Keyword	Type	Analysis
	<u>International awareness of the East Timor issue</u> continued to <u>increase</u>		
(a)	<u>Describing</u> <u>1991 Santa Cruz massacre</u>		
(b)	<u>Showing</u> <u>Amos Wako</u> <u>did not witness</u> the massacre		
(c)	<u>Highlighting</u> that the <u>Nobel Peace Prize</u> awarded in recognition of the <u>Timorese cause</u>		
(d)	<u>Arguing</u> <u>Indonesian occupation of East Timor</u> was <u>ignored</u>		

5. In examining how zero energy buildings relate to sustainability as a whole, we must first understand the reasons behind the need for more energy-efficient buildings in our world. It comes as no surprise that the energy use of buildings has a significant impact on the environment. Data from

5 the 2012 U.S. Energy Information Administration Annual Review indicate that commercial and residential buildings used a total of 39.4% of the total fossil fuel energy in the United States and European Union, roughly a 7% increase from three decades ago, and approximately 70% of the electricity consumption in the United States.

10 Electricity consumption in the commercial building sector doubled between 1980 and 2000, and is expected to increase another 50% by 2025, primarily because new buildings are constructed faster than old ones are demolished or retired. Until buildings are designed to produce more energy than they use to offset the growing burden on worldwide energy demands,

15 energy consumption in the commercial building sector will continue to

increase to levels that are ultimately unsustainable; further compounding the unpredictable and devastating impacts of global warming.

Author: Darell Koh

The author shows that <u>energy use of buildings</u> have a <u>significant impact</u> on the <u>environment</u> by
a) <u>arguing</u> that we must <u>first understand the reasons</u> behind the need for more energy-efficient buildings
b) <u>comparing fossil fuel energy</u> use in the <u>United States</u> and <u>European Union</u>
c) <u>describing</u> how much <u>fossil fuel energy</u> is used by <u>commercial and residential buildings</u>
d) <u>identifying</u> that <u>worldwide energy demands</u> are <u>growing</u>

	Keyword	Type	Analysis
	Energy use of buildings have a significant impact on the environment		
(a)	Arguing that we must first understand the reasons for more energy-efficient buildings		
(b)	Comparing fossil fuel energy use in the United States and European Union		
(c)	Describing how much fossil fuel energy is used by commercial and residential buildings		
(d)	Identifying that worldwide energy demands are growing		

Answers:

1. In most European countries and parts of America, zero energy buildings have come to be seen as the next frontier or gold standard for new construction across all sectors of the building industry. This constant push for the highest level of sustainability in buildings, for the most part, comes as a result of
5   the growing burden on worldwide energy demands and the increasingly unpredictable effects of climate change, which in turn makes zero energy

buildings a very attractive solution to help mitigate the devastating impacts of global warming on our world.

The author explains that <u>zero energy buildings</u> have come to be seen as the <u>next frontier for new construction</u> by

a) <u>describing</u> the <u>growing burden</u> on <u>worldwide energy demands</u> and the effects of <u>climate change</u>
b) <u>stating</u> that <u>zero energy buildings</u> are the "<u>gold standard</u>"
c) <u>showing</u> how <u>devastating</u> the impact of <u>global warming</u> can be
d) <u>comparing European</u> countries' views with <u>America</u>'s views

	Keyword	Type	Analysis
	Zero energy buildings — the next frontier	Cause/effect	The answer must prove that zero energy buildings are important
(a)	Describing growing burden on worldwide energy demands; effects of climate change	Cause/effect	Correct — This shows that zero energy buildings are important because there is growing burden on worldwide energy demands
(b)	Stating zero energy buildings are the "gold standard"	Classification	Incorrect — Merely stating that zero energy buildings are the "gold standard" does not explain why they are important
(c)	Showing devastating impact of global warming	Cause/effect	Incorrect — This does not link global warming with zero energy buildings
(d)	Comparing European views with America's	Compare/contrast	Incorrect — There is no mention of this in the passage.

The answer is (a) because it summarizes the reasons as to why zero energy buildings have grown in importance.

2. Little is known about the few individual designers who have worked with Mies van der Rohe during the transitional stage of his career, which took place shortly after World War I. Even less is known about the German-born female designer Lilly Reich who received little recognition for her
5   immense contribution to the success of Mies's domestic dwellings such as

the Tugendhat House (1928–1930) despite being Mies' constant collaborator and companion from 1925 till he left for the United States in 1938.

An intensely private man by nature, Mies maintained this image of himself in public light, only letting those who had studied or worked with
10   him observe the development of his creative process. While their fourteen years of correspondence represented only a fraction of Mies's sixty-two year career, the extent of Reich's influence on Mies can be considered in the words of Albert Pfeiffer, "Mies did not fully develop any contemporary furniture successfully before or after his collaboration with Reich." It is not
15   preposterous to argue that Mies's success in exhibition and home design, generally regarded as the most experimental and fruitful time of his career, began and ultimately flourished because of his relationship with Reich.

The author shows what an <u>important role Lilly Reich</u> played in Mies van der Rohe's life by

a) <u>stating</u> that <u>few individual designers</u> have <u>worked with Mies van der Rohe</u> during the <u>transitional</u> stage of his career

b) <u>describing</u> Mies van der Rohe as <u>"an intensely private man by nature"</u>

c) <u>highlighting</u> that Mies van der Rohe <u>did not fully develop</u> any <u>contemporary furniture successfully</u> before or after his collaboration with <u>Reich</u>

d) <u>describing</u> the <u>success</u> of Mies van der Rohe's <u>domestic dwellings</u> such as <u>Tugendhat House</u>

	Keyword	Type	Analysis
	The <u>important role Lilly Reich</u> in Mies van der Rohe's life	Cause/effect	The answer must show how Lilly Reich played an important role in Mies van der Rohe's life
(a)	Stating <u>few individual designers worked with Mies van der Rohe</u> during his career's <u>transitional</u> stage	Classification	Incorrect — Few individual designers does not single out Reich's importance
(b)	Describing Mies van der Rohe as <u>"an intensely private man by nature"</u>	Classification	Incorrect — This is an informational description of Mies van der Rohe

(c)	Highlighting that Mies van der Rohe did not fully develop any contemporary furniture successfully before or after his collaboration with Reich	Compare/contrast	Correct — The author compares/contrast Mies van der Rohe's success in developing contemporary furniture during the time he collaborated with Reich and the time he did not
(d)	Describing the success of Mies van der Rohe's domestic dwellings such as Tugendhat House	Classification	Incorrect — This does not show how Reich directly contributed to Mies van der Rohe's success

The answer is (c) because it demonstrates how reliant Mies van der Rohe was on Lilly Reich, such that he did not develop any contemporary furniture successfully when she was absent.

3.   Urban renewal in ancient times was closely associated with the politics of a city or nation. The dependence of ancient urban renewal on the ruler's will is often interpreted as a mechanism to prevent citizens from rebelling against the rise of a new national power. Some of the most common methods
5   of early urban renewal include the demolition of monuments and statues from the preceding ruler's reign to make way for the installation of new ones exulting the current king's newfound power.

   The idea of clearing up crowded streets and overgrowth to create an open public space for ceremonial processions was also popular in early urban
10   renewal. Though these little changes may seem insignificant, they reinforce the omnipresence and power of the king when implemented throughout the whole city. This accumulation of power expressed in physical terms also indicates the growth and wealth of a city.

   Despite the different cultures and governmental structure of these
15   early cities, the universal idea of ancient urban renewal suggests that of destruction, impermanence and potential displacement of history. The sense of frustration that rises from this limited and vicious template of city renewal is best expressed by Aldo Rossi who once wrote that "one is forced to look beyond (an urban monument) to the present-day actions that modify
20   it" in order to understand its significance.

The author shows that <u>urban renewal</u> was <u>closely associated</u> with the <u>politics of a city</u> by

a) <u>describing</u> how the ruler could install <u>new monuments</u> and <u>statues</u> to <u>exult</u> the current king's <u>newfound power</u>
b) <u>arguing</u> that <u>citizens</u> may <u>rebel</u> against the rise of a <u>new national power</u>
c) <u>comparing</u> the different <u>cultures</u> and <u>governmental structure</u> of early cities
d) <u>describing</u> the sense of <u>frustration</u> expressed by <u>Aldo Rossi</u>

	Keyword	Type	Analysis
	<u>Urban renewal closely associated</u> with <u>politics of a city</u>	Cause/effect	The answer must show why urban renewal is closely associated with the politics of a city
(a)	<u>Describing new monuments</u> and <u>statues</u> to <u>exult</u> current king's <u>newfound power</u>	Cause/effect	Correct — This shows how new monuments and statues can exult the current king's newfound power
(b)	<u>Arguing citizens</u> may <u>rebel</u> against <u>new national power</u>	Problem/solution	Incorrect — This states the problem that new rulers face, not why urban renewal is important in countering it
(c)	<u>Comparing</u> different <u>cultures</u> and <u>governmental structure</u> of early cities	Compare/contrast	Incorrect — Comparisons do not show why urban renewal is important as urban renewal is supposed to be important in every country
(d)	<u>Describing frustration</u> expressed by <u>Aldo Rossi</u>	Classification	Incorrect — Aldo Rossi states: "one is forced to look beyond (an urban monument) to the present-day actions that modify it." This merely identifies that one must analyze urban monuments before being able to understand its deeper meaning

The answer is (a) because it is the only cause/effect type option that matches the nature of the question. It provides an example of how urban renewal is used to further political ambitions.

4.   For many years, the Indonesian occupation of East Timor was ignored, until the 1991 Santa Cruz massacre in Dili. On 12 November 1991, several hundred mourners attended the services for a student activist, Sebastião Gomes. Over 1,000 demonstrators followed the family of mourners with
5   banners that called for independence. However, upon reaching the cemetery, the mourners and protesters were mowed down by automatic weapons operated by the Indonesian army. What made this massacre different was that a British journalist captured it on film and smuggled the footage out of East Timor and into televisions across the world. The massacre occurred
10 during a visit to Indonesia and East Timor, UN Special Rapporteur Amos Wako. However, he did not witness it. On 8 January 1992, Wako published a report concluding that torture was commonplace in East Timor and made eleven recommendations to help address the problem.

      International awareness of the East Timor issue continued to increase.
15 In 1996, the Nobel Peace Prize was awarded to Sydney-based José Ramos-Horta and Dili-based Bishop Carlos Ximenes Belo in recognition of the Timorese cause. Between 1997 and 1998, there were numerous riots and public protests by activists in Indonesia.

The author shows that <u>international awareness of the East Timor issue</u> continued to <u>increase</u> by
a) <u>describing</u> the <u>1991 Santa Cruz massacre</u>
b) <u>showing</u> that <u>Amos Wako</u> <u>did not witness</u> the massacre
c) <u>highlighting</u> that the <u>Nobel Peace Prize</u> was awarded to José Ramos-Horta and Bishop Carlos Ximenes Belo in recognition of the <u>Timorese cause</u>
d) <u>arguing</u> that the <u>Indonesian occupation of East Timor</u> was <u>ignored</u>

	Keyword	Type	Analysis
	<u>International awareness of the East Timor issue</u> continued to <u>increase</u>	Cause/effect	The answer must show evidence that supports increasing international awareness of the East Timor issue
(a)	<u>Describing</u> <u>1991 Santa Cruz massacre</u>	Classification	Incorrect — The Santa Cruz massacre was one of the events that led to growing international awareness, but is not a sign that international awareness grew

(b)	Showing <u>Amos Wako</u> <u>did not</u> <u>witness</u> the massacre	Classification	Incorrect — This does not support the author's argument as it shows lack of international awareness
(c)	<u>Highlighting</u> that the <u>Nobel</u> <u>Peace Prize</u> awarded in recognition of the <u>Timorese</u> <u>cause</u>	Cause/effect	Correct — This shows that the world became aware of the Timorese cause because the prestigious Nobel Prize was awarded to individuals involved in the cause
(d)	<u>Arguing Indonesian</u> <u>occupation of East Timor</u> was <u>ignored</u>	Classification	Incorrect — This does not support the author's argument as it shows lack of international awareness

The answer is (c) because the Nobel Peace Prize is reflective of international awareness. The word "prestigious" emphasizes the importance of the prize.

5. In examining how zero energy buildings relate to sustainability as a whole, we must first understand the reasons behind the need for more energy-efficient buildings in our world. It comes as no surprise that the energy use of buildings has a significant impact on the environment. Data from

5   the 2012 U.S. Energy Information Administration Annual Review indicate that commercial and residential buildings used a total of 39.4% of the total fossil fuel energy in the United States and European Union, roughly a 7% increase from three decades ago, and approximately 70% of the electricity consumption in the United States.

10   Electricity consumption in the commercial building sector doubled between 1980 and 2000, and is expected to increase another 50% by 2025, primarily because new buildings are constructed faster than old ones are demolished or retired. Until buildings are designed to produce more energy than they use to offset the growing burden on worldwide

15 energy demands, energy consumption in the commercial building sector will continue to increase to levels that are ultimately unsustainable; further compounding the unpredictable and devastating impacts of global warming.

The author shows that <u>energy use of buildings</u> have a <u>significant impact</u> on the <u>environment</u> by

a) <u>arguing</u> that we must <u>first understand the reasons</u> behind the need for more energy-efficient buildings

b) <u>comparing fossil fuel energy</u> use in the <u>United States</u> and <u>European Union</u>

c) <u>describing</u> how much <u>fossil fuel energy</u> is used by <u>commercial and residential buildings</u>

d) <u>identifying</u> that <u>worldwide energy demands</u> are <u>growing</u>

	Keyword	Type	Analysis
	<u>Energy use of buildings</u> have a <u>significant impact</u> on the <u>environment</u>	Cause/effect	The answer must show how energy use of buildings have a significant impact on the environment
(a)	<u>Arguing</u> that we must <u>first understand the reasons</u> for <u>more energy-efficient buildings</u>	Problem/solution	Incorrect — This just poses a solution: that we must first understand the reasons for more energy-efficient buildings
(b)	<u>Comparing fossil fuel energy</u> use in the <u>United States</u> and <u>European Union</u>	Compare/contrast	Incorrect — Comparing fossil fuel energy usage in the United States and European union does not show how energy use of buildings have impacted the environment
(c)	<u>Describing</u> how much <u>fossil fuel energy</u> is used by <u>commercial and residential buildings</u>	Classification	Correct — This shows specifically that buildings consume a significant amount of energy and therefore have a significant on the environment
(d)	<u>Identifying</u> that <u>worldwide energy demands</u> are <u>growing</u>	Classification	Incorrect — This shows that energy demands are growing but not specifically why buildings are a key contributor to environmental pollution

The answer is (c) because it explains the direct impact that buildings have on the environment in terms of fossil fuel energy usage.

Perfect Paraphrasing

In the TOEFL, you will also be tested on your ability to paraphrase parts of the text. This means you must know how to rewrite sentences by using other words and phrases without changing the original meaning. The TOEFL tests your ability in this area because when you do research in college, you are not allowed to copy and paste scholars' works directly. Instead, you should paraphrase and integrate the scholars' works with your own.

Common Mistake 1:

Here is an example of poor paraphrasing that can result in you being penalized for academic dishonesty:

Original:

> The key drivers for the food and beverage industry's rise in the United States are growing household income, which increased by more than 10% every year for the past decade, and shifting consumer preferences towards eating out.

Poor paraphrasing:

> The <u>important</u> drivers for the food and beverage industry's rise in the United States are <u>increasing</u> household income, which <u>grew</u> by more than 10% every year for the past decade, and <u>changing</u> consumer preferences towards eating out.

The paraphrased version is different from the original, but as you can see, only a few words were changed. This means the paraphrased version is nearly the same as the original, which is a sign of poor paraphrasing.

Common Mistake 2:

Here's another example of how students often get it wrong:

Poor paraphrasing:

> The American food and beverage industry was fuelled by growing household income and changes in consumer preferences.

The problem with the above paraphrasing is that while it has varied sentence structure and also used different vocabulary, the original meaning is lost. Refer to the original version and you will see that more information is given, such as the 10 percent increase in household income and how consumers are moving towards eating out.

The TOEFL will test you more on your ability to avoid Common Mistake 2. Since the questions are multiple choice, you will not be tested on your ability to paraphrase in writing. Rather, you will be asked to select the answer option that best paraphrases a certain portion of the passage.

Simple Steps

In order to answer paraphrasing questions correctly, put these simple steps into practice:

1. List down essential information in the original sentence point by point.
2. List down essential information in each answer option point by point.
3. Eliminate answer options that do not possess all essential information. Then, analyze the remaining options and select the best choice.

Elaboration with Examples

Refer to the following example:

Sample passage:

After serving as the last director of the Bauhaus for a short period of time, Mies van der Rohe left Germany for good and emigrated to the United States in 1938. The Nazis' rejection of his architecture as not being "German" enough in style and character frustrated him immensely, making the allure of the secure academic post in the Illinois Institute of Technology in Chicago and private commission in Wyoming impossible to resist. **The move to America marked the end of Mies's period of experimentation, signaling the beginning of many profound changes that would impact his personal philosophy and body of work.** Mies had mostly worked on residential dwellings and interiors in Germany, but he only ever designed two private houses (one of them being the noteworthy Farnsworth House) after coming to the States.

Author: Darell Koh

Sample question:

Which of the sentences below best expresses the essential information in the following sentence?

The move to America marked the end of Mies's period of experimentation, signaling the beginning of many profound changes that would impact his personal philosophy and body of work.

Incorrect choices change the meaning in important ways or leave out essential information.

a) America was a life-changing experience for Mies and it had a profound impact on him.

b) Mies experimented in America but it was only after he left that he became a changed man.

c) Moving to America caused Mies to reflect on his life and to change his personal philosophy as well as body of work.

d) A milestone in Mies's life was when he moved to America, as it marked the start of various changes that influenced his work as well as personal philosophy.

1. *List down essential information in the original sentence point by point*

The key is to read the original sentence very carefully and list down the key points. This will help you draw comparisons in a more efficient manner. It is especially helpful because the TOEFL can sometimes confuse you by providing answer options that are very similar.

If you have trouble doing this, try breaking up the sentence and analyzing each portion individually just like what you did for vocabulary.

Original Sentence	Essential Information
The move to America marked the end of Mies' period of experimentation, signaling the beginning of many profound changes that would impact his personal philosophy and body of work.	• Mies moved to America • The move marked the end of his period of experimentation • It was also the start of many profound changes • These changes would impact his personal philosophy • It would also impact his body of work

2. List down essential information in each answer option point by point

	Answer Option	Essential Information
(a)	America was a life-changing experience for Mies and it had a profound impact on him.	• America was a life-changing experience • America impacted Mies profoundly
(b)	Mies experimented in America but it was only after he left that he became a changed man.	• Mies experimented in America. • After he left America, he became a changed man
(c)	Moving to America caused Mies to reflect on his life and to change his personal philosophy as well as body of work.	• Moving to America caused Mies to reflect on his life • It also caused him to change his personal philosophy and his body of work
(d)	A milestone in Mies's life was when he moved to America, as it marked the start of various changes that influenced his work as well as personal philosophy.	• A milestone in Mies' life was when he moved to America. • It marked the start of various changes • These changes influenced his work • These changes also influenced his personal philosophy

3. Eliminate answer options that do not possess all essential information. Then, analyze the remaining options and select the best choice

Original Sentence	Essential Information
The move to America marked the end of Mies's period of experimentation, signaling the beginning of many profound changes that would impact his personal philosophy and body of work.	• Mies moved to America • The move marked the end of his period of experimentation • It was also the start of many profound changes • These changes would impact his personal philosophy • It would also impact his body of work

	Essential Information	**Analysis**
(a)	• America was a lifechanging experience • America impacted Mies profoundly	• Incorrect — America did not impact Mies. Rather, it marked the end of his period of experimentation
(b)	• Mies experimented in America • After he left America, he became a changed man	• Incorrect — Mies moved to America. He did not leave America.
(c)	• Moving to America caused Mies to reflect on his life • It also caused him to change his personal philosophy and his body of work	• Incorrect — The move did not cause the changes but merely marked the start of the changes
(d)	• A milestone in Mies' life was when he moved to America • It marked the start of various changes • These changes influenced his work • These changes also influenced his personal philosophy	• Correct — The only piece of essential information this is missing is that moving to America marked the end of the experimentation period

As you may have noticed, there were some very similar answers, especially (c) and (d). How do you select the best one? Use the essential information as a guide. You may not always get the perfect answer in the answer options, but you need to learn how to select the best one possible in order to secure the marks.

Let's go through this again with another example:

Sample passage:

Despite any constraints that domestic pressures may have placed on American military commitment in Vietnam, it cannot be argued that the cause of American defeat was due to lack of firepower. The tons of munitions per man during the Vietnam War were 26 times greater than the 1941–45 period. In World War II, seven million tons of munitions were used — a small amount compared to the fifteen million tons used during 1964–72.

Sample question:

Which of the sentences below best expresses the essential information in the following sentence?

Despite any constraints that domestic pressures may have placed on American military commitment in Vietnam, it cannot be argued that the cause of American defeat was due to lack of firepower.

Incorrect choices change the meaning in important ways or leave out essential information.

a) American defeat in Vietnam was due to a lack of firepower.

b) American defeat in Vietnam was definitely not due to a lack of firepower despite whatever constraints domestic pressures may have placed on the American army.

c) Domestic pressures restrained American involvement in Vietnam and contributed to its defeat.

d) American defeat was due to restrained military commitment and lack of firepower, among other reasons.

List down essential information in the original sentence point by point.

Original Sentence	Essential Information
Despite any constraints that domestic pressures may have placed on American military commitment in Vietnam, it cannot be argued that the cause of American defeat was due to lack of firepower.	• There may have been domestic pressures on American military commitment in Vietnam • However, we cannot say that Americans lost because of a lack of firepower

----

List down essential information in each answer option point by point.

	Answer Option	Essential Information
(a)	American defeat in Vietnam was due to a lack of firepower.	• Americans lost in Vietnam due to a lack of firepower

(b)	American defeat in Vietnam was definitely not due to a lack of firepower despite whatever constraints domestic pressures may have placed on the American army.	• American did not lose in Vietnam due to a lack of firepower • This is despite whatever constraints that domestic pressures may have placed on the American army
(c)	Domestic pressures restrained American involvement in Vietnam and contributed to its defeat.	• Domestic pressures restrained American involvement in Vietnam • Domestic pressures contributed to America's defeat
(d)	American defeat was due to restrained military commitment and lack of firepower, among other reasons.	• America lost because of restrained military commitment • America also lost because of a lack of firepower • There are other reasons as to why America lost

Eliminate answer options that do not possess all essential information.
Then, analyze the remaining options and select the best choice.

Original Sentence	Essential Information
Despite any constraints that domestic pressures may have been placed on American military commitment in Vietnam, it cannot be argued that the cause of American defeat was due to lack of firepower.	• There may have been domestic pressures on American military commitment in Vietnam • However, we cannot say that Americans lost because of a lack of firepower

	Essential Information	Analysis
(a)	• Americans lost in Vietnam due to a lack of firepower	• Incorrect — America did not lose due to a lack of firepower
(b)	• American did not lose in Vietnam due to a lack of firepower • This is despite whatever constraints that domestic pressures may have placed on the American army	• Correct

(c)	• Domestic pressures restrained American involvement in Vietnam • Domestic pressures contributed to America's defeat	• Incorrect — The statements are true but they leave out essential information such as the fact that America did not lose due to a lack of firepower
(d)	• America lost because of restrained military commitment • America also lost because of a lack of firepower • There are other reasons as to why America lost	• Incorrect — America did not lose due to a lack of firepower

Now, it's your turn. Sharpen your skills with the *TOEFL Trainer*.

TOEFL Trainer

Step I: *List down essential information in the original sentence point by point*

1. **The enormous publicity garnered by "The Dwelling" exhibit and the 1932 International Style Exhibition curated by Philip Johnson and Henry-Russell Hitchcock at the Museum of Modern Art, New York had elevated Mies van der Rohe's status to that of a well-regarded celebrity.** Naturally,
5   this meant an increase in the size and financial power of his clientele as well as the scale of his commissions. Mies's American clients were huge corporate figures with a propensity for modern capitalism. They demanded modular-type mega structures coupled with the advanced technology of massive steel constructions that had been gaining rapid momentum since
10   the advent of Louis Sullivan's development of the high-rise.

Author: Darell Koh

Which of the sentences below best expresses the essential information in the following sentence?

The enormous publicity garnered by "The Dwelling" exhibit and the 1932 International Style Exhibition curated by Philip Johnson and Henry-Russell Hitchcock at the Museum of Modern Art, New York had elevated Mies van der Rohe's status to that of a well-regarded celebrity.

Incorrect choices change the meaning in important ways or leave out essential information.

a) Two successful exhibitions attracted many people's attention and made Mies van der Rohe a respected public figure.

b) Mies van der Rohe's, a well-regarded celebrity, attracted many people to see his exhibitions.

c) The Museum of Modern Art drew a large crowd because it hosted the famous celebrity, Mies van der Rohe.

d) Philip Johnson and Henry-Russell Hitchcock's exhibition drew large crowds, including the artist Mies van der Rohe.

Original Sentence	Essential Information
The enormous publicity garnered by "The Dwelling" exhibit and the 1932 International Style Exhibition curated by Philip Johnson and Henry-Russell Hitchcock at the Museum of Modern Art, New York had elevated Mies van der Rohe's status to that of a well-regarded celebrity.	• •

2. The problem therefore did not lie in the amount of military commitment, but the efficacy of any military aid given. Divisions within the American army had their own interests to look out for, causing intra-military wrangling. The Marines, for example, saw Vietnam as a chance to "save their antiquated
5   amphibious functions, boost their reputation among congressmen, and even add another division to their forces." **They had their own logistics and tactical aviation, which they used as a costly substitute for heavy artillery and which they refused to relinquish any control over until early 1968.** Again, this was no isolated case — the army and the air force were also at
10 loggerheads over the army's fixed-wing aircraft and helicopters, a dispute that was not resolved until April 1966.

Which of the sentences below best expresses the essential information in the following sentence?

They had their own logistics and tactical aviation, which they used as a costly substitute for heavy artillery and which they refused to relinquish any control over until early 1968.

Incorrect choices change the meaning in important ways or leave out essential information.

a) Logistics and tactical aviation were a costly substitute for heavily artillery, and were still used until early 1968.

b) They refused to give up control of their own logistics and tactical aviation until early 1968, even though these were very expensive compared to heavy artillery.

c) In early 1968, they used heavy artillery because having their own logistics and tactical aviation were too costly.

d) Heavy artillery is a costly substitute for logistics and tactical aviation, and no one was willing to give up control until after 1968.

Original Sentence	Essential Information
They had their own logistics and tactical aviation, which they used as a costly substitute for heavy artillery and which they refused to relinquish any control over until early 1968.	• •

3. Because the nature of American commitment to its partners in East Asia was uncertain and poorly defined, the communists' interpretation of American policy rested heavily on the individual leaders' psychology. **Secretary of State Dean Acheson's National Press Club speech in January 1950 seemed**
5 **to indicate that the United States had abandoned commitments to both South Korea and Taiwan, which subsequently prompted the Korean invasion of June 1950.** Robert Pollard points out that this may be too unfair an assessment, for Acheson's intended audience was the American public, and thus Acheson understandably devoted most of his remarks to
10 an explanation of the American failure in China. Regardless of Acheson's intentions, what is clear is that this highlights the role that individual leaders' psychology plays especially when interpreting unclear signals.

Which of the sentences below best expresses the essential information in the following sentence?

Secretary of State Dean Acheson's National Press Club speech in January 1950 seemed to indicate that the United States had abandoned

commitments to both South Korea and Taiwan, which subsequently prompted the Korean invasion of June 1950.

Incorrect choices change the meaning in important ways or leave out essential information.

a) The Korean invasion of June 1950 inspired Secretary of State Dean Acheson's National Press Club speech.

b) The United States appointed Secretary of State Dean Acheson to give a speech at the National Press Club to prevent the Korean invasion.

c) After the United States abandoned commitments to South Korea and Taiwan, Secretary of State Dean Acheson gave a speech at the National Press Club.

d) The Korean invasion of June 1950 was triggered by Secretary of State Dean Acheson's National Press Club speech which implied that the United States had abandoned commitments to both South Korea and Taiwan.

Original Sentence	Essential Information
Secretary of State Dean Acheson's National Press Club speech in January 1950 seemed to indicate that the United States had abandoned commitments to both South Korea and Taiwan, which subsequently prompted the Korean invasion of June 1950.	• •

4. On August 9, 1974, President Richard Nixon became the first and only U.S. President to resign. Even for the most powerful man in America, the backlash that broke out over the Watergate scandal proved far too much.

5   But Watergate was not immediately perceived as a scandal. **In fact, the Watergate Scandal only surfaced in June 1972 — almost two years before Nixon's resignation — beginning with the arrest of five men breaking and entering into the Democratic National Committee (DNC) headquarters at the Watergate complex.**

Which of the sentences below best expresses the essential information in the following sentence?

In fact, the Watergate Scandal only surfaced in June 1972 — almost two years before Nixon's resignation — beginning with the arrest of five men breaking and entering into the Democratic National Committee (DNC) headquarters at the Watergate complex.

Incorrect choices change the meaning in important ways or leave out essential information.

a) After the Watergate Scandal surfaced, five men broke and entered into the Democratic National Committee (DNC) headquarters at the Watergate complex.

b) Although the Watergate Scandal came to light in June 1972 after the arrest of five men breaking and entering into the Watergate complex, Nixon only resigned two years later.

c) Nixon resigned two years before the Watergate scandal surfaced in June 1972 following the arrest of five men breaking and entering into the Democratic National Committee (DNC) headquarters at the Watergate complex.

d) After Nixon resigned in 1972 over the Watergate scandal, five men broke and entered into the Democratic National Committee (DNC) headquarters at the Watergate complex.

Original Sentence	Essential Information
In fact, the Watergate Scandal only surfaced in June 1972 — almost two years before Nixon's resignation — beginning with the arrest of five men breaking and entering into the Democratic National Committee (DNC) headquarters at the Watergate complex.	• •

5. "Containment" and "peaceful coexistence" were two policies that were frequently touted during the Cold War. These terms are misleading for two reasons. First, it suggests a period of peace under these policies. On the contrary, the period 1953–1968 was actually a period of high tension,
5   most notably with the shooting down of the American U2 plane, the Bay of

Pigs, the Cuban Missile Crisis and American military escalation in Vietnam. **Second, the "policy" label implies a principle that will lead to more or less consistent action, but what happened in practice was that different interpretations were often made and lines were blurred.**

Which of the sentences below best expresses the essential information in the following sentence?

Second, the "policy" label implies a principle that will lead to more or less consistent action, but what happened in practice was that different interpretations were often made and lines were blurred.

Incorrect choices change the meaning in important ways or leave out essential information.

a) Although the "policy" label suggests that consistent action would follow, varying interpretations were often made and there was a lack of clarity.

b) The "policy" label led to different interpretations and blurry lines in practice.

c) The principle of having a "policy" label means that we should see consistent action, and not different interpretations with blurry lines.

d) The "policy" label caused several different interpretations instead of consistent action.

Original Sentence	Essential Information
Second, the "policy" label implies a principle that will lead to more or less consistent action, but what happened in practice was that different interpretations were often made and lines were blurred.	• •

6. Adult tissue in multicellular organisms contains self-renewing cells, which are known as somatic stem cells, and are found in small clusters in a variety of tissues. Some examples of tissues containing stem cells are the epithelia, hematopoietic system and even the central nervous system. Stem cells asymmetrically replicate to produce one stem cell and one progenitor cell, whereas progenitor cells often undergo symmetrical replication, forming two identical cells which eventually undergo differentiation to form various tissues. Pepper et al. (2007) termed this process as "serial differentiation".

The process of symmetric and asymmetric replication has been observed
10   in colon tissue and transplantations with animal models.

Author: Flora Wong

Which of the sentences below best expresses the essential information in the following sentence?

The process of symmetric and asymmetric replication has been observed in colon tissue and transplantations with animal models.

Incorrect choices change the meaning in important ways or leave out essential information.

a)   Colon tissue has gone through the process of symmetric and asymmetric replication.

b)   Colon tissue has been transplanted with animal models via the process of symmetric and asymmetric replication.

c)   Both colon tissue and transplantations with animal models have involved symmetric and asymmetric replication.

d)   Colon tissue has been processed by symmetric and asymmetric replication.

Original Sentence	Essential Information
The process of symmetric and asymmetric replication has been observed in colon tissue and transplantations with animal models.	• •

Answers:

1.

Original Sentence	Essential Information
The enormous publicity garnered by "The Dwelling" exhibit and the 1932 International Style Exhibition curated by Philip Johnson and Henry-Russell Hitchcock at the Museum of Modern Art, New York had elevated Mies van der Rohe's status to that of a well-regarded celebrity.	• "The Dwelling" and the 1932 Exhibition attracted a lot of publicity • The 1932 Exhibition was curated by Philip Johnson and Henry-Russell Hitchcock at the Museum of Modern Art, New York • These exhibitions boosted Mies van der Rohe's status • Thereafter, he became a well-regarded celebrity

2.

Original Sentence	Essential Information
They had their own logistics and tactical aviation, which they used as a costly substitute for heavy artillery and which they refused to relinquish any control over until early 1968.	• They had their own logistics and tactical aviation • The logistics and tactical aviation was an expensive substitute for heavy artillery • They refused to give up control over logistics and tactical aviation until early 1968

3.

Original Sentence	Essential Information
Secretary of State Dean Acheson's National Press Club speech in January 1950 seemed to indicate that the United States had abandoned commitments to both South Korea and Taiwan, which subsequently prompted the Korean invasion of June 1950.	• Secretary of State Dean Acheson gave a National Press Club speech in January 1950 • The speech suggested that the United States had abandoned commitments to both South Korea and Taiwan • The speech prompted the Korean invasion of June 1950

4.

Original Sentence	Essential Information
In fact, the Watergate Scandal only surfaced in June 1972 — almost two years before Nixon's resignation — beginning with the arrest of five men breaking and entering into the Democratic National Committee (DNC) headquarters at the Watergate complex.	• The Watergate Scandal surfaced in June 1972 • The scandal occurred almost two years before Nixon's resignation • The revelation of the scandal began with the arrest of five men breaking and entering into the Democratic National Committee (DNC) headquarters at the Watergate complex.

5.

Original Sentence	Essential Information
Second, the "policy" label implies a principle that will lead to more or less consistent action, what happened in practice was that different interpretations were often made and lines were blurred.	• The "policy" label implies a principle that will lead to more or less consistent action • However, what happened in practice was that different interpretations were often made • Lines were also often blurred

6.

Original Sentence	Essential Information
The process of symmetric and asymmetric replication has been observed in colon tissue and transplantations with animal models.	• The process of symmetric and asymmetric replication has been observed in colon tissue • The same has also been observed in transplantations with animal models

Step II: *List down essential information in each answer option point by point*

1.

	Answer Option	Essential Information
(a)	Two successful exhibitions attracted many people's attention and made Mies van der Rohe a respected public figure.	•
(b)	Mies van der Rohe's, a well-regarded celebrity, attracted many people to see his exhibitions.	•
(c)	The Museum of Modern Art drew a large crowd because it hosted the famous celebrity, Mies van der Rohe.	•
(d)	Philip Johnson and Henry-Russell Hitchcock's exhibition drew large crowds, including the artist Mies van der Rohe.	•

2.

	Answer Option	Essential Information
(a)	Logistics and tactical aviation were a costly substitute for heavily artillery, and were still used until early 1968.	•
(b)	They refused to give up control of their own logistics and tactical aviation until early 1968, even though these were very expensive compared to heavy artillery.	•
(c)	In early 1968, they used heavy artillery because having their own logistics and tactical aviation were too costly.	•
(d)	Heavy artillery is a costly substitute for logistics and tactical aviation, and no one was willing to give up control until after 1968.	•

3.

	Answer Option	Essential Information
(a)	The Korean invasion of June 1950 inspired Secretary of State Dean Acheson's National Press Club speech.	•
(b)	The United States appointed Secretary of State Dean Acheson to give a speech at the National Press Club to prevent the Korean invasion.	•
(c)	After the United States abandoned commitments to South Korea and Taiwan, Secretary of State Dean Acheson gave a speech at the National Press Club.	•
(d)	The Korean invasion of June 1950 was triggered by Secretary of State Dean Acheson's National Press Club speech which implied that the United States had abandoned commitments to both South Korea and Taiwan.	•

4.

	Answer Option	Essential Information
(a)	After the Watergate Scandal surfaced, five men broke and entered into the Democratic National Committee (DNC) headquarters at the Watergate complex.	•
(b)	Although the Watergate Scandal came to light in June 1972 after the arrest of five men breaking and entering into the Watergate complex, Nixon only resigned two years later.	•
(c)	Nixon resigned two years before the Watergate scandal surfaced in June 1972 following the arrest of five men breaking and entering into the Democratic National Committee (DNC) headquarters at the Watergate complex.	•
(d)	After Nixon resigned in 1972 over the Watergate scandal, five men broke and entered into the Democratic National Committee (DNC) headquarters at the Watergate complex.	•

5.

	Answer Option	Essential Information
(a)	Although the "policy" label suggests that consistent action would follow, varying interpretations were often made and there was a lack of clarity.	•
(b)	The "policy" label led to different interpretations and blurry lines in practice.	•
(c)	The principle of having a "policy" label means that we should see consistent action, and not different interpretations with blurry lines.	•
(d)	The "policy" label caused several different interpretations instead of consistent action.	•

6.

	Answer Option	Essential Information
(a)	Colon tissue has gone through the process of symmetric and asymmetric replication.	•
(b)	Colon tissue has been transplanted with animal models via the process of symmetric and asymmetric replication.	•
(c)	Both colon tissue and transplantations with animal models have involved symmetric and asymmetric replication.	•
(d)	Colon tissue has been processed by symmetric and asymmetric replication.	•

Answers:

1.

	Answer Option	Essential Information
(a)	Two successful exhibitions attracted many people's attention and made Mies van der Rohe a respected public figure.	• Two successful exhibitions attracted many people's attention • The exhibitions made Mies van der Rohe a respected public figure
(b)	Mies van der Rohe, a well-regarded celebrity, attracted many people to see his exhibitions.	• Mies van der Rohe is a well-regarded celebrity • He attracted many people to see his exhibitions
(c)	The Museum of Modern Art drew a large crowd because it hosted the famous celebrity, Mies van der Rohe.	• The Museum of Modern Art drew a large crowd • This is because it hosted the famous celebrity, Mies van der Rohe
(d)	Philip Johnson and Henry-Russell Hitchcock's exhibition drew large crowds, including the artist Mies van der Rohe.	• Philip Johnson and Henry-Russell Hitchcock's exhibition drew large crowds • The crowd included the artist Mies van der Rohe

2.

	Answer Option	Essential Information
(a)	Logistics and tactical aviation were a costly substitute for heavily artillery, and were still used until early 1968.	• Logistics and tactical aviation were a costly substitute for heavily artillery • Logistics and tactical aviation were still used until early 1968
(b)	They refused to give up control of their own logistics and tactical aviation until early 1968, even though these were very expensive compared to heavy artillery.	• They refused to give up control of their own logistics and tactical aviation until early 1968 • This was even though these were very expensive compared to heavy artillery
(c)	In early 1968, they used heavy artillery because having their own logistics and tactical aviation were too costly.	• In early 1968, they used heavy artillery • This was because having their own logistics and tactical aviation were too costly
(d)	Heavy artillery is a costly substitute for logistics and tactical aviation, and no one was willing to give up control until after 1968.	• Heavy artillery is a costly substitute for logistics and tactical aviation • No one was willing to give up control until after 1968

3.

	Answer Option	Essential Information
(a)	The Korean invasion of June 1950 inspired Secretary of State Dean Acheson's National Press Club speech.	• The Korean invasion of June 1950 inspired Secretary of State Dean Acheson • This was reflected in his National Press Club speech
(b)	The United States appointed Secretary of State Dean Acheson to give a speech at the National Press Club to prevent the Korean invasion.	• The United States appointed Secretary of State Dean Acheson to give a speech at the National Press Club • This was done to prevent the Korean invasion
(c)	After the United States abandoned commitments to South Korea and Taiwan, Secretary of State Dean Acheson gave a speech at the National Press Club.	• The United States abandoned commitments to South Korea and Taiwan • Following this, Secretary of State Dean Acheson gave a speech at the National Press Club

(d)	The Korean invasion of June 1950 was triggered by Secretary of State Dean Acheson's National Press Club speech which implied that the United States had abandoned commitments to both South Korea and Taiwan.	• Secretary of State Dean Acheson gave the National Press Club speech • The speech implied that the United States had abandoned commitments to both South Korea and Taiwan • This triggered the Korean invasion of June 1950

4.

	Answer Option	**Essential Information**
(a)	After the Watergate Scandal surfaced, five men broke and entered into the Democratic National Committee (DNC) headquarters at the Watergate complex.	• The Watergate Scandal surfaced • Following this, five men broke and entered into the Democratic National Committee (DNC) headquarters at the Watergate complex
(b)	Although the Watergate Scandal came to light in June 1972 after the arrest of five men breaking and entering into the Watergate complex, Nixon only resigned two years later.	• The Watergate Scandal came to light in June 1972 • This was after the arrest of five men breaking and entering into the Watergate complex • However, Nixon only resigned two years later
(c)	Nixon resigned two years before the Watergate scandal surfaced in June 1972 following the arrest of five men breaking and entering into the Democratic National Committee (DNC) headquarters at the Watergate complex.	• Nixon resigned two years before the Watergate scandal surfaced in June 1972 • The scandal surfaced following the arrest of five men breaking and entering into the Democratic National Committee (DNC) headquarters at the Watergate complex
(d)	After Nixon resigned in 1972 over the Watergate scandal, five men broke and entered into the Democratic National Committee (DNC) headquarters at the Watergate complex.	• Nixon resigned in 1972 over the Watergate scandal • After this, five men broke and entered into the Democratic National Committee (DNC) headquarters at the Watergate complex

5.

	Answer Option	Essential Information
(a)	Although the "policy" label suggests that consistent action would follow, varying interpretations were often made and there was a lack of clarity.	• The "policy" label suggests that consistent action would follow • However, varying interpretations were often made • There was also a lack of clarity
(b)	The "policy" label led to different interpretations and blurry lines in practice.	• The "policy" label led to different interpretations • It also led to blurry lines in practice
(c)	The principle of having a "policy" label means that we should see consistent action, and not different interpretations with blurry lines.	• The principle of having a "policy" label means that we should see consistent action • It should not result in different interpretations with blurry lines
(d)	The "policy" label caused several different interpretations instead of consistent action.	• The "policy" label caused several different interpretations • This was instead of consistent action

6.

	Answer Option	Essential Information
(a)	Colon tissue has gone through the process of symmetric and asymmetric replication.	• Colon tissue has gone through symmetric and asymmetric replication
(b)	Colon tissue has been transplanted with animal models via the process of symmetric and asymmetric replication.	• Colon tissue was transplanted with animal models • This was done with symmetric and asymmetric replication
(c)	Both colon tissue and transplantations with animal models have involved symmetric and asymmetric replication.	• Colon tissue has involved symmetric and asymmetric replication • Transplantations with animal models have also involved symmetric and asymmetric replication
(d)	Colon tissue has been processed by symmetric and asymmetric replication.	• Colon tissue was processed by symmetric and asymmetric replication

Step III: *Eliminate answer options that do not possess all essential information. Then, analyze the remaining options and select the best choice*

1.

Original Sentence	Essential Information
The enormous publicity garnered by "The Dwelling" exhibit and the 1932 International Style Exhibition curated by Philip Johnson and Henry-Russell Hitchcock at the Museum of Modern Art, New York had elevated Mies van der Rohe's status to that of a well-regarded celebrity.	• "The Dwelling" and the 1932 Exhibition attracted a lot of publicity • The 1932 Exhibition was curated by Philip Johnson and Henry-Russell Hitchcock at the Museum of Modern Art, New York • These exhibitions boosted Mies van der Rohe's status • Thereafter, he became a well-regarded celebrity

	Essential Information	Analysis
(a)	• Two successful exhibitions attracted many people's attention • The exhibitions made Mies van der Rohe a respected public figure	• Correct
(b)	• Mies van der Rohe is a well-regarded celebrity • He attracted many people to see his exhibitions	• Incorrect — Mies van der Rohe only became a well-regarded celebrity after the exhibitions
(c)	• The Museum of Modern Art drew a large crowd • This is because it hosted the famous celebrity, Mies van der Rohe	• Incorrect — Mies van der Rohe only became a well-regarded celebrity after the exhibitions
(d)	• Philip Johnson and Henry-Russell Hitchcock's exhibition drew large crowds • The crowd included the artist Mies van der Rohe	• Incorrect — Mies van der Rohe was featured in the exhibition. He was not part of the crowd attending the exhibition.

2.

Original Sentence	Essential Information
They had their own logistics and tactical aviation, which they used as a costly substitute for heavy artillery and which they refused to relinquish any control over until early 1968.	• They had their own logistics and tactical aviation • The logistics and tactical aviation was an expensive substitute for heavy artillery • They refused to give up control over logistics and tactical aviation until early 1968

	Essential Information	Analysis
(a)	• Logistics and tactical aviation were a costly substitute for heavily artillery • Logistics and tactical aviation were still used until early 1968	• Correct, but option (b) is better
(b)	• They refused to give up control of their own logistics and tactical aviation until early 1968 • This was even though these were very expensive compared to heavy artillery	• Correct — Not only states that they refused to give up control of their own logistics and tactical aviation until early 1968, but also compares these against heavy artillery
(c)	• In early 1968, they used heavy artillery • This was because having their own logistics and tactical aviation were too costly	• Incorrect — The passage did not state why they replaced logistics and tactical aviation with heavy artillery
(d)	• Heavy artillery is a costly substitute for logistics and tactical aviation • No one was willing to give up control until after 1968	• Incorrect — They gave up control of logistics and tactical aviation after 1968

3.

Original Sentence	Essential Information
Secretary of State Dean Acheson's National Press Club speech in January 1950 seemed to indicate that the United States had abandoned commitments to both South Korea and Taiwan, which subsequently prompted the Korean invasion of June 1950.	• Secretary of State Dean Acheson gave a National Press Club speech in January 1950 • The speech suggested that the United States had abandoned commitments to both South Korea and Taiwan • The speech prompted the Korean invasion of June 1950

	Essential Information	Analysis
(a)	• The Korean invasion of June 1950 inspired Secretary of State Dean Acheson • This was reflected in his National Press Club speech	• Incorrect — The speech prompted the Korean invasion of June 1950, not vice versa
(b)	• The United States appointed Secretary of State Dean Acheson to give a speech at the National Press Club • This was done to prevent the Korean invasion	• Incorrect — The sentence does not state that the United States appointed Secretary of State Dean Acheson to give a speech at the National Press Club. Further, the speech prompted the Korean invasion of June 1950, and was not given to prevent it
(c)	• The United States abandoned commitments to South Korea and Taiwan • Following this, Secretary of State Dean Acheson gave a speech at the National Press Club	• Incorrect — The speech suggested that the United States had abandoned commitments to both South Korea and Taiwan
(d)	• Secretary of State Dean Acheson gave the National Press Club speech • The speech implied that the United States had abandoned commitments to both South Korea and Taiwan • This triggered the Korean invasion of June 1950	• Correct

4.

Original Sentence	Essential Information
In fact, the Watergate Scandal only surfaced in June 1972 — almost two years before Nixon's resignation — beginning with the arrest of five men breaking and entering into the Democratic National Committee (DNC) headquarters at the Watergate complex.	• The Watergate Scandal surfaced in June 1972 • The scandal occurred almost two years before Nixon's resignation • The revelation of the scandal began with the arrest of five men breaking and entering into the Democratic National Committee (DNC) headquarters at the Watergate complex.

	Essential Information	Analysis
(a)	• The Watergate Scandal surfaced • Following this, five men broke and entered into the Democratic National Committee (DNC) headquarters at the Watergate complex	• Incorrect — The revelation of the scandal began with the arrest of five men breaking and entering into the Democratic National Committee (DNC) headquarters at the Watergate complex
(b)	• The Watergate Scandal came to light in June 1972 • This was after the arrest of five men breaking and entering into the Watergate complex • However, Nixon only resigned two years later	• Correct
(c)	• Nixon resigned two years before the Watergate scandal surfaced in June 1972 • The scandal surfaced following the arrest of five men breaking and entering into the Democratic National Committee (DNC) headquarters at the Watergate complex	• Incorrect — The scandal occurred almost two years before Nixon's resignation
(d)	• Nixon resigned in 1972 over the Watergate scandal • After this, five men broke and entered into the Democratic National Committee (DNC) headquarters at the Watergate complex	• Incorrect — The scandal occurred almost two years before Nixon's resignation

5.

Original Sentence	Essential Information
Second, the "policy" label implies a principle that will lead to more or less consistent action, but what happened in practice was that different interpretations were often made and lines were blurred.	• The "policy" label implies a principle that will lead to more or less consistent action • However, what happened in practice was that different interpretations were often made • Lines were also often blurred

	Essential Information	Analysis
(a)	• The "policy" label suggests that consistent action would follow • However, varying interpretations were often made • There was also a lack of clarity	• Correct
(b)	• The "policy" label led to different interpretations • It also led to blurry lines in practice	• Incorrect — The "policy" label did not cause different interpretations and blurry lines in practice
(c)	• The principle of having a "policy" label means that we should see consistent action • It should not result in different interpretations with blurry lines	• Incorrect — The "policy" label only implies a principle that will lead to more or less consistent action
(d)	• The "policy" label caused several different interpretations • This was instead of consistent action	• Incorrect — The "policy" label only implies a principle that will lead to more or less consistent action

6.

Original Sentence	Essential Information
The process of symmetric and asymmetric replication has been observed in colon tissue and transplantations with animal models.	• The process of symmetric and asymmetric replication has been observed in colon tissue • The same has also been observed in transplantations with animal models

	Essential Information	Analysis
(a)	• Colon tissue has gone through symmetric and asymmetric replication	• Incorrect — Left out transplantations with animal models
(b)	• Colon tissue was transplanted with animal models • This was done with symmetric and asymmetric replication	• Incorrect — Colon tissue was not transplanted with animal models

(c)	• Colon tissue has involved symmetric and asymmetric replication • Transplantations with animal models have also involved symmetric and asymmetric replication	• Correct
(d)	• Colon tissue was processed by symmetric and asymmetric replication	• Incorrect — Left out transplantations with animal models; colon tissue was not processed by symmetric and asymmetric replication

Succinct Summaries

One of the most important things you will have to do in life — and not just for the TOEFL — is to summarize documents. These documents can range from one-pagers to thick stacks of paper, so the better you are at summarizing, the more efficiently you'll be able to do the job.

The TOEFL tests your summarizing skills in another way. This is part of the third level of reading, which the TOEFL calls "reading to learn."

However, instead of asking you to write a summary of a passage, it provides multiple choice questions.

These questions will ask you to select three answer choices that best represent the important ideas within the passage. On the bright side, half the work is already done for you. All you have to do is to pick and choose from a selection of answer choices that have already been prepared. On the not-so-bright side, which answer options do you choose? Like paraphrasing, summarizing can also be tricky.

We like to keep it simple. Thus, as always, here are the three simple steps that you need to do in order to master the art of summarizing.

Simple Steps

1. Underline keywords in the introductory sentence and identify the key points.
2. Underline keywords in the remaining answer options. Eliminate answer choices that are not part of the introductory sentence's main idea or that are only very minor points.
3. Match the answer options' key points to the introductory sentence. If still unsure, then analyze relevant portions of the passage and determine if they are important enough to be part of the summary.

Elaboration with Examples

Let's first look at a shorter passage, followed by a longer one.

Sample passage:

Nuclear Weapons

Whether or not nuclear weapons contributed to keeping the peace between East and West is debatable. Mutually Assured Destruction (MAD) predicts that if both sides have enough power to wipe out the other, then there is no rational incentive to initiate a conflict. In this sense, nuclear weapons made deterrence (discouragement by fear) the key strategy for the superpowers by encouraging prudence. With MAD, the superpowers had a common interest in avoiding nuclear war. There are certainly examples that attest to this, or seem to, such as Russia's refrain from interfering in the airlift at the height of the Berlin blockade crisis in the summer of 1948. But what is it exactly about nuclear weapons that make them so different? Destructive power is nothing new, and the fire-bombing of Tokyo and Dresden shows us that conventional weapons are just as lethal on a large scale. Rather, it is the psychological edge of nuclear weapons — with the swift and certain destruction that they guarantee — that sets them apart.

During the early years of the Cold War, under President Truman and in the aftermath of Hiroshima, there was a strong sense of shock and outrage at nuclear weapons. This was picked up on by American leaders, who frequently made references to Hiroshima. According to John Emerson in November 1950, who was in the State Department's Bureau of Far Eastern Affairs, "The A-bomb has the status of a peculiar monster conceived by American cunning." John Foster Dulles also recognized, "Any nation that is first to make use of a new and terrible weapon is likely to bear — both in the eyes of its own citizens and those of the rest of the world as well — a particularly moral responsibility." Truman himself described the atomic bomb as "terrible" and that "it should not be used on innocent men, women, and children who have nothing whatever to do with this military aggression."

Against this backdrop of strong sentiment regarding the effects of the nuclear bomb, the United States entered the Korean War and came close to defeat more than once, particularly after Chinese intervention in 1950. Using the atomic bomb was certainly on the cards. General MacArthur recommended bombing China, which later led to his removal. But why was there such restraint? It can certainly be argued that part of it was due to the stigma attached to the use of nuclear weapons. From that aspect, nuclear weapons contributed to peace in the sense that their promised destruction led leaders to work towards restraint.

But this assessment would not be whole. There were other strategic considerations and contingencies that could similarly have prevented the United States from escalating the conflict. A close reading of the quotes extracted from Emerson, Dulles and Truman implicitly suggests that the concern is not entirely with the horror of nuclear weapons, but the reaction that it will elicit. Domestically, there was the concern for public opinion backlash. Internationally, there was the fear that escalating with the atomic bomb could break apart the United Nations coalition that was fighting in Korea. Furthermore, there was also the danger of dragging the Soviet Union into the war.

Sample question:

An introductory sentence for a brief summary of the passage is provided below.

Complete the summary by selecting the THREE answer choices that express the most important ideas in the passage.

Some sentences do not belong in the summary because they express ideas that are not presented in the passage or are minor ideas in the passage. **This question is worth 2 points.**

Write your answer choices in the spaces where they belong. You can write in the number of the answer choice or the whole sentence.

It is the psychological edge of nuclear weapons — with the swift and certain destruction that they guarantee — that set them apart from conventional weapons.
•
•
•

Answer choices:

a) According to the theory of Mutually Assured Destruction (MAD), there is no reason why both sides will clash if both sides have enough power to destroy each other.

b) There was a strong sense of shock and outrage at nuclear weapons during the early years of the Cold War, and American leaders frequently made references to the Hiroshima nuclear attack.

c) Russia decided not to interfere in the airlift when tensions rose during the Berlin blockade crisis in the summer of 1948.

d) Despite coming close to defeat more than once, the United States did not use the atomic bomb and General MacArthur, who recommended bombing China, was even removed.

e) However, there are other aspects and factors that could have prevented the United States from using nuclear weapons, such as the fear of public opinion backlash or the possibility that this could drag the Soviet Union into the war.

f) Nuclear weapons have been described as a "peculiar monster conceived by American cunning."

1. Underline keywords in the introductory sentence and identify the key points

Introductory Sentence	Key Points
It is the <u>psychological edge</u> of nuclear weapons — with the <u>swift</u> and <u>certain destruction</u> that they guarantee — that set them apart from conventional weapons.	• Nuclear weapons have a psychological edge • Key features of this psychological edge are the swift and certain destruction that they guarantee • These features make nuclear weapons very different from conventional weapons

If you recall what you learnt in "Top Tip 4: Structure and Organization II," you would be able to identify this introductory sentence as a compare/contrast type question. The summary should essentially be a detailed comparison of why nuclear weapons are different from conventional weapons.

2. Underline keywords in the remaining answer options. Eliminate answer choices that are not part of the introductory sentence's main idea or that are only very minor points

You can use a framework similar to the one used in "Top Tip 5: Perfect Paraphrasing" to extract the key points from the answer options. In practice, summarizing is like putting numerous paraphrased sentences together.

By doing this, you can clearly see the answers (a) and (c) have nothing to do with what makes nuclear weapons different from conventional weapons. Thus, you can eliminate them.

You will then be left with (b), (d), (e) and (f).

	Answer Option	Essential Information
(a)	According to the <u>theory</u> of <u>Mutually Assured Destruction (MAD)</u>, there is no reason why both sides will clash if both sides have enough power to destroy each other.	• The theory of Mutually Assured Destruction (MAD) stipulates that if both sides have enough power to destroy each other, then they will not clash
(b)	There was a strong sense of <u>shock</u> and <u>outrage</u> at nuclear weapons during the early years of the <u>Cold War</u>, and <u>American leaders</u> frequently made <u>references</u> to the <u>Hiroshima nuclear attack.</u>	• People were generally shocked and outraged at nuclear weapons during the early years of the Cold War • This is also reflected in how American leaders made frequent references to the Hiroshima nuclear attack
(c)	<u>Russia</u> decided <u>not to interfere</u> in the <u>airlift</u> when tensions rose during the <u>Berlin blockade crisis</u> in the summer of 1948.	• Russia did not intervene in the airlift during the Berlin blockade crisis • This occurred in the summer of 1948
(d)	Despite coming close to defeat more than once, the United States did not use the atomic bomb and <u>General MacArthur,</u> who recommended bombing China, was even <u>removed.</u>	• The United States came close to defeat more than once • But it did not use the atomic bomb • Conversely, General MacArthur who recommended bombing China, was removed
(e)	However, there are <u>other aspects and factors</u> that could have prevented the United States from using nuclear weapons, such as the fear of <u>public opinion backlash</u> or the possibility that this could <u>drag the Soviet Union into the war.</u>	• There could be other reasons as to why United States did not use nuclear weapons • These reasons include the fear of public opinion backlash • It also includes the fear of dragging the Soviet Union into the war
(f)	Nuclear weapons have been described as a "<u>peculiar monster</u> conceived by American cunning."	• Nuclear weapons: "peculiar monster conceived by American cunning"

3. *Match the answer options' key points to the introductory sentence. If still unsure, then analyze relevant portions of the passage and determine if they are important enough to be part of the summary*

Have a systematic way of analyzing each option. What happens to most students is that they often get confused by similar answer options — not all of them are accurate. Usually, they end up guessing, which means you may lose out on crucial marks.

Introductory Sentence	Key Points
It is the <u>psychological edge</u> of nuclear weapons — with the <u>swift</u> and <u>certain destruction</u> that they guarantee — that set them apart from conventional weapons.	• Nuclear weapons have a psychological edge • Key features of this psychological edge are the swift and certain destruction that they guarantee • These features make nuclear weapons very different from conventional weapons

	Essential Information	Analysis
(b)	• People were generally shocked and outraged at nuclear weapons during the early years of the Cold War • This is also reflected in how American leaders made frequent references to the Hiroshima nuclear attack	• Correct — Nuclear weapons caused shock and outrage. The fact that American leaders made frequent references to the Hiroshima nuclear attack also shows that nuclear weapons are different from conventional weapons
(d)	• The United States came close to defeat more than once • But it did not use the atomic bomb • Conversely, General MacArthur who recommended bombing China, was removed	• Incorrect — This does not explain why nuclear weapons are different
(e)	• There could be other reasons as to why United States did not use nuclear weapons • These reasons include the fear of public opinion backlash • It also includes the fear of dragging the Soviet Union into the war	• Correct — This provides other viewpoints as to why the United States did not want to use nuclear weapons. Public opinion backlash is related to the psychological effect of nuclear weapons
(f)	• Nuclear weapons: "peculiar monster conceived by American cunning"	• Correct — The description of nuclear weapons as a "peculiar monster" sets it apart from other weapons

However, what if you come across a particularly difficult question that requires you to refer back to the original passage?

Let's take a look at another example:

Sample passage:

Détente between the United States and the Soviet Union

Détente between the Soviet Union and the United States refers to a thawing of tension during the Cold War. It must not be confused with friendship or alliance; it is "rooted in a recognition of difference, and inspired by a premonition of disaster. The word can be applied only to an adversarial relationship." Some pinpoint the start of détente with the conclusion of the Strategic Arms Limitation Talks (SALT I) in 1972. However, there were already events signaling the shift towards détente in the 1960s, especially with the final signature of the Nuclear Non-Proliferation Treaty in July 1968.

In order to understand the period of détente, the changes in the structural backdrop must first be identified. There were two very important changes in the world system in the late 1960s and early 1970s. First, the Soviet Union had achieved parity with the United States. This is reflected in the shift in Soviet behavior. In 1964, Khrushchev's First Deputy Premier, Kosygin, rejected President Johnson's proposal for a verified freeze on strategic arms. However, soon after, the Soviet Union gained superiority in megatonnage and numbers of strategic missiles. Domestic factors were intertwined here as Soviet leaders had a doctrinal change, where "avoiding the nuclear devastation of Russia became the governing objective." Entering into agreements with the United States would not only ensure that the United States did not engage in "ambitious strategic modernization programs," but would also freeze the Soviet Union into a position of seeing eye-to-eye with the United States. In this sense, entering into détente was a strategic move that was only acceptable under the condition of power parity.

The second important change in the structural system was the rise of China as a communist power and the Sino-Soviet split. This caused a shift in the overall balance of power. Cracks in the Sino-Soviet relationship appeared as early as 1960 and were exacerbated by Khrushchev's denunciation of

Stalin. It eroded the legitimacy of the Soviet leadership of the communist bloc. Mao's claims over Russian territory also sparked deep concern in the Soviet Union. According to Mao, "A hundred years ago they [the Russians] incorporated the territory to the East of Lake Baikal, including Khabarovsk, Vladivostok and the Kamchatka Peninsula ... We have not settled these accounts with them." This fear was reflected in the rapid proliferation of Soviet forces along the Eastern frontier. The 12 Soviet divisions in 1961 were transformed into 25 in 1969, and 45 by 1973. China also had a huge army, second in size only to the Soviet Army itself, and a huge population to back it up.

Losing China as an ally therefore struck a blow to the balance of power. Worse, there was the fear that China might join the United States against the Soviet Union. Indeed, the progress in Sino-American relations following President Nixon's first visit in 1972 certainly gave the Soviet Union a cause for concern. In February 1973, Kissinger made his fifth visit to China, which resulted in the establishment of official liaison offices in Beijing and Washington. Trade between the two countries had also leapt from $5 million in 1970 to $900 million in 1973. It was not in the Soviet Union's strategic interest to allow China to get close to the West; increased trade and technology transfers from the West would make China a more formidable adversary right next door.

Sample question:

An introductory sentence for a brief summary of the passage is provided below.

Complete the summary by selecting the THREE answer choices that express the most important ideas in the passage.

Some sentences do not belong in the summary because they express ideas that are not presented in the passage or are minor ideas in the passage. **This question is worth 2 points.**

Write your answer choices in the spaces where they belong. You can write in the number of the answer choice or the whole sentence.

> During the period of détente between the United States and the Soviet Union, there were structural changes in the backdrop.
>
> -
> -
> -

Answer choices:

a) There are some who argue that the period of détente began with the completion of the Strategic Arms Limitation Talks (SALT I) in 1972.

b) The first structural change was when the Soviet Union achieved parity with the United States, which marked a change in Soviet behavior.

c) The rise of China as a communist power and the following Sino-Soviet split that occurred also caused a structural shift in the overall balance of power.

d) The Soviet army along the Eastern frontier expanded in the 1960s, going from 12 divisions in 1961 into 25 in 1969.

e) When President Nixon first visited China in 1972, this dealt an even deeper blow to the balance of power as the Soviet Union became fearful that China might set up an alliance with the United States.

f) Trade between China and the United States increased dramatically from $5 million in 1970 to $900 million in 1973.

Underline keywords in the introductory sentence and identify the key points.

Introductory Sentence	Key Points
During the period of <u>détente</u> between the United States and the Soviet Union, there were <u>structural changes in the backdrop</u>.	• During détente, there were structural changes in the backdrop

This is a cause/effect question, testing you on whether you can accurately summarize what caused the author to say there were structural changes in the backdrop.

Underline keywords in the remaining answer options.
Eliminate answer choices that are not part of the introductory sentence's main idea or that are only very minor points.

A quick elimination of the unlikely answers will leave you with fewer to ponder over. This means quicker and more accurate answers.

By doing so, you can eliminate (a) because it focuses on when détente began, and not the "structural changes in the backdrop."

	Answer Option	Essential Information
(a)	There are some who argue that the period of <u>détente began</u> with the <u>completion</u> of the <u>Strategic Arms Limitation Talks (SALT I) in 1972</u>.	• Détente began with the completion of the Strategic Arms Limitation Talks (SALT I) in 1972
(b)	The <u>first structural change</u> was when the <u>Soviet Union achieved parity</u> with the United States, which marked a <u>change in Soviet behavior</u>.	• The first structural change was when the Soviet Union achieved parity with the United States • This marked a change in Soviet behavior
(c)	The <u>rise of China</u> as a communist power and the following <u>Sino-Soviet split</u> that occurred also caused a <u>structural shift</u> in the overall <u>balance of power</u>.	• There was a structural shift in the overall balance of power • This was caused by the rise of China • The other factor was the Sino-Soviet split that occurred after the rise of China
(d)	The <u>Soviet army</u> along the <u>Eastern frontier expanded</u> in the 1960s, going from 12 divisions in 1961 into 25 in 1969.	• The Soviet army along the Eastern frontier expanded in the 1960s • To give a clearer picture, it went from 12 divisions in 1961 to 25 in 1969
(e)	When <u>President Nixon first visited China</u> in 1972, this dealt an even <u>deeper blow to the balance of power</u> as the <u>Soviet Union became fearful</u> that <u>China might set up an alliance with the United States</u>.	• President Nixon first visited China in 1972 • This dealt an even deeper blow to the balance of power • This was because the Soviet Union became fearful that China might ally with the United States
(f)	<u>Trade</u> between <u>China</u> and the <u>United States increased dramatically</u> from $5 million in 1970 to $900 million in 1973.	• Trade between China and the United States increased dramatically • It went from $5 million in 1970 to $900 million in 1973

Match the answer options' key points to the introductory sentence.
If still unsure, then analyze relevant portions of the passage and
determine if they are important enough to be part of the summary.

Refer to the key points that you extracted from the introductory sentence while doing your analysis.

Introductory Sentence	Key Points
During the period of <u>détente</u> between the United States and the Soviet Union, there were <u>structural changes in the backdrop</u>.	• During détente, there were structural changes in the backdrop

Suppose, however, that while you are sure about some answers, there are other options that are more ambiguous. These require you to search for the relevant portions in the passage. This will provide you with more information on which you can base your decision.

By doing so, you spend more time focusing on the more challenging questions that require more thought. This is called strategic management of time.

Let's see how this works by digging deeper into answer options (d), (e) and (f):

	Essential Information	Analysis
(b)	• The first structural change was when the Soviet Union achieved parity with the United States • This marked a change in Soviet behavior	• Correct — This is a clear reference to a structural change
(c)	• There was a structural shift in the overall balance of power • This was caused by the rise of China • The other factor was the Sino-Soviet split that occurred after the rise of China	• Correct — This is also a clear reference to a structural change
(d)	• The Soviet army along the Eastern frontier expanded in the 1960s • To give a clearer picture, it went from 12 divisions in 1961 to 25 in 1969	• Relevant portion in passage: Mao's claims over Russian territory also sparked deep concern in the Soviet Union... This fear was reflected in the rapid proliferation of Soviet forces along the Eastern frontier. The 12 Soviet divisions in 1961 were transformed into 25 in 1969, and 45 by 1973. China also had a huge army, second in size only to the Soviet Army itself, and a huge population to back it up. • Incorrect — This focuses on what happened after Mao made claims over Russian territory. While relevant, it is a minor point

(e)	• President Nixon first visited China in 1972 • This dealt an even deeper blow to the balance of power • This was because the Soviet Union became fearful that China might ally with the United States	• Relevant portion: Losing China as an ally therefore struck a blow to the balance of power. Worse, there was the fear that China might join the United States against the Soviet Union. Indeed, the progress in Sino-American relations following President Nixon's first visit in 1972 certainly gave the Soviet Union a cause for concern. • Correct — Recall that in option (c) there was a reference to the balance of power as a structural shift. Answer option (e) expands on why and how this structural shift worsened.
(f)	• Trade between China and the United States increased dramatically • It went from $5 million in 1970 to $900 million in 1973	• Relevant portion in passage: It was not in the Soviet Union's strategic interest to allow China to get close to the West; increased trade and technology transfers from the West would make China a more formidable adversary right next door. • Incorrect — This focuses on why the Soviet Union should be concerned about increased trade and technology transfers between China and the West, not on the structural change

Now that you've seen how it works, it's time for you to put it into practice.

TOEFL Trainer

This "Top Tip" *TOEFL Trainer* will be arranged slightly differently due to the lengthiness of the passages. Instead of separating out the *Simple Steps* so that you practice each "Simple Step" progressively, this section will test your ability to apply the full set of *Simple Steps* at one go. Good luck!

1. **Urban Renewal in Ancient Times**

   Urban renewal in ancient times was closely associated with the politics of a city or nation. The dependence of ancient urban renewal on the ruler's will is often interpreted as a mechanism to prevent citizens from rebelling against the rise of a new national power. Some of the most common methods
5 of early urban renewal include the demolition of monuments and statues

from the preceding ruler's reign to make way for the installation of new ones exulting the current king's newfound power. This is what is called "destructive urban renewal."

A prime example of an ancient city shaped by the destructive forces of early urban renewal would be no other than ancient Rome. During the reign of Julius Caesar in 45 BC, great terrains were cleared for the building of a wall all around the city of Rome known as the Pomerium. The purpose of the wall's construction was to differentiate areas allocated for the ceremonial functions of the ruling class and the menial activities of the peasants. Caesar's propagation of the belief that the empire of Rome only exists within the Pomerium and no other person could enter certain areas except for him due to its sanctity served its purpose well — it elevated his status from an emperor to that of a God's.

In addition, Caesar also ordered the removal of the undergrowth surrounding the Capitoline Hill to form the Sacred Way, a route encircling the hill that ends at the temple of Jupiter. The Sacred Way was ancient Rome's main processional route for the endless parades held by the emperor and his generals to celebrate war victories. Soldiers would deposit war spoils in protruding "piles" along the length of the Sacred Way, symbolizing the growing wealth and sovereignty of the emperor. In AD 205, the steps from the ancient level of the Roman forum were demolished for the archway of Septimius Severus to be built. This tributary memorial in commemoration of Emperor Severus and sons' victory in the Parthian War was destroyed when Caracalla destroyed all images and inscriptions associated with Geta after the former murdered the latter. Hence, one can say that the notion of destruction is essential in the development of urban renewal and documentation of historical events in ancient Rome.

Apart from ancient Rome, the enclaves of medieval Paris presented another opportunity for destructive urban renewal. In the extremely hierarchical society of medieval Paris, the masses are driven by desperation and destitution to form cult-like groups where every member can enjoy the mutual sustenance and safety benefits from the numerous ties and associations with other members of the enclave. With their enclosed walls and surrounding gates, these fortress-like enclaves are an exact microcosm of the bigger city as a whole.

When King Henri the IV came into power, he worried about how the citizens' enormous private stake on the city's territory was a potential danger

to the societal status quo. His fear of the immense amount of liberty and freedom possessed by the underclass propagated the breaking down of the
45 damp, festering and diseased enclave-slums sprawled all over the left bank of Paris. The "opening up" of these enclaves does not only symbolize the collapse of these walled enclosures, but that of medieval Paris's rigid social structure as well. Hence, the loss of the citizens' physical space and identity as a form of urban renewal is just another opportunity for the monarch to
50 impose his authority over them in a subliminal way.

Author: Darell Koh

An introductory sentence for a brief summary of the passage is provided below.

Complete the summary by selecting the THREE answer choices that express the most important ideas in the passage.

Some sentences do not belong in the summary because they express ideas that are not presented in the passage or are minor ideas in the passage. **This question is worth 2 points.**

Write your answer choices in the spaces where they belong. You can write in the number of the answer choice or the whole sentence.

Urban renewal in ancient times was closely associated with the politics of a city or nation, and is sometimes used by the new ruler to consolidate and establish his newfound power.
•
•
•

Answer choices:

a) Julius Caesar, for example, used urban renewal to elevate his status from an emperor to that of a God's by building a wall around Rome known as the Pomerium,

b) King Henri the IV often worried about the threat his citizens posed to him due to their large private stake on the city's territory.

c) Citizens lost a large amount of physical space and identity in medieval France.

d) Some other methods of early urban renewal include the demolition of monuments and statues from the preceding ruler's reign to make way for the installation of new ones exulting the current king's newfound power.

e) Urban renewal was also used in medieval Paris, where King Henri the IV broke down the Parisian underclass' enclaves and imposed his authority over them in a subliminal way.

f) Emperor Severus and sons were respected army generals who managed to gain victory in the Parthian War.

Step I: *Underline keywords in the introductory sentence and identify the key points*

Introductory Sentence	Key Points
Urban renewal in ancient times was closely associated with the politics of a city or nation, and is sometimes used by the new ruler to consolidate and establish his newfound power.	•

Step II: *Underline keywords in the remaining answer options. Eliminate answer choices that are not part of the introductory sentence's main idea or that are only very minor points*

	Answer Option	Essential Information
(a)	Julius Caesar, for example, used urban renewal to elevate his status from an emperor to that of a God's by building a wall around Rome known as the Pomerium.	•
(b)	King Henri the IV often worried about the threat his citizens posed to him due to their large private stake on the city's territory.	•
(c)	Citizens lost a large amount of physical space and identity in medieval France.	•
(d)	Urban renewal was also used in medieval Paris, where King Henri the IV broke down the Parisian underclass' enclaves and imposed his authority over them in a subliminal way.	•
(e)	Some other methods of early urban renewal include the demolition of monuments and statues from the preceding ruler's reign to make way for the installation of new ones exulting the current king's newfound power.	•
(f)	Emperor Severus and sons were respected army generals who managed to gain victory in the Parthian War.	•

Step III: *Match the answer options' key points to the introductory sentence. If still unsure, then analyze relevant portions of the passage and determine if they are important enough to be part of the summary*

	Essential Information	Analysis
(a)	• Julius Caesar elevated his status • This was done by building a wall around Rome (the Pomerium)	•
(b)	• King Henri the IV worried about the threat his citizens posed • They had a large private stake on the city's territory	•
(c)	• Citizens lost physical space and identity	•
(d)	• King Henri the IV broke down the Parisian underclass' enclaves • He imposed his authority in a subliminal way	•
(e)	• Other methods of early urban renewal include the demolition of monuments and statues to install new ones exulting the current king's newfound power	•
(f)	• Emperor Severus and sons were respected army generals from the Parthian War	•

Answers:

Step I: *Underline keywords in the introductory sentence and identify the key points*

Introductory Sentence	Key Points
Urban renewal in ancient times was closely associated with the politics of a city or nation, and is sometimes used by the new ruler to consolidate and establish his newfound power.	• Urban renewal was closely associated with politics, as a new ruler could use it to consolidate newfound power.

Step II: *Underline keywords in the remaining answer options. Eliminate answer choices that are not part of the introductory sentence's main idea or that are only very minor points*

	Answer Option	Essential Information
(a)	Julius Caesar, for example, used urban renewal to elevate his status from an emperor to that of a God's by building a wall around Rome known as the Pomerium.	• Julius Caesar elevated his status • This was done by building a wall around Rome (the Pomerium)
(b)	King Henri the IV often worried about how the threat his citizens posed to him due to their large private stake on the city's territory.	• King Henri the IV worried about the threat his citizens posed • They had a large private stake on the city's territory
(c)	Citizens lost a large amount of physical space and identity in medieval France.	• Citizens lost physical space and identity
(d)	Urban renewal was also used in medieval Paris, where King Henri the IV broke down the Parisian underclass' enclaves and imposed his authority over them in a subliminal way.	• King Henri the IV broke down the Parisian underclass' enclaves • He imposed his authority in a subliminal way
(e)	Some other methods of early urban renewal include the demolition of monuments and statues from the preceding ruler's reign to make way for the installation of new ones exulting the current king's newfound power.	• Other methods of early urban renewal include the demolition of monuments and statues to install new ones exulting the current king's newfound power
(f)	Emperor Severus and sons were respected army generals who managed to gain victory in the Parthian War.	• Emperor Severus and sons were respected army generals from the Parthian War

Step III: *Match the answer options' key points to the introductory sentence. If still unsure, then analyze relevant portions of the passage and determine if they are important enough to be part of the summary*

Introductory Sentence	Key Points
Urban renewal in ancient times was closely associated with the politics of a city or nation, and is sometimes used by the new ruler to consolidate and establish his newfound power.	• Urban renewal was closely associated with politics, as a new ruler could use it to consolidate newfound power.

	Essential Information	Analysis
(a)	• Julius Caesar elevated his status • This was done by building a wall around Rome (the Pomerium)	• Correct — "Elevated status" is related to "consolidate newfound power"
(b)	• King Henri the IV worried about the threat his citizens posed • They had a large private stake on the city's territory	• Incorrect — This shows why rulers felt under threat
(c)	• Citizens lost physical space and identity	• Incorrect — This only states a consequence of urban renewal
(d)	• King Henri the IV broke down the Parisian underclass' enclaves • He imposed his authority in a subliminal way	• Correct — Details how King Henri the IV used urban renewal to consolidate his power
(e)	• Other methods of early urban renewal include the demolition of monuments and statues to install new ones exulting the current king's newfound power	• Correct — Explains some methods of early urban renewal
(f)	• Emperor Severus and sons were respected army generals from the Parthian War	• Incorrect — Unrelated to urban renewal or consolidating a ruler's newfound power

2. Development: A Brief History

The root of the word "development" can be generally defined as the process of realizing a potential or bringing something into activity. In the context of resource development, the term comes to mean the process of bringing a resource into use instead of being "wasted." "Development" is also commonly
5   used synonymously with the notion of "growth," though as Daly (1990) points out, the two are not the same. "Development" should be understood as a qualitative change or improvement, while "growth" is a quantitative increase in physical scale.

Nowadays, the term "development" is often used in relation to economics,
10   referring to the processes that increase an economy's potential to organize and to respond to outside factors. In a nutshell, the economy is a complex system based on the division of labor, specialization and the production of goods or services for markets instead of for personal consumption.

In economic development, the ultimate purpose is often growth, to
15 increase the capacity to produce surpluses and to accumulate wealth. In
this system of specialization, the market determines the value of products
and indirectly the ability of individuals to buy and consume. A belief then
develops that if development can increase the potential of a market's economy
for growth, it can also increase an individual's ability to consume and gain
20 wealth. In relation to this, another widely held belief is that development
is good for everyone. The rationale for this is that development brings
"untapped" resources (including physical, intellectual, human etc.) into
production that adds to the services or products available to the market.
As a result, these services or products increase in value and individuals
25 directly involved in the production process benefit first. These benefits will
eventually "trickle down" to other individuals in the market indirectly, so
theoretically even the poorest people in the community will benefit from
a development project given sufficient time.

The beliefs that "development" can profit everyone and that we want
30 to be wealthy are a couple of reasons that made "economic development"
such a powerful force for national movements. Another reason could be
the success that major European nations achieved since the colonial times,
so much so that other nations became convinced that the same process
of "development" could bring them equal affluence. These power nations
35 were emulated for their success, although the exploitative nature and often
the negative societal impacts of these "development" processes were often
overlooked. Economic growth and the accumulation of wealth have remained
an important goal for many nations to this day.

Author: Flora Wong

An introductory sentence for a brief summary of the passage is provided below.

Complete the summary by selecting the THREE answer choices that express the most important ideas in the passage.

Some sentences do not belong in the summary because they express ideas that are not presented in the passage or are minor ideas in the passage. **This question is worth 2 points.**

Write your answer choices in the spaces where they belong. You can write in the number of the answer choice or the whole sentence.

Nowadays, the term "development" is often used in relation to economics, and economic development is an attractive goal that is widely sought after.

-
-
-

Answer choices:

a) The root of the word "development" can be generally defined as the process of realizing a potential or bringing something into activity.

b) "Development" is also commonly used synonymously with the notion of "growth."

c) In economic development, the ultimate purpose is often growth, to increase the capacity to produce surpluses and to accumulate wealth.

d) The economy is a complex system based on the division of labor, specialization and the production of goods or services for markets instead of for personal consumption.

e) The beliefs that "development" can profit everyone and that we want to be wealthy are a couple of reasons that made "economic development" such a powerful force for national movements.

f) Furthermore, European nations have achieved so much since colonial times that other countries now believe "economic development" can bring them the same wealth.

Step I: *Underline keywords in the introductory sentence and identify the key points*

Introductory Sentence	Key Points
Nowadays, the term "development" is often used in relation to economics, and economic development is an attractive goal that is widely sought after.	•

Step II: *Underline keywords in the remaining answer options. Eliminate answer choices that are not part of the introductory sentence's main idea or that are only very minor points*

	Answer Option	Essential Information
(a)	The root of the word "development" can be generally defined as the process of realizing a potential or bringing something into activity.	•
(b)	"Development" is also commonly used synonymously with the notion of "growth."	•
(c)	In economic development, the ultimate purpose is often growth, to increase the capacity to produce surpluses and to accumulate wealth.	•
(d)	The economy is a complex system based on the division of labor, specialization and the production of goods or services for markets instead of for personal consumption.	•
(e)	The beliefs that "development" can profit everyone and that we want to be wealthy are a couple of reasons that made "economic development" such a powerful force for national movements.	•
(f)	Furthermore, European nations have achieved so much since colonial times that other countries now believe "economic development" can bring them the same wealth.	•

Step III: *Match the answer options' key points to the introductory sentence. If still unsure, then analyze relevant portions of the passage and determine if they are important enough to be part of the summary*

	Essential Information	Analysis
(a)	• Development means realizing potential	•
(b)	• Development is synonymous with growth	•
(c)	• Economic development's purpose is growth, increasing capacity, surpluses and wealth	•

(d)	• The economy is a complex system to produce goods and services for markets	•
(e)	• "Economic development" is a powerful force because of the beliefs that it can profit everyone and we want to be wealthy	•
(f)	• European nations' success caused other countries to believe that "economic development" can bring the same wealth	•

Answers:

Step I: *Underline keywords in the introductory sentence and identify the key points*

Introductory Sentence	Key Points
Nowadays, the term "development" is often used in relation to economics, and economic development is an attractive goal that is widely sought after.	• Economic development is an attractive goal that is widely sought after

Step II: *Underline keywords in the remaining answer options. Eliminate answer choices that are not part of the introductory sentence's main idea or that are only very minor points*

	Answer Option	Essential Information
(a)	The root of the word "development" can be generally defined as the process of realizing a potential or bringing something into activity.	• Development means realizing potential
(b)	"Development" is also commonly used synonymously with the notion of "growth."	• Development is synonymous with growth
(c)	In economic development, the ultimate purpose is often growth, to increase the capacity to produce surpluses and to accumulate wealth.	• Economic development's purpose is growth, increasing capacity, surpluses and wealth
(d)	The economy is a complex system based on the division of labor, specialization and the production of goods or services for markets instead of for personal consumption.	• The economy is a complex system to produce goods and services for markets

(e)	The beliefs that "development" can profit everyone and that we want to be wealthy are a couple of reasons that made "economic development" such a powerful force for national movements.	• "Economic development" is a powerful force because of the beliefs that it can profit everyone and we want to be wealthy
(f)	Furthermore, European nations have achieved so much since colonial times that other countries now believe "economic development" can bring them the same wealth.	• European nations' success caused other countries to believe that "economic development" can bring the same wealth

Step III: *Match the answer options' key points to the introductory sentence. If still unsure, then analyze relevant portions of the passage and determine if they are important enough to be part of the summary*

Introductory Sentence	Key Points
Nowadays, the term "development" is often used in relation to economics, and economic development is an attractive goal that is widely sought after.	• Economic development is an attractive goal that is widely sought after

	Essential Information	Analysis
(a)	• Development means realizing potential	• Incorrect — This is merely a definition
(b)	• Development is synonymous with growth	• Incorrect — This is merely a definition
(c)	• Economic development's purpose is growth, increasing capacity, surpluses and wealth	• Correct — Describes the main goal of development, which readers must understand before they can see why economic development is an attractive goal
(d)	• The economy is a complex system to produce goods and services for markets	• Incorrect — A minor detail about the economy, unrelated as to why economic development is so popular

(e)	• "Economic development" is a powerful force because of the beliefs that it can profit everyone and we want to be wealthy	• Correct — Explains why economic development is powerful
(f)	• European nations' success caused other countries to believe that "economic development" can bring the same wealth	• Correct — Explains another reason why economic development caught the eye of other nations

3. **The Origins of UNESCO**

   To understand why the United Nations Educational, Scientific and Cultural Organization (UNESCO) prizes cultural diversity, it is necessary to consider its origins. Founded in 1946, UNESCO was formed against a historical backdrop very different from today. Having just emerged from the shadow
5 of World War II, what was key in the minds of its founders was the need to build and maintain peace. The underlying logic was that cultural diversity is often the cause of conflict, or at least the excuse for it. When faced with strange cultures, humans react too easily with hostility, rather than seeking to understand, accommodate, negotiate, and compromise. The desire to build
10 peace through intercultural dialogue and understanding is reflected in the preamble of UNESCO's constitution: "That since wars begin in the minds of men, it is in the minds of men that the defenses of peace must be constructed."

   It was UNESCO's 1972 World Heritage Convention that brought the "little known international organization out of the wilderness and made it a
15 household name the world over." The Convention sought to identify, protect, and preserve "World Heritage sites," realized primarily through the World Heritage List that includes both cultural and natural sites of "outstanding universal value." Any State Party can nominate a site for inscription. A technical advisor sent by one of the Advisory Bodies will then evaluate
20 the nominated site. If it is a natural heritage site, the technical evaluator will come from the International Union for Conservation of Nature (IUCN). If it is a cultural heritage site, the technical evaluator will come from the International Council on Monuments and Sites (ICOMOS). However, it is the World Heritage Committee, consisting of representatives from 21
25 State Parties, which has the final say. This means that even if the technical evaluators do not recommend a site for inscription, the Committee may overturn the recommendation and inscribe the site nonetheless.

The Convention also provides for a World Heritage Fund to lend international assistance to threatened sites. However, the annual budget is
30 extremely low — in 2012, only US$4 million was given to support activities requested by the State Parties in need of international assistance. This effectively means that UNESCO has virtually no resources for enforcement.

The idea of an international fund to subsidize the maintenance and restoration work of monuments and sites had actually been around since
35 1946, but was twice rejected due to opposition from both developed and developing countries. The United States, for one, did not want an obligation to finance projects that could not be easily controlled. Correspondingly, developing countries were wary of possible Western intrusion into internal affairs. Up until 1964, the consensus was still that the preservation of ancient
40 sites should remain beyond UNESCO's competence and that "each state ought to ensure the preservation of its monuments at the national level."

An introductory sentence for a brief summary of the passage is provided below.

Complete the summary by selecting the THREE answer choices that express the most important ideas in the passage.

Some sentences do not belong in the summary because they express ideas that are not presented in the passage or are minor ideas in the passage. **This question is worth 2 points.**

Write your answer choices in the spaces where they belong. You can write in the number of the answer choice or the whole sentence.

UNESCO is an international body that aims to promote and protect cultural diversity.
•
•
•

Answer choices:

a) To understand why UNESCO prizes cultural diversity, it is necessary to consider its origins.

b) The desire to build peace through intercultural dialogue and understanding is reflected in the preamble of UNESCO's constitution.

c) It was UNESCO's 1972 World Heritage Convention that made the organization famous.

d) UNESCO's 1972 World Heritage Convention is a tool used to identify, protect, and preserve "World Heritage sites."

e) Furthermore, UNESCO also provides for a World Heritage Fund to lend international assistance to threatened sites.

f) The idea of an international fund to subsidize the maintenance and restoration work of monuments and sites had actually been around since 1946.

Step I: *Underline keywords in the introductory sentence and identify the key points*

Introductory Sentence	Key Points
UNESCO is an international body that aims to promote and protect cultural diversity.	•

Step II: *Underline keywords in the remaining answer options. Eliminate answer choices that are not part of the introductory sentence's main idea or that are only very minor points*

	Answer Option	Essential Information
(a)	To understand why UNESCO prizes cultural diversity, it is necessary to consider its origins.	•
(b)	The desire to build peace through intercultural dialogue and understanding is reflected in the preamble of UNESCO's constitution.	•
(c)	It was UNESCO's 1972 World Heritage Convention that made the organization famous.	•
(d)	UNESCO's 1972 World Heritage Convention is a tool used to identify, protect, and preserve "World Heritage sites."	•
(e)	Furthermore, UNESCO also provides for a World Heritage Fund to lend international assistance to threatened sites.	•
(f)	The idea of an international fund to subsidize the maintenance and restoration work of monuments and sites had actually been around since 1946.	•

Step III: *Match the answer options' key points to the introductory sentence. If still unsure, then analyze relevant portions of the passage and determine if they are important enough to be part of the summary*

	Essential Information	Analysis
(a)	• Consider UNESCO's origins to understand why it prizes cultural diversity	•
(b)	• The desire to build peace through intercultural dialogue and understanding is in the preamble of UNESCO's constitution	•
(c)	• UNESCO's 1972 World Heritage Convention made it famous	•
(d)	• UNESCO's 1972 World Heritage Convention is a tool • It is used to identify, protect and preserve "World Heritage Sites"	•
(e)	• UNESCO's World Heritage Fund lends international assistance to threatened sites	•
(f)	• The idea of an international fund had been around since 1946	•

Answers:

Step I: *Underline keywords in the introductory sentence and identify the key points*

Introductory Sentence	Key Points
UNESCO is an international body that aims to promote and protect cultural diversity.	• UNESCO is an international body • It promotes and protects cultural diversity

Step II: *Underline keywords in the remaining answer options. Eliminate answer choices that are not part of the introductory sentence's main idea or that are only very minor points*

	Answer Option	Essential Information
(a)	To <u>understand why UNESCO prizes cultural diversity</u>, it is necessary to <u>consider its origins</u>.	• Consider UNESCO's origins to understand why it prizes cultural diversity
(b)	<u>The desire to build peace</u> through <u>intercultural dialogue</u> and <u>understanding</u> is reflected in the <u>preamble</u> of <u>UNESCO's constitution</u>.	• The desire to build peace through intercultural dialogue and understanding is in the preamble of UNESCO's constitution
(c)	It was <u>UNESCO's 1972 World Heritage Convention</u> that made the organization <u>famous</u>.	• UNESCO's 1972 World Heritage Convention made it famous
(d)	<u>UNESCO's 1972 World Heritage Convention</u> is a <u>tool</u> used to <u>identify, protect, and preserve "World Heritage sites."</u>	• UNESCO's 1972 World Heritage Convention is a tool • It is used to identify, protect and preserve "World Heritage Sites"
(e)	Furthermore, <u>UNESCO</u> also provides for a <u>World Heritage Fund</u> to <u>lend international assistance to threatened sites</u>.	• UNESCO's World Heritage Fund lends international assistance to threatened sites
(f)	<u>The idea of an international fund</u> to subsidize the maintenance and restoration work of monuments and sites had actually <u>been around since 1946</u>.	• The idea of an international fund had been around since 1946

Step III: *Match the answer options' key points to the introductory sentence. If still unsure, then analyze relevant portions of the passage and determine if they are important enough to be part of the summary*

Introductory Sentence	Key Points
<u>UNESCO</u> is an <u>international body</u> that aims to <u>promote and protect cultural diversity</u>.	• UNESCO is an international body • It promotes and protects cultural diversity

	Essential Information	Analysis
(a)	• Consider UNESCO's origins to understand why it prizes cultural diversity	• Incorrect — This sentence merely tells you what you should consider in order to understand why it prizes cultural diversity, and not how UNESCO promotes and protects cultural diversity
(b)	• The desire to build peace through intercultural dialogue and understanding is in the preamble of UNESCO's constitution	• Correct — This shows proof that UNESCO promotes intercultural dialogue which is a way to support cultural diversity
(c)	• UNESCO's 1972 World Heritage Convention made it famous	• Incorrect — Stating how UNESCO became famous has nothing to do with its aims
(d)	• UNESCO's 1972 World Heritage Convention is a tool • It is used to identify, protect and preserve "World Heritage Sites"	• Correct — This explains the way in which UNESCO identifies, protects and preserves "World Heritage Sites," which are part of cultural diversity
(e)	• UNESCO's World Heritage Fund lends international assistance to threatened sites	• Correct — This explains how UNESCO can assist threatened sites from a financial aspect
(f)	• The idea of an international fund had been around since 1946	• Incorrect — This is irrelevant to UNESCO's aims

4. **Germany and the Weimar Republic**

There is a lot of historical debate on Germany, concerning in particular the period during the 1920s and 1930s. Many question whether the Weimar Republic (formed late in 1918) was "doomed from the outset" or whether it was just the victim of the Great Depression.

5   Underneath the surface of an orderly transfer of power, the situation looked bleak for the Weimar Republic from the beginning. The parliamentary democracy that was set up was more of a reaction, "not the deliberate choice of a majority." While the president had the power to rule by decrees, the government was weak because of the electoral system of strict proportional

10   representation, which made coalitions a necessity. Furthermore, the defeat of 1918 which "hit the German public with brutal suddenness" and the harshness of the Treaty of Versailles put the already unpopular "November Criminals" government in an uncomfortable situation.

Politically, the government was also under threat. The 1919 Spartacist
15 (communist) uprising in Berlin forced Ebert, the president at that time, to
fall back on the Ebert–Groener Pact. Were it not for the army's help, the
government would have been overthrown. In this way, the Weimar Republic
was never really a republic because it was "too reliant on the old imperial
officers." Just one year later, in 1920, monarchists Kapp and von Luttwitz
20 who, ironically, "had been instrumental in suppressing the Spartacists," led
the Kapp Putsch. The Putsch failed, but the government "barely punished
the leaders for fear of losing valuable support." These two major uprisings
highlight how unstable the government was, even in the early years.

Economically, the Weimar Republic was far from sound. The republic
25 suffered from the inflation leftover from the war, and the huge amount of
reparations was a burden that she struggled to carry. Moreover, the Republic
lost 75% of its iron ore and 25% of its coal reserves to the Allies, which dealt
another blow to her economy. The fact that one-third of the budget was spent
on families of dead or wounded soldiers did not help. The 1923 Ruhr Crisis
30 "knocked the bottom out of the German currency" when France occupied the
Ruhr, thinking it would force Germany to pay the reparations since the Ruhr
was resource-rich. Implementing "passive resistance" eventually cost Germany
even more as she had to pay the wages of the workers who were on strike.

By the summer of 1923, hyper-inflation almost destroyed the Republic.
35 Separatist uprisings broke out from both sides across Germany and it was the
1924 Dawes Plan that rescued the Republic, in the form of loans from the USA.
While the Dawes Plan contributed to Weimar's "Golden Age" (1924–1929), it
was seen as "enslavement" by many Germans and made Germany too reliant
on the USA. These fears materialized when the Wall Street crashed in October
40 1929. Germany's economy, which "had already shown signs of sluggishness
earlier in 1929," suffered tremendously and struggled to recover. By 1933, the
Nazis rose to power and marked the end of the Weimar Republic.

The Weimar Republic had survived many severe crises and was doing
well in light of the circumstances. It was also one of the most democratic
45 constitutions of that period. "The Golden Age" signified hope and the
Republic seemed to be gaining in popularity. Perhaps the Great Depression,
a stroke of bad luck, was what killed the Republic, but in the end its inability
to overcome its fundamental weaknesses made its downfall inevitable.

An introductory sentence for a brief summary of the passage is provided below.

Complete the summary by selecting the THREE answer choices that express the most important ideas in the passage.

Some sentences do not belong in the summary because they express ideas that are not presented in the passage or are minor ideas in the passage. **This question is worth 2 points.**

Write your answer choices in the spaces where they belong. You can write in the number of the answer choice or the whole sentence.

The Weimar Republic, which was formed in 1918, was an unstable government from many aspects.
•
•
•

Answer choices:

a) There is a lot of historical debate on Germany, concerning in particular the period during the 1920s and 1930s.

b) The government was weak because of the electoral system of strict proportional representation, which made coalitions a necessity.

c) Two major uprisings — the 1919 Spartacist uprising and the 1920 Kapp Putsch — further highlighted how unstable the government was.

d) Economically, the Weimar Republic was also far from sound. The republic suffered from the inflation leftover from the war, and the huge amount of reparations was a burden that she struggled to carry.

e) By 1933, the Nazis rose to power and marked the end of the Weimar Republic.

f) Perhaps the Great Depression, a stroke of bad luck, was what killed the Republic, but in the end its inability to overcome its fundamental weaknesses made its downfall inevitable.

Step I: *Underline keywords in the introductory sentence and identify the key points*

Introductory Sentence	Key Points
The Weimar Republic, which was formed in 1918, was an unstable government from many aspects.	•

Step II: *Underline keywords in the remaining answer options. Eliminate answer choices that are not part of the introductory sentence's main idea or that are only very minor points*

	Answer Option	Essential Information
(a)	There is a lot of historical debate on Germany, concerning in particular the period during the 1920s and 1930s.	•
(b)	The government was weak because of the electoral system of strict proportional representation, which made coalitions a necessity.	•
(c)	Two major uprisings — the 1919 Spartacist uprising and the 1920 Kapp Putsch — further highlighted how unstable the government was.	•
(d)	Economically, the Weimar Republic was also far from sound. The republic suffered from the inflation leftover from the war, and the huge amount of reparations was a burden that she struggled to carry.	•
(e)	By 1933, the Nazis rose to power and marked the end of the Weimar Republic.	•
(f)	Perhaps the Great Depression, a stroke of bad luck, was what killed the Republic, but in the end its inability to overcome its fundamental weaknesses made its downfall inevitable.	•

Step III: *Match the answer options' key points to the introductory sentence. If still unsure, then analyze relevant portions of the passage and determine if they are important enough to be part of the summary*

	Essential Information	Analysis
(a)	• There is historical debate about Germany in the 1920s and 1930s	•
(b)	• The government was weak • The electoral system of strict proportional representation made coalitions a necessity	•

(c)	• Two major uprisings highlighted how unstable the government was	•
(d)	• The Weimar Republic also had economic problems • It had inflation and a huge amount of reparations to pay	•
(e)	• The Nazis took over power from the Weimar Republic by 1933	•
(f)	• The Great Depression and bad luck could have caused the Republic's downfall • But its inability to overcome fundamental weaknesses made its downfall inevitable	•

Answers:

Step I: *Underline keywords in the introductory sentence and identify the key points*

Introductory Sentence	Key Points
The Weimar Republic, which was formed in 1918, was an unstable government from many aspects.	• The Weimar Republic was an unstable government

Step II: *Underline keywords in the remaining answer options. Eliminate answer choices that are not part of the introductory sentence's main idea or that are only very minor points*

	Answer Option	Essential Information
(a)	There is a lot of historical debate on Germany, concerning in particular the period during the 1920s and 1930s.	• There is historical debate about Germany in the 1920s and 1930s
(b)	The government was weak because of the electoral system of strict proportional representation, which made coalitions a necessity.	• The government was weak • The electoral system of strict proportional representation made coalitions a necessity

(c)	Two major uprisings — the 1919 Spartacist uprising and the 1920 Kapp Putsch — further highlighted how unstable the government was.	• Two major uprisings highlighted how unstable the government was
(d)	Economically, the Weimar Republic was also far from sound. The republic suffered from the inflation leftover from the war, and the huge amount of reparations was a burden that she struggled to carry.	• The Weimar Republic also had economic problems • It had inflation and a huge amount of reparations to pay
(e)	By 1933, the Nazis rose to power and marked the end of the Weimar Republic.	• The Nazis took over power from the Weimar Republic by 1933
(f)	Perhaps the Great Depression, a stroke of bad luck, was what killed the Republic, but in the end its inability to overcome its fundamental weaknesses made its downfall inevitable.	• The Great Depression and bad luck could have caused the Republic's downfall • But its inability to overcome fundamental weaknesses made its downfall inevitable

Step III: *Match the answer options' key points to the introductory sentence. If still unsure, then analyze relevant portions of the passage and determine if they are important enough to be part of the summary*

Introductory Sentence	Key Points
The Weimar Republic, which was formed in 1918, was an unstable government from many aspects.	The Weimar Republic was an unstable government

	Essential Information	Analysis
(a)	• There is historical debate about Germany in the 1920s and 1930s	• Incorrect — This merely states there is historical debate about Germany and is unrelated to why the Weimar Republic was unstable
(b)	• The government was weak • The electoral system of strict proportional representation made coalitions a necessity	• Correct — "Weak" is a synonym for "unstable." This explains why the government was weak

(c)	• Two major uprisings highlighted how unstable the government was	• Correct — This provides evidence that the government was politically unstable
(d)	• The Weimar Republic also had economic problems • It had inflation and a huge amount of reparations to pay	• Correct — This shows the government was also economically unstable
(e)	• The Nazis took over power from the Weimar Republic by 1933	• Incorrect — This shows the government was also economically unstable
(f)	• The Great Depression and bad luck could have caused the Republic's downfall • But its inability to overcome fundamental weaknesses made its downfall inevitable	• Incorrect — This focuses on what caused the Weimar Republic's downfall, not about why it was unstable

5. **Tsar Alexander II of Russia**

Also known as the "Tsar Liberator," Alexander II is one of Russia's more well-known Tsars for the series of reforms he introduced during his reign, most notably the Emancipation Edict of 1861 which legally freed more than 23 million serfs, followed by other reforms such as in the local government,
5   law, army and education. The causes for these reforms draw back to the growing awareness for free labor instead of serfdom, the Crimean War in 1854 and the civil unrest that threatened to crumble Russia from within. Sensing that he was facing a crisis, Alexander "believed that attack was the best form of defense" and these attacks came in the form of reforms.
10 Whether or not these reforms were effective is highly debatable, with some believing that the only result he had was in making Russia "an incomplete and uncomfortable dwelling."

The main causes for the reforms are interlinked. Russia in the 1800s was very behind compared to the other major countries. According to statistics,
15 the comparative density of their railway network compared to Germany and Britain was one to twelve. Furthermore, their natural resources were poorly managed and far apart, which hindered her growth. A major cause of Russia's economic problems was her serfdom. "A minority of educated Russians had argued since the eighteenth century that serfdom was an
20 inefficient way of using labor." However, most Russian nobles were unable

to understand why they should pay serfs for their labor when they could get it for free. Hence, for years, serfdom remained until the Crimean War forced Alexander II to reconsider.

As Alexander II's Minister of War, Dmitrii Miliutin, told him in 1867:
25 "Thanks to the army, Russia became a first class European power and only by maintaining the army can Russia uphold the position it has acquired." Prior to the army reforms, the army numbered over 1 million with conscripts serving for 25 years. Discipline was fierce; soldiers could face up to 12,000 lashings a day, which caused dread in Russians. While the army won most
30 of its victories against weaker opponents, the Crimean War exposed its weaknesses. Most of the army consisted of nobles who despised formal military training and the soldiers still concentrated on bayonets rather than firearms. Furthermore, the lack of railways also contributed to their defeat, which drove the government to the verge of bankruptcy; it was saved only
35 by rising revenue in vodka sales.

Hence serfdom posed another problem, not only an economic one but also a military one. Although military officials knew that a more efficient and less costly army would mean recruiting serfs, they were reluctant because traditionally recruits were freed at the end of service, which would mean a
40 gradual yet automatic emancipation for male serfs. While serfdom existed, the government was also reluctant to encourage large-scale construction of railways. Threats of serf rebellions were also surfacing all over Russia. "It is better to begin abolishing serfdom from above than to wait for it to begin to abolish itself from below," said Alexander II in 1856 — it was clear that
45 the abolition of serfdom was inevitable.

Following the Emancipation Edict in 1861, the other reforms that followed came mainly in the form of the legal system, the army and the local government. With 23 million new peasants there emerged a need for a new legal system to govern them. Open courts, jury trials and an independent
50 judiciary based on the concept of equality before the law for all citizens were introduced. In the local government, special bodies were created as elected local government assemblies representing all classes. The reforms had deprived the nobles of their traditional authority and the special bodies were seen as a way to restore it.

An introductory sentence for a brief summary of the passage is provided below.

Complete the summary by selecting the THREE answer choices that express the most important ideas in the passage.

Some sentences do not belong in the summary because they express ideas that are not presented in the passage or are minor ideas in the passage. **This question is worth 2 points.**

Write your answer choices in the spaces where they belong. You can write in the number of the answer choice or the whole sentence.

Tsar Alexander II introduced a series of reforms during his reign for several reasons.
•
•
•

Answer choices:

a) The causes for these reforms draw back to the growing awareness for free labor instead of serfdom, the Crimean War in 1854 and civil unrest, which threatened to crumble Russia from within.

b) Whether or not these reforms were effective is highly debatable, with some believing that the only result he had was in making Russia "an incomplete and uncomfortable dwelling."

c) Most Russian nobles were unable to understand why they should pay serfs for their labor when they could get it for free.

d) Most of the army consisted of nobles who despised formal military training and the soldiers still concentrated on bayonets rather than firearms.

e) The traditional system of serfdom posed both economic as well as military problems, and needed to be reformed.

f) After 23 million new peasants emerged following the reform of serfdom, there was further need for new legal reforms to govern this new group of people.

Step I: *Underline keywords in the introductory sentence and identify the key points*

Introductory Sentence	Key Points
Tsar Alexander II introduced a series of reforms during his reign for several reasons.	•

Step II: *Underline keywords in the remaining answer options. Eliminate answer choices that are not part of the introductory sentence's main idea or that are only very minor points*

	Answer Option	Essential Information
(a)	The causes for these reforms draw back to the growing awareness for free labor instead of serfdom, the Crimean War in 1854 and civil unrest, which threatened to crumble Russia from within.	•
(b)	Whether or not these reforms were effective is highly debatable, with some believing that the only result he had was in making Russia "an incomplete and uncomfortable dwelling."	•
(c)	Most Russian nobles were unable to understand why they should pay serfs for their labor when they could get it for free.	•
(d)	Most of the army consisted of nobles who despised formal military training and the soldiers still concentrated on bayonets rather than firearms.	•
(e)	The traditional system of serfdom posed both economic as well as military problems, and needed to be reformed.	•
(f)	After 23 million new peasants emerged following the reform of serfdom, there was further need for new legal reforms to govern this new group of people.	•

Step III: *Match the answer options' key points to the introductory sentence. If still unsure, then analyze relevant portions of the passage and determine if they are important enough to be part of the summary*

Introductory Sentence	Key Points
Tsar Alexander II introduced a series of reforms during his reign for several reasons.	Tsar Alexander II introduced reforms for several reasons

	Essential Information	Analysis
(a)	• The causes of the reforms include growing awareness for free labor, the Crimean War and civil unrest	•
(b)	• The efficacy of the reforms is debatable • Some believe it only made Russia "an incomplete and uncomfortable dwelling"	•
(c)	• Russian nobles could not understand why they should pay serfs for labor	•
(d)	• Most of the army consisted of nobles who despised formal military training • The soldiers still concentrated on bayonets, not firearms	•
(e)	• The traditional system of serfdom posed economic and military problems • The serfdom system needed to be reformed	•
(f)	• After the reform of serfdom, there was further need for new legal reforms to govern the 23 million new peasants	•

Answers:

Step I: *Underline keywords in the introductory sentence and identify the key points*

Introductory Sentence	Key Points
<u>Tsar Alexander II</u> introduced a series of <u>reforms</u> during his reign for <u>several reasons</u>.	• Tsar Alexander II introduced reforms for several reasons

Step II: *Underline keywords in the remaining answer options. Eliminate answer choices that are not part of the introductory sentence's main idea or that are only very minor points*

	Answer Option	Essential Information
(a)	The <u>causes for these reforms</u> draw back to the <u>growing awareness for free labor</u> instead of serfdom, the <u>Crimean War</u> in 1854 and <u>civil unrest</u>, which threatened to crumble Russia from within.	• The causes of the reforms include growing awareness for free labor, the Crimean War and civil unrest
(b)	Whether or not these <u>reforms</u> were <u>effective</u> is highly <u>debatable</u>, with some believing that the only result he had was in making Russia "<u>an incomplete and uncomfortable dwelling.</u>"	• The efficacy of the reforms is debatable • Some believe it only made Russia "an incomplete and uncomfortable dwelling"
(c)	Most <u>Russian nobles</u> were <u>unable to understand why they should pay serfs</u> for their <u>labor</u> when they could get it for free	• Russian nobles could not understand why they should pay serfs for labor
(d)	<u>Most of the army</u> consisted of <u>nobles</u> who <u>despised formal military training</u> and the <u>soldiers</u> still <u>concentrated on bayonets</u> rather than firearms.	• Most of the army consisted of nobles who despised formal military training • The soldiers still concentrated on bayonets, not firearms
(e)	The <u>traditional system of serfdom</u> posed both <u>economic</u> as well as <u>military problems</u>, and needed to be <u>reformed</u>.	• The traditional system of serfdom posed economic and military problems • The serfdom system needed to be reformed

(f)	After 23 million new peasants emerged following the reform of serfdom, there was further need for new legal reforms to govern this new group of people.	• After the reform of serfdom, there was further need for new legal reforms to govern the 23 million new peasants

Step III: *Match the answer options' key points to the introductory sentence. If still unsure, then analyze relevant portions of the passage and determine if they are important enough to be part of the summary*

Introductory Sentence	Key Points
Tsar Alexander II introduced a series of reforms during his reign for several reasons.	Tsar Alexander II introduced reforms for several reasons

	Essential Information	Analysis
(a)	• The causes of the reforms include growing awareness for free labor, the Crimean War and civil unrest	• Correct — This details the general causes for the reforms
(b)	• The efficacy of the reforms is debatable • Some believe it only made Russia "an incomplete and uncomfortable dwelling."	• Incorrect — This questions the efficacy of the reforms, not the causes for the reforms
(c)	• Russian nobles could not understand why they should pay serfs for labor	• Incorrect — Minor, irrelevant point relating to serfdom
(d)	• Most of the army consisted of nobles who despised formal military training • The soldiers still concentrated on bayonets, not firearms	• Incorrect — Minor, irrelevant point relating to the army
(e)	• The traditional system of serfdom posed economic and military problems • The serfdom system needed to be reformed	• Correct — This explains why serfdom in particular needed to be reformed
(f)	• After the reform of serfdom, there was further need for new legal reforms to govern the 23 million new peasants	• Correct — This explains how the reform of serfdom led to the further need for legal reforms

Intelligent Inferences

In the TOEFL, you will come across inference-type questions. Inference-type questions will often include one of the following keywords:

- **Infer** — Which of the following can be <u>inferred</u> from paragraph 2 about why we drink coffee with milk?
- **Imply** — In paragraph 1, the author <u>implies</u> that eating boiled vegetables is nutritious because...
- **Suggest** — What does paragraph 4 <u>suggest</u> about high-starch diets?

In order to receive a score at the "high" level, one of the things you have to do is to make correct inferences even when the passage is complex and difficult. Making an "inference" means the ability to understand an idea that is suggested, but not stated explicitly. For example, suppose you see a friend sweating and panting. Although your friend does not say anything, your mind automatically *infers* that your friend has just been running or gone through another form of physical exertion.

For most students, this is probably the hardest part of the TOEFL because the answer cannot be directly found in the passage. However, don't let that get in the way of a high TOEFL score. In *Top the TOEFL*, we don't just teach you how to make inferences. We want you to make intelligent inferences — and that means getting the right answer more quickly and effectively. To do so, just use the *Simple Steps* as your guiding compass.

Simple Steps

1. Understand and subsequently rephrase the question in a more straightforward manner.
2. Underline keywords within each answer option.
3. Analyze each answer option by considering whether it is directly relevant to the question and whether there is evidence in the passage to support the claim.

Elaboration with Examples

Let's take a look at a sample passage to see how it works.

Sample passage:

Tuberculosis in South African Gold Mines

The South African gold mining sector faces a serious epidemic of infections with tuberculosis (TB). Many factors are involved in facilitating the spread of the infection, including the HIV/AIDS epidemic, silicosis as well as crowded living and working conditions in ultra-deep mines. This situation is further complicated by the emergence of multidrug-resistant tuberculosis (MDR-TB) and its transmission. Recent developments, specifically new systems such as the GeneXpert, have made TB and MDR-TB diagnosis radically faster and cheaper while maintaining a good level of sensitivity and specificity. Despite these accomplishments, current measures fail to detect 40% of estimated TB cases and 75% of estimated MDR-TB cases every year. Furthermore, according to a WHO TB financing tool, the cost of treating an MDR-TB patient in South Africa exceeds 9,000 USD per patient treated. Finally, the long duration of treatment makes it difficult to prevent patients from defaulting on the treatment regimen, despite the new DOTS TB treatment framework implemented by the World Health Organization. This epidemic is therefore becoming a threat not only to the health of the citizens of high-burden countries but also poses a risk to their economies.

One of the most effective tools of preventing the spread of disease and therefore mitigating its high cost is immunization. Allowing the body to develop antibodies that would recognize and clear a pathogen and therefore prevent the disease from developing is generally preferred to spending large amounts of money on subsequent treatment. However, developing vaccines against bacteria capable of immune escape has been notoriously difficult, and despite focused research, advances in the field of TB vaccine design have been slow. In spite of such obstacles, there are several concurrent trials of novel TB vaccines that could yield successful immunizations. Nevertheless, the literature studying the impact of vaccination on the dynamics of mining-related TB and MDR TB is scarce, even though such predictions can offer results for vaccine developers as well as policymakers.

Author: Veronika Lipkova

Sample question:

The author implies that diagnostic systems like GeneXpert still have room for more improvement because ...

a) Technology develops rapidly and there may be advanced tools that can make more effective diagnoses.

b) The current diagnostic systems are not readily equipped to deal with complex epidemics such as the one occurring in the South Africa gold mining sector.

c) Every year, a significant number of TB as well as MDR-TB cases go undetected, which means that patients do not get a chance at treatment.

d) Treating patients with TB or MDR-TB is a long and costly process.

1. *Understand and subsequently rephrase the question in a more straightforward manner*

When dealing with inferential questions, it is very important that you first understand what the question is asking. This is because the question may be phrased in a roundabout way, and the answers may also be very similar. Having a clear understanding of the question is a crucial first step, and you can ensure this by rewriting the question in simpler terms.

For example:

Original question: The author implies that diagnostic systems like GeneXpert still have room for more improvement because ...

Rephrased question: Why does the author believe that current diagnostic systems still have weaknesses?

If you study these two methods of posing the questions, you will see that the former is indirect because it requires you to understand what "have room for more improvement" means.

On the other hand, the rephrased question directly states that you should look out for the weaknesses in the current diagnostic systems. Once you have this in mind, you can zoom in on the correct answer by targeting key points in the passage where the current diagnostic systems' flaws are mentioned.

2. *Underline keywords within each answer option*

Next, after you have a clear understanding of the question, you must focus on understanding the key points of each answer option. This is particularly important for inferential questions because students often get caught when there are too many answers that appear to be correct.

a) Technology develops rapidly and <u>there may be advanced tools</u> that can make more effective diagnoses.

b) The <u>current diagnostic systems are not readily equipped to deal with complex epidemics</u> such as the one occurring in the South Africa gold mining sector.

c) Every year, <u>a significant number of TB as well as MDR-TB cases go undetected</u>, which means that patients do not get a chance at treatment.

d) Treating patients with TB or MDR-TB is a <u>long and costly process</u>.

3. *Analyze each answer option by considering whether it is directly relevant to the question and whether there is evidence in the passage to support the claim*

As a final step, analyze each answer option by asking yourself two key questions.

First, is the answer option relevant to the question? If it is not, then you can eliminate the answer option immediately.

Second, is there any evidence at all in the passage to support the answer option? How can you infer that the answer option is correct? This is the final and most key consideration because an answer may be relevant in the mind of the reader, but it may be completely incorrect in the context of the passage.

Rephrased question: Why does the author believe that current diagnostic systems still have weaknesses?

	Relevance	Evidence
(a)	Low — The possibility of having advanced tools in the future is not a criticism of the current diagnostic systems	Not applicable
(b)	Relevant — States that the current systems are not compatible to deal because some epidemics are exceptionally complex	The South African gold mining sector faces a serious epidemic of infections with tuberculosis (TB). Many factors are involved in facilitating the spread of the infection including the HIV/AIDS epidemic, silicosis as well as crowded living and working conditions in ultra-deep mines.

(c)	Relevant — The current systems are flawed because a significant number of cases remain undetected	Despite these accomplishments, current measures fail to detect 40% of estimated TB cases and 75% of estimated MDR-TB cases every year.
(d)	Low — The time and money required for treatment has nothing to do with the diagnostic process	Not applicable

The answer now boils down to either (b) or (c). Which one should you choose?

In such situations, always pick the answer that is most specific and accurate. Based on the evidence, answer option (b) is less specific because a complex endemic is not necessarily a flaw or something that current diagnostic systems can improve on. It is a feature of the environment, which is out of the control of the diagnostic systems.

Answer option (c), on the other hand, is more specific because it highlights the failure of diagnostic systems in detecting TB as well as MDR-TB cases. This is a clear flaw on the part of the diagnostic systems, and therefore answer option (c) is the correct option.

Let's take a look at another example.

Sample passage:

Prime Minister Clement Atlee's Government

When the Labor Party was swept to power in 1945 many people believed that this would be the start of many years of Labor dominance. They thought that the British people were actively voting for a more socialist ideology and this represented a true change in public opinion. Yet six years later Labor was out of power again, and would remain that way for the next 13 years. Many people have heralded Prime Minister Clement Atlee's government as one of the most successful and important of the 20th century and there is no question that they achieved what very few governments do — keeping the promises that they made in their election campaign. How then, with all these things going for it, did the Atlee government end up losing the 1951 election?

The vast majority of the reasons for Labor's defeat in 1951 are external factors that any post-war government would have had to face. The most important of these is the economy. The Second World War left the British economy in a terrible state with a huge deficit. The Atlee government was completely dependent on a significant loan from the United States to be able to carry out any of the welfare reforms they had promised. The British economy had already been in trouble before the start of the war, as it was just coming out of a decade of depression. Industry had not had enough time to recover and was in desperate need of modernizing. The costs of the war did not end when peace was declared, blocking many of the government's attempted plans.

Author: Lydia Levy

Sample question:
According to paragraph 1, what can you infer about the general expectations of the Labor Party when it came to power in 1945?
a) The Labor Party deserved to lose and it was only a matter of time before it did so.
b) The Labor Party could stay in power, but only if it were extremely lucky and fortunate.
c) The Labor Party would implement true socialist ideology.
d) The Labor Party would be able to retain power for a significant period of time.

Understand and subsequently rephrase the question
in a more straightforward manner.

Original question: According to paragraph 1, what can you infer about the general expectations of the Labor Party when it came to power in 1945?
Rephrased question: What did people think of the Labor Party in 1945?

Underline keywords within each answer option.
---

a) The Labor Party <u>deserved to lose</u> and it was only a matter of time before it did so.

b) The Labor Party <u>could stay in power</u>, but only if it were <u>extremely lucky</u> and fortunate.

c) The Labor Party would implement <u>true socialist ideology</u>.

d) The Labor Party would be able to <u>retain power</u> for a <u>significant period of time</u>.

Analyze each answer option by considering whether it is directly relevant to the question and whether there is evidence in the passage to support the claim.

Rephrased question: What did people think of the Labor Party in 1945?

	Relevance	Evidence
(a)	Relevant — The Labor Party deserved to lose	None available
(b)	Relevant — The Labor Party could stay in power if it were lucky	None available
(c)	Relevant — The Labor Party would implement true socialist ideology	They thought that the British people were actively voting for a more socialist ideology and this represented a true change in public opinion.
(d)	Relevant — The Labor Party would retain power for some time	Yet six years later Labor was out of power again, and would remain that way for the next 13 years.

Compared to the previous sample question, this passage is trickier in the sense that all the answer options are relevant. This is why the "Evidence" portion is important. It helps you channel your analysis in a more structured way, allowing you to eliminate answer options more efficiently.

By attempting to fill in the "Evidence" section, you will realize that there is no possible corresponding evidence for answer options (a) and (b).

There is possible supporting evidence for answer options (c) and (d). But a closer look will quickly reveal to you that answer option (c) is less accurate in comparison to answer option (d). Paragraph 1 does state that the British people were voting for socialist ideology. However, answer option (d) is more compelling because nearly the whole of paragraph 1 focuses on bolstering the point that no one in 1945 could foresee that the Labor Party would lose the elections in just six years. Clues like "Yet six years later Labor was out of power again," with the emphasis on "yet" help you infer this.

Therefore, answer option (d) is the correct answer. Answer option (c) is not entirely wrong, but it is simply not as good as answer option (d).

TOEFL Trainer

Step I: *Understand and subsequently rephrase the question in a more straightforward manner*

Rephrase and rewrite the following questions in a more straightforward manner. Infer what the question is asking you before you move onto the second step of analyzing the answer options. Try to complete each question within three minutes so that you can work under pressure when it comes to the real examination.

1. According to paragraph 3, what can be inferred about the material that is used to make rucksacks?
2. Paragraph 2 suggests that Ding made slanderous comments about numerous innocent students because …
3. What does the President's latest speech imply about his attitude towards public healthcare?
4. Based on paragraph 1, what does the school's refusal to investigate the issue suggest?
5. What do nutritionists imply about the importance of potassium in our diets?
6. Judging from the amount of damage, what can be inferred about the latest terrorist attack?
7. Paragraph 4 implies that honey is the best antibacterial substance because …
8. The military general decided not to invade the neighboring country even though it was a great threat because …
9. What is implied by the hotel manager's decision to resign from his position?
10. What does the fact that many counterfeit products remain in existence today suggest?
11. Paragraph 1 implies that not all of W.E.B. Du Bois's ideas were worthwhile accepting because …
12. What does paragraph 2 imply about the success of Du Bois's efforts?
13. What does paragraph 1 suggest about how long fascist and communist ideologies lasted?

14. What similarity does paragraph 1 suggest Germany, Italy and the Soviet Union had in common in interwar Europe?
15. Based on paragraph 3, what can be inferred about why defeat in the Second World War was so detrimental to the fascist regimes?

Answers:

1. What is so special about the material that is used to make rucksacks?
2. Why did Ding make slanderous comments about numerous innocent students?
3. How does the President view public healthcare?
4. Why didn't the school investigate the issue?
5. Why is potassium important?
6. Judging from the amount of damage, what can be inferred about the latest terrorist attack?
7. Why is honey the best antibacterial substance?
8. Why didn't the military general decide not to invade the neighboring country even though it was a great threat?
9. Why did the hotel manager's decide to resign from his position?
10. Why do many counterfeit products remain in existence today?
11. Why weren't all of W.E.B. Du Bois's ideas worth accepting?
12. Were Du Bois's efforts successful?
13. How long did fascist and communist ideologies last?
14. What was something Germany, Italy and the Soviet Union had in common?
15. Why was defeat in the Second World War so detrimental to the fascist regimes?

Step II: *Underline keywords within each answer option*

1. Paragraph 1 implies that not all of W.E.B. Du Bois's ideas were worthwhile accepting because …
   a) Some ideas, such as the "Talented Tenth" were too elitist.
   b) He plays far too many different roles but his key expertise lies in the realm of education.
   c) His does not think that black Americans managed to achieve complete freedom after the Civil War.
   d) Du Bois advocated rights that are taken for granted today.

2. What does paragraph 2 imply about the success of Du Bois's efforts?
   a) Du Bois was less successful than Booker T. Washington, another black activist of the late 19th century.
   b) Du Bois did not manage to directly solve many of the problems that he sought to address while he was still alive.
   c) Du Bois managed to cooperate with Washington to allow black people to "race with the world."
   d) Du Bois could solve all problems except the "Negro Problem."

3. What does paragraph 1 suggest about how long fascist and communist ideologies lasted?
   a) Both these ideologies prevail even until this day.
   b) These ideologies collapsed at the same time as they were positioned in opposition towards each other.
   c) Communist ideology collapsed before fascist ideology.
   d) Fascist ideology collapsed before communist ideology.

4. What similarity does paragraph 1 suggest Germany, Italy and the Soviet Union had in common in interwar Europe?
   a) They had an ideology that was closely related to Italian fascism.
   b) They had a similar ideological origins.
   c) They aimed to control every aspect of its citizens' lives.
   d) Their governments managed to survive the impact of the Second World War.

5. Based on paragraph 3, what can be inferred about why defeat in the Second World War was so detrimental to the fascist regimes?
   a) Fascist regimes viewed war as the ultimate test of a nation, and failure in war caused the regime to lose legitimacy.
   b) The Second World War absorbed a large amount of economic resources.
   c) War involves aggression and the potential loss of many lives.
   d) Fascist regimes were very heavily dependent on the military.

Answers:

1. Paragraph 1 implies that not all of W.E.B. Du Bois's ideas were worthwhile accepting because ...
   a) Some ideas, such as the "Talented Tenth" were too elitist.

b) He plays <u>far too many different roles</u> but his <u>key expertise</u> lies in the realm of <u>education</u>.

c) His <u>does not think</u> that <u>black Americans</u> managed to achieve <u>complete freedom</u> after the <u>Civil War</u>.

d) Du Bois advocated <u>rights</u> that are <u>taken for granted today</u>.

2. What does paragraph 2 imply about the success of Du Bois's efforts?

   a) <u>Du Bois was less successful than Booker T. Washington</u>, another black activist of the late 19th century.

   b) <u>Du Bois did not manage to directly solve many of the problems</u> that he sought to address while he was still alive.

   c) <u>Du Bois</u> managed to <u>cooperate with Washington</u> to <u>allow black people to "race with the world."</u>

   d) Du Bois could <u>solve</u> all problems <u>except</u> the <u>"Negro Problem."</u>

3. What does paragraph 1 suggest about how long fascist and communist ideologies lasted?

   a) <u>Both</u> these <u>ideologies prevail</u> even until this day.

   b) These ideologies <u>collapsed at the same time</u> as they were <u>positioned in opposition towards each other</u>.

   c) <u>Communist</u> ideology <u>collapsed before fascist</u> ideology.

   d) <u>Fascist</u> ideology <u>collapsed before communist</u> ideology.

4. What similarity does paragraph 1 suggest Germany, Italy and the Soviet Union had in common in interwar Europe?

   a) They had an <u>ideology</u> that was <u>closely related to Italian fascism</u>.

   b) They had a <u>similar ideological origins</u>.

   c) They aimed to <u>control</u> every aspect of its <u>citizens' lives</u>.

   d) Their <u>governments</u> managed to <u>survive</u> the <u>impact</u> of the <u>Second World War</u>.

5. Based on paragraph 3, what can be inferred about why defeat in the Second World War was so detrimental to the fascist regimes?

   a) Fascist regimes viewed war as the <u>ultimate test of a nation</u>, and <u>failure</u> in war caused the regime to <u>lose legitimacy</u>.

   b) The Second World War <u>absorbed</u> a large amount of <u>economic resources</u>.

   c) War involves <u>aggression</u> and the <u>potential loss of many lives</u>.

   d) Fascist regimes were very heavily <u>dependent on the military</u>.

Step III: *Analyze each answer option by considering whether it is directly relevant to the question and whether there is evidence in the passage to support the claim*

Questions 1 and 2 are based on the passage below:

On W.E.B. Du Bois

W.E.B. Du Bois was among the most prominent of black intellectuals in the late 19th and early 20th century. He has been described variously as "radical activist," "pristine idealist," "elitist integrationist" and even as a Communist and Pan-Africanist. Among his many contributions was his role as a historian in the rise of sociology as an academic discipline in the United States. As a sociologist, Du Bois undertook many of the studies that shaped his belief in solving what he called the "Negro Problem." This was the failure of black Americans to achieve complete freedom after the Civil War. To him, the solution lay in "systematic investigation and intelligent understanding." Du Bois published numerous volumes of prose on his theories for solving the "Negro Problem," most notably including *The Souls of Black Folk* (1903). The early 20th century saw Du Bois's rise in stature as "race leader" and "black activist." As a leader of black political thought, Du Bois advocated rights that are taken for granted today. Meanwhile, his ideas influenced activists through the 1920s, 1960s and 1980s; his conception of "two-ness" and the "double consciousness" of the African American have since dominated the discourse of African American thought. Of interest to us today are Du Bois's thoughts on the role of education, much of which seems to be remarkably modern in outlook. At the same time, some of his ideas have been quite rightly forgotten. Particularly deserving of this fate was his ruthlessly pragmatic but dangerously elitist idea of a "Talented Tenth."

In spite of the Fifteenth Amendment and the voting rights it conferred, by the time Du Bois wrote *The Souls of Black Folk*, there still existed segregation, reduced rights, and poverty, which he equated to a form of "economic slavery" and which he sought to address. His theories are best viewed in contrast to Booker T. Washington, probably the most prominent of black activists in the late 19th century. Washington advocated a policy of what Du Bois declared as "submission." As Du Bois notes, such policies did nothing to stem the disenfranchisement of blacks, the loss of financial support for their educational institutions and the "legal creation of a distinct status of civil inferiority." Instead, his solution to the "Negro Problem" had three main foci: the pursuit of education both technical and at a higher level, civil rights and black suffrage. Only a concerted effort in all three areas, rather than just in the popular ballot or within Washington's circumscriptions, would allow the black people to "race with the world."

Du Bois was remarkably modern in his belief that public education would lead to the advancement of the black community in America. To him, education was the best means by which to "keep [black Americans] from brooding over the wrongs of the past and the difficulties of the present, so that all their energies may be bent toward a cheerful striving and co-operation with their white neighbors toward a larger, more just, and fuller future." Du Bois's ideas covered a range of educational institutions: from the public schools to black colleges and universities. Du Bois noted the underfunding of the black schools — in Georgia, just 20 percent of the state spending on education was allocated to them. Yet, he strongly believed in government assistance of these schools, so as to ensure the "training [of] decent self-respecting citizens." Such ideas are, of course, not alien to us in the 21st century. Parallels to Du Bois's forward-thinking ideas can be found in strategies implemented to foster the social and economic advancement of disadvantaged communities through education, and we can see the possibilities of their positive impact on society.

Author: Arjun Naidu

1. Paragraph 1 implies that not all of W.E.B. Du Bois's ideas were worthwhile accepting because …
   a) Some ideas, such as the "Talented Tenth" were too elitist.
   b) He plays far too many different roles but his key expertise lies in the realm of education.
   c) His does not think that black Americans managed to achieve complete freedom after the Civil War.
   d) Du Bois advocated rights that are taken for granted today.

2. What does paragraph 2 imply about the success of Du Bois's efforts?
   a) Du Bois was less successful than Booker T. Washington, another black activist of the late 19th century.
   b) Du Bois did not manage to directly solve many of the problems that he sought to address while he was still alive.
   c) Du Bois managed to cooperate with Washington to allow black people to "race with the world."
   d) Du Bois could solve all problems except the "Negro Problem."

Questions 3, 4 and 5 are based on the passage below:

Fascism and Communism

Fascism and communism were two of the most influential ideologies that rose to prominence in interwar Europe. The Russian Revolution of 1917 turned Russia into a socialist state, while in Italy Mussolini and the fascists seized power in 1922, after their March on Rome. In Germany, meanwhile, Hitler's Nazi party came to power in 1933, with an ideology (National Socialism) closely related to Italian fascism. Fascism and communism may have had very different ideological origins — indeed, fascism positioned itself in opposition to communism — but both fascist and communist regimes were unique in that they were totalitarian regimes in which the state aimed to control every aspect of its citizens' lives. Crucially, the Second World War saw these two ideologies come into conflict with each other — expansionist Nazi Germany and fascist Italy on the side of the Axis powers, and the communist Soviet Union with the Allies. But whereas communism weathered this storm, defeat in war spelt the end of fascism, both as a regime in Italy and Germany, as well as a political movement.

Yet, by 1991, communism would join fascism as an exhausted ideology, as the regimes that clung to it collapsed. The prime difference between the collapses of the two great interwar totalitarian ideologies was that whereas fascism collapsed as a result of war, communism's collapse was peaceful. That communism itself would collapse was surprising. The aftermath of the Second World War saw a variety of Soviet satellite communist regimes being set up: in a newly partitioned East Germany, Czechoslovakia, Poland and Hungary, among others. For a period, it seemed that communism as an ideology would last for a long time. By the 1980s, however, the legitimacy of communist regimes were beginning to come under increasing challenges — with the rise of movements like Solidarity in Poland. As the decade drew to a close, regimes in East Germany, Czechoslovakia and Hungary joined Poland in repudiating communism, a process completed by the dissolution of the USSR in 1991.

Although fascist and communist regimes collapsed in very different ways, both regimes collapsed due to a loss of legitimacy, on their own terms. Fascist and communist regimes had different bases for legitimacy. On one hand, fascist regimes were aggressive nationalist regimes that viewed war as the ultimate test of a nation. Facing imminent defeat in the Second World War, it was therefore clear that both the Italian and Nazi regime had failed on this account. Collapse was the only viable option for these illegitimate regimes. On the other hand, war was not at all central to communist states. These regimes believed in the superiority of communism over capitalism as a political and economic system, and were content to wait until the inevitable transition of other regimes to communism. Yet, by that same token, communist regimes had proven themselves to be far inferior to capitalist regimes, both on economic and political grounds. As a result, shorn of legitimacy, communist regimes were forced to concede reforms (*perestroika* and *glasnost* in the USSR, for instance) that ultimately led to their collapse.

Author: Arjun Naidu

3. What does paragraph 1 suggest about how long fascist and communist ideologies lasted?
    a) Both these ideologies prevail even until this day.
    b) These ideologies collapsed at the same time as they were positioned in opposition towards each other.
    c) Communist ideology collapsed before fascist ideology.
    d) Fascist ideology collapsed before communist ideology.

4. What similarity does paragraph 1 suggest Germany, Italy and the Soviet Union had in common in interwar Europe?
    a) They had an ideology that was closely related to Italian fascism.
    b) They had a similar ideological origins.

c) They aimed to control every aspect of its citizens' lives.

d) Their governments managed to survive the impact of the Second World War.

5. Based on paragraph 3, what can be inferred about why defeat in the Second World War was so detrimental to the fascist regimes?

a) Fascist regimes viewed war as the ultimate test of a nation, and failure in war caused the regime to lose legitimacy.

b) The Second World War absorbed a large amount of economic resources.

c) War involves aggression and the potential loss of many lives.

d) Fascist regimes were very heavily dependent on the military.

Answers:

1. Rephrased question: Why weren't all of W.E.B. Du Bois's ideas worth accepting?

	Relevance	Evidence
(a)	Relevant — Elitism is a possible reason	At the same time, some of his ideas have been quite rightly forgotten. Particularly deserving of this fate was his ruthlessly pragmatic but dangerously elitist idea of a "Talented Tenth."
(b)	Low — This is a general criticism about Du Bois's expertise, not about a specific idea	Not applicable
(c)	Low — There is no clear link between Du Bois's thinking and whether or not his ideas are worth accepting	Not applicable
(d)	Low — This is again a general criticism (if it is indeed a criticism) about Du Bois, and not about a specific idea	Not applicable

Answer: (a)

The answer is clearly answer option (a) because it is the only answer option that highlights weaknesses about a specific idea or ideas. In this question, you can clearly see that taking a step back and first asking yourself whether an answer option is relevant or not is worthwhile. It saves you a lot of time as you will not have to spend precious time carefully analyzing the remaining answers.

2. Rephrased question: Were Du Bois's efforts successful?

	Relevance	Evidence
(a)	Relevant — This answer option compares Du Bois against another black activist, Washington, and claims Du Bois was less successful	His theories are best viewed in contrast to Booker T. Washington, probably the most prominent of black activists in the late 19th century. Washington advocated a policy of what Du Bois declared as "submission."
(b)	Relevant — Du Bois had some success but did not manage to directly solve many of the problems that he sought to address while he was still alive	In spite of the Fifteenth Amendment and the voting rights it conferred, by the time Du Bois wrote *The Souls of Black Folk*, there **still** existed segregation, reduced rights, and poverty, which he equated to a form of "economic slavery."
(c)	Relevant — Du Bois achieved a certain degree of success and managed to allow black people to "race with the world"	Only a concerted effort in all three areas, rather than just in with the popular ballot or within Washington's circumscriptions, would allow the black people to "race with the world."
(d)	Relevant — Du Bois could solve all problems except the "Negro Problem," which means not all his efforts were successful	Instead, his solution to the "Negro Problem" had three main foci: the pursuit of education both technical and at a higher level, civil rights and black suffrage.

Answer: (b)

This question is more complex because all of the answers seem possible. After isolating the evidence, analyze each one carefully to infer which is the correct answer.

Answer option (a) sounds relevant but there is no evidence in paragraph 2 to support it. Answer option (c) also sounds fine but again, there is no evidence to say that Du Bois did succeed in allowing the black people to "race with the world." The same goes for answer option (d). While the "Negro Problem" is mentioned, there is no clear evidence to prove that Du Bois could solve all problems except the "Negro Problem." The passage only suggests that the "Negro Problem" remains unsolved.

*You will then see that answer option (b) is the most plausible because it quotes Du Bois in stating that certain problems that he sought to solve **still** exist.*

3. Rephrased question: How long did fascist and communist ideologies last?

	Relevance	Evidence
(a)	Relevant — Both ideologies have lasted until now	None available
(b)	Relevant — Both collapsed at the same time	None available
(c)	Relevant — Communist ideology collapsed before fascist ideology	But whereas communism weathered this storm, defeat in war spelt the end of fascism, both as a regime in Italy and Germany, as well as a political movement.
(d)	Relevant — Fascist ideology collapsed before communist ideology	None available

Answer: (c)

Answer option (c) is the clear answer in this case. Although every answer option seems relevant, only answer option (c) has evidence to support its claim.

4. Rephrased question: What was something Germany, Italy and the Soviet Union had in common?

	Relevance	Evidence
(a)	Relevant — Ideology that was related to Italian fascism	Hitler's Nazi party came to power in 1933, with an ideology (National Socialism) closely related to Italian fascism.
(b)	Relevant — Similar ideological origins	Fascism and communism may have had very different ideological origins — indeed, fascism positioned itself in opposition to communism.
(c)	Relevant — They aimed to control every aspect of its citizens' lives	Both fascist and communist regimes were unique in that they were totalitarian; regimes in which the state aimed to control every aspect of its citizens' lives.
(d)	Relevant — They survived the Second World War	But whereas communism weathered this storm, defeat in war spelt the end of fascism, both as a regime in Italy and Germany, as well as a political movement.

Answer: (c)

Because all answer options seem relevant, the evidence is again very crucial. To do so properly, you must first go a step further and associate Germany, Italy and Soviet Union with their respective ideologies. This is because nearly each answer option directly or indirectly mentions ideology.

Once you do that, the evidence clearly shows that every answer option is false except for answer option (c).

For answer option (a), only Germany had ideology closely related to Italian fascism. Therefore, it is false.

For answer option (b), the passage clearly states that fascism and communism had very different origins. Germany and Italy were fascist while the Soviet Union was communist. Therefore, answer option (b) is also false.

Lastly, answer option (d) is also false because it states that fascism did not survive the Second World War.

5. Rephrased question: Why was defeat in the Second World War so detrimental to the fascist regimes?

	Relevance	Evidence
(a)	Relevant — Failure in war caused the regime to lose legitimacy	On one hand, fascist regimes were aggressive nationalist regimes that viewed war as the ultimate test of a nation. Facing imminent defeat in the Second World War, it was therefore clear that both the Italian and Nazi regime had failed on this account.
(b)	Relevant — The Second World War absorbed a large amount of economic resources	None available
(c)	Relevant — It caused the potential loss of many lives	None available
(d)	Relevant — Fascist regimes were very heavily dependent on the military	None available

Answer: (a)

The answer for this question is quite straightforward because there simply does not exist any evidence to support the remaining three options. On the other hand, you have strong evidence from the passage that states that fascist regimes viewed war as the ultimate test of a nation. From this, you can infer that failing in war could cause a fascist regime to lose legitimacy.

Topping the Independent Writing Section

Introduction

Most people think that the TOEFL writing section only tests your English language abilities in terms of grammar and vocabulary. This is false. It is not just a test of the English language, but also a test of your ability to express clear and logical reasoning. This is why the essay topics, in general, require you to express and defend an opinion. They do not ask you to write personal stories or stories that are based on fantasy.

There are two types of writing tasks. The first is the Independent Writing section, where you will be asked to write two essays. You will only be allowed 25 minutes for each essay. The second is the Integrated Writing section, which will be covered in the last portion of this book.

The two main types of essay questions that you will be asked are:

1. Directly express your opinion about a certain topic
For this essay question, you will be asked to directly express your opinion about something.

Sample Topic A:
How can technology help make your school a better place? Use specific reasons and examples to support your choice.

Sample Topic B:
If you could change one thing about how the world works, what would you change? Why? Use specific reasons and details to support your choice.

Sample Topic C:
Choose **one** of the following inventions and explain why you think it has changed people's everyday lives:

- Light bulbs
- Telephones

Use specific reasons and examples to support your answer.

2. Compare and contrast two or more different items
This type of question requires you to pit one stance against another. You will have to know how to support your view as well as how to debunk the opposing view.

Sample Topic A:
Do you agree or disagree with the following statement? Children should be allowed to use smartphones in school. Use specific reasons and examples to support your answer.

Sample Topic B:
It has been said, "Gifts that are handmade are better than gifts that are bought from the store." Compare and contrast gifts that are handmade with gifts that are bought from the store. In your opinion, which gift is better? Why?

Sample Topic C:
What do you want **most** in a car — a car that is spacious, or fuel-efficient or with a powerful engine? Which **one** of these aspects is most important to you? Use reasons and specific examples to explain your choice.

Top the TOEFL's Approach

At this juncture, you may feel worried about how you are going to effectively tackle these essay topics. We're here to tell you that you don't have worry. These essays are simple to write — all you have to do is to apply the correct strategies. The best part is, our strategies are not just effective but are also general enough to be applied to the different types of questions.

In this section, we will cover the following "Top Tips."

Top Tip 8: Toning the Tone
Top Tip 9: Skeletons to Success
Top Tip 10: Bridging Ideas
Top Tip 11: Introductions Made Easy
Top Tip 12: Topic Sentences
Top Tip 13: Stitching the Essay Together

Toning the Tone

You have probably heard it time and time again: tone is important. Guidebooks mention it everywhere. But few pause to properly say what it means. Luckily for you, *Top the TOEFL* can explain it *and* show you how to use tone effectively.

What is tone? Well, let's take a step back. First, let's think of something common that you would use in everyday conversation. The example that we are using is very simple:

"Goodbye"

Now, think about how you would say goodbye to different people. We'll demonstrate a few scenarios just to get you started.

Scenario 1:

The Prime Minister makes a surprise visit to your classroom and has a brief chat with you. Before he leaves, you want to say goodbye in respectful manner.

What do you say to the Prime Minister? If you aren't too tongue-tied and nervous, you might say: "Goodbye, sir."

Scenario 2:

You are the last to leave the classroom. You wish to say goodbye to your teacher.

What are you likely to say? Instinctively, you would probably say something along these lines: "Thank you and goodbye, Mr. Lim."

Scenario 3:

You have been playing in the playground with your friends. It is getting late and it is time to go home. You want to say goodbye to your friends.

This seems a bit easier. You may not even think too hard about it. There are so many ways you might say goodbye, and one of the ways is probably: "Bye! See you tomorrow!"

Scenario 4:

Now let's jump to the final scenario.

You are getting out of the car to go to school. You want to say goodbye to your parents.

You would probably say something like this: "Bye mum and dad! I love you and see you later!"

Now, let's compile all these different responses into a table:

Scenario	Response	What's special?
Prime Minister	"Goodbye, Sir."	"Sir" implies deep respect, as well as formality
Teacher	"Goodbye, Mr. Lim."	"Mr." (or Ms./Madam/Mrs.) is the appropriate way to address a teacher
Friends	"Bye! See you tomorrow!"	The usage of exclamation marks, on top of shortening "goodbye" to "bye"
Parents	"Bye mum and dad! I love you and see you later!"	An expression of closeness and love as seen through "I love you," as well as the shortening of "goodbye" to "bye"

Have you noticed something? In each scenario, you are saying the same thing: Goodbye. But in each scenario, you have had to say goodbye in a different way. The differences are very subtle (meaning not immediately obvious), but they are there and they are important.

Why? Imagine saying "I love you" to the Prime Minister! Conversely, imagine calling your father "Sir" or "Mr. Tan." It just does not sound right, and the reason for this is because it is not the right *tone*. Can you see how using the wrong tone would be disastrous for any essay? It could make your grade drop from an A to an E!

The literal definition of tone implies a gradient, or a scale along which there are different quantities or qualities of the same thing. For example, there is the color green. But there are also different shades (or one could even say "tones") of green. Similarly, there are many musical tones — but it is all music!

In the case of writing, tone refers to the audience you are addressing. Let us map out the gradient for you:

Prime Minister	Extremely formal and respectful
Teacher	Formal, but with a degree of familiarity (as you both know each other)
Friend	Familiar, informal
Parent	Familiar, informal, with respect

Now that it is clear what tone means, let's establish the tone that you need to maintain for the TOEFL. In short, you need to be formal, professional and polite. You are a student attempting to apply to a university abroad, and your audience is a grader. Therefore, there are formal conventions that you must adhere to. But the more crucial question is: *how can you maintain a formal, professional and polite tone in English?*

Simple Steps

1. Avoid contractions.
2. Avoid casual or informal slang.
3. Avoid revealing personal information.
4. Do not use exclamation marks unless absolutely necessary.

Elaboration with Examples

1. *Avoid contractions*

Contractions are words that you join together with an apostrophe for convenience. For example, sometimes, instead of saying "I do not want to eat rice," people say "I don't want to eat rice."

As you can see, contractions are used when people speak quickly. They are not usually used under formal circumstances. Just browse through the websites of some top companies and you will see that they do not use contractions on the website, unless of course they want to be informal.

2. *Avoid casual or informal slang*

You may think this goes without saying, but we have received some TOEFL essays written by students with informal slang such as "geez" and "oh my God." Here is an example of writing that is riddled with casual or informal slang:

Living without electricity is like hell. You'd start to starve, as you wouldn't even be able to cook something to eat. You wouldn't even be able to get your peeps to help you!

The TOEFL is not Facebook or a chatting application you can download on your phone. Once you start using informal slang, the grader can only arrive at two conclusions. The first conclusion is that you do not know how to appropriately use these words. The second conclusion is that you do not know how to write essays with the correct tone.

To avoid this, always use proper words that you have learnt from credible sources such as textbooks and official websites. If you are not sure, try to find a substitute for the word you have in mind. Once you do this, you can rewrite the paragraph and it could look something like this:

> Living without electricity is <u>very challenging</u>. You <u>would</u> start to starve, as you <u>would not</u> even be able to cook something to eat. You <u>would not</u> even be able to get your <u>friends</u> to help you!

3. *Avoid revealing personal information*

Have you ever seen the CEO of a multinational company reveal personal information about himself or herself on their website biography? Probably not, and this is because it is unprofessional to do so. Imagine your teacher suddenly spilling her most heartfelt secrets to you, and how uncomfortable or shocked you would feel. Indeed, emotions as well as personal information are seen as overly informal and may overstep professional boundaries.

Here's an example of how a student included personal information in an essay:

> I believe that parents are more important than friends because my mother used to take care of me when I was sick. I will never forget her soft and tender touch, and how much effort she spent just to make sure I could be as comfortable as possible. I love my mother very much.

As a reader, perhaps you can also sense that the personal information revealed is a little too much. First, it does not fulfill one of the core requirements of TOEFL essays, and that is to be reasoned out logically. To be logical, this means providing general examples that everyone can accept. If you give personal examples, these have less persuasive power because these are only examples personal to you. It is not strong enough evidence to sway the grader.

Second, personal information can also cause the reader to feel uncomfortable. For example, how would you feel if you had to watch a couple that would not stop expressing their love openly? The same goes for your grader. Telling the grader that you love your parents does not add value to your logical argument and neither is it professional.

A better way to present the student's essay would have been like this:

> I believe that parents are more important than friends because parents are always there for you even when you are sick. They will go to any length to

make sure that you are as comfortable as can be. Even though they are not doctors, their love and care goes a long way in comforting a sick person.

4. *Do not use exclamation marks unless absolutely necessary*

In familiar and informal scenarios the exclamation mark can be an effective way of conveying excitement and enthusiasm. However, when it comes to formal and professional writing, exclamation marks can come across as immature or rude. You may be able to use exclamation marks in an effective manner, but if you are unsure, do avoid using them.

Here is an example of how an exclamation mark can make you seem immature:

> Theme parks are important contributors to every nation's economy. More importantly, they are fun!

As you can see, the exclamation mark emphasizes the fact that theme parks are fun, thereby making it seem as though that is the only thing you are concerned about.

Let's take a look at an example whereby the exclamation mark can be seen as rude:

> The TOEFL examination is very complex and comprehensive. It takes a significant amount of time!

Here, the exclamation mark makes it seem as though the writer is against how the TOEFL examination is run, especially the amount of time it takes up.

If the student avoided using exclamation marks in these two sentences, the tone would be a lot more neutral:

> Theme parks are important contributors to every nation's economy. More importantly, they are fun.

> The TOEFL examination is very complex and comprehensive. It takes a significant amount of time.

Therefore, when unsure, try not to use exclamation marks. They can be used to great effect under some circumstances but it is always better to err on the side of safety.

TOEFL Trainer

I. *Avoid contractions*

Convert the following sentences into sentences without contractions.

1. They'll take steps to prevent the problem from happening again.
2. The typhoon won't affect the shopping mall's operations.
3. Headmasters shouldn't be doing teachers' jobs.
4. The plan should be executed whenever the timing's perfect.
5. Drinking coffee for the sake of caffeine isn't a very good idea.
6. Handmade gifts are definitely better than gifts bought in the store because they're made with love and care.
7. With a more powerful engine, we'll be able to drive the car at a higher speed more quickly.
8. Laptops these days don't come with a disc drive any longer.
9. Toddlers won't understand what you are saying if you speak too fast.
10. The students daren't break the rules anymore after they were severely punished for the mistakes.

Answers:

1. They will take steps to prevent the problem from happening again.
2. The typhoon will not affect the shopping mall's operations.
3. Headmasters should not be doing teachers' jobs.
4. The plan should be executed whenever the timing is perfect.
5. Drinking coffee for the sake of caffeine is not a very good idea.
6. Handmade gifts are definitely better than gifts bought in the store because they are made with love and care.
7. With a more powerful engine, we will be able to drive the car at a higher speed more quickly.
8. Laptops these days do not come with a disc drive any longer.
9. Toddlers will not understand what you are saying if you speak too fast.
10. The students dare not break the rules anymore after they were severely punished for the mistakes.

II. *Avoid casual or informal slang*

Convert the following sentences into sentences without casual or informal slang.

1. Sometimes, students deserve a good whacking for the mischief they get up to.
2. Most people wanna know how they can get rich quickly.
3. You can make loads of cash just by getting an Internet job.
4. Students who slander other students should be kicked out of school.
5. It makes sense to wear enough clothes when it is freezing outside.
6. Chitchatting with strangers can sometimes be beneficial because you never know what you can learn.
7. Motorcyclists who drive at high speeds are crazy because they are risking their lives when they do so.
8. Nobody should give up even when things get sticky and tough because there is always light at the end of the tunnel.
9. History is really boring but it is a necessary subject and something that all students need to learn.
10. Those who are super smart should be given more opportunities to move forward faster in life.

Answers:

1. Sometimes, students deserve <u>to be punished</u> for the mischief they get up to.
2. Most people <u>want to</u> know how they can get rich quickly.
3. You can make a <u>large amount of money</u> just by getting an Internet job.
4. Students who slander other students should be <u>expelled from</u> school.
5. It makes sense to wear enough clothes when it is <u>cold</u> outside.
6. <u>Having conversations</u> with strangers can sometimes be beneficial because you never know what you can learn.
7. Motorcyclists who drive at high speeds are <u>not thinking straight</u> because they are risking their lives when they do so.
8. Nobody should give up even when things get <u>challenging</u> because there is always light at the end of the tunnel.
9. History <u>can be dry</u> but it is a necessary subject and something that all students need to learn.
10. Those who are <u>very intelligent</u> should be given more opportunities to move forward faster in life.

III. *Avoid revealing personal information*

Remove the personal information from the following sample paragraphs.

1. Cycling is a much better sport than walking. The intensity of the exercise that cycling can bring is much higher, especially if you cycle up slopes and hills. I remember cycling up a hill once and it nearly killed my thighs. I could barely walk for a week, but it was in hindsight good for me as it really gave my legs a good workout. On the other hand, walking is fairly low-key and may be more suitable for the older generation. It can help raise your heart rate but cannot help you tone your muscles or burn fat.

2. Students should be encouraged to participate in extracurricular activities even if their examinations grades are not the best. This is because everyone has different strengths, and they may be able to find their strengths through extracurricular activities. Although I have personally hated some of the extracurricular activities I was made to participate in, I do admit that they have helped me developed into a better person.

3. Healthcare should not be free for everyone because some people may end up abusing the system by visiting the doctor when it is unnecessary. When I was in high school, I heard of a senior who went to the hospital on purpose just to make full use of her healthcare benefits. I cannot really understand why anyone would do that, but it proves that these things happen. If the country loses valuable resources due to wastage, then other important public goods such as education may also suffer.

4. Elders are the pillars of our society and we should always respect them. Because of their experience, they may be able to predict things that we cannot. I realized this when I was talking to my grandmother about smartphones one day. Even though she didn't know how to use a smartphone, she commented that these may soon replace newspapers. Sure enough, I found myself beginning to read news articles on my smartphone instead of buying the paper copy.

5. I disagree with the statement that children should be allowed to make the decisions that they want. While I respect the freedom to choose, children are not mature enough yet and they may not know what is best for them. It is best to let the parents to decide until the children are of a certain age. Even though my parents made all the decisions for me since I was young, I never blamed them and in fact I appreciate their help because in hindsight their decisions were always the best. Besides, parents would also want the best for their children and would never choose something that is detrimental towards their children.

Answers:

1. Cycling is a much better sport than walking. The intensity of the exercise that cycling can bring is much higher, especially if you cycle up slopes and hills. <u>I remember cycling up a hill once and it nearly killed my thighs. I could barely walk for a week, but it was in hindsight good for me as it really gave my legs a good workout.</u> On the other hand, walking is fairly low-key and may be more suitable for the older generation. It can help raise your heart rate but cannot help you tone your muscles or burn fat.

2. Students should be encouraged to participate in extracurricular activities even if their examinations grades are not the best. This is because everyone has different strengths, and they may be able to find their strengths through extracurricular activities. <u>Although I have personally hated some of the extracurricular activities I was made to participate in, I do admit that they have helped me developed into a better person.</u>

3. Healthcare should not be free for everyone because some people may end up abusing the system by visiting the doctor when it is unnecessary. <u>When I was in high school, I heard of a senior who went to the hospital on purpose just to make full use of her healthcare benefits. I cannot really understand why anyone would do that, but it proves that these things happen.</u> If the country loses valuable resources due to wastage, then other important public goods such as education may also suffer.

4. Elders are the pillars of our society and we should always respect them. Because of their experience, they may be able to predict things that we cannot. <u>I realized this when I was talking to my grandmother about smartphones one day. Even though she didn't know how to use a smartphone, she commented that these may soon replace newspapers. Sure enough, I found myself beginning to read news articles on my smartphone instead of buying the paper copy.</u>

5. I disagree with the statement that children should be allowed to make the decisions that they want. While I respect the freedom to choose, children are not mature enough yet and they may not know what is best for them. It is best to let the parents to decide until the children are of a certain age. <u>Even though my parents made all the decisions for me since I was young, I never blamed them and in fact I appreciate their help because in hindsight their decisions were always the best.</u> Besides, parents would also want the best for their children and would never choose something that is detrimental towards their children.

Skeletons to Success

A common mistake that students often make in the TOEFL is that they rush into the essay writing before they are ready. They think that with only 25 minutes for each essay assignment, time is of the essence.

That is true, but you must also remember that clear logical reasoning is also extremely crucial in the TOEFL exam. It is not good enough to simply write an essay that is free from grammatical and vocabulary errors. You must also write something that is logically sound.

To be logically sound, you must first start with a logical structure. That means you have to sketch a brief skeleton before you begin writing. Having this rough guide to follow will help you write a more successful essay.

This "Top Tip" focuses on teaching you how to create the best structure for your essay and how to train your brain to think in a logical manner.

Simple Steps

1. State your opinion in response to the general question.
2. Generate key points and sub-bullet points for each paragraph.
3. Think of possible counter-arguments.

Elaboration with Examples

In the TOEFL, we use what we call a "funnel technique." This means helping to channel your thoughts from broad thoughts to more specific points. In effect, you are linking ideas together to support a certain opinion and this is the key to producing a logically sound essay.

We always start from the broadest question, and that is the TOEFL essay question. Once you state your opinion, the universe of possibilities shrinks by half. You only need to focus on your side of the argument.

Next, think of some key points to support your argument and number them accordingly. Again, notice how you are going to increasingly specific levels. Now, you begin to organize your thoughts into point form.

The subsequent step is to think of sub-bullet points to support each point you are trying to make. Building a solid argument is like building a house. The key points are the foundation, while each sub-bullet point is like the rest of the material required to build the house, such as brick and mortar.

Finally, you want to make sure that your argument does not have holes. This is why we require you to think of counter-arguments. Most students choose to ignore the counter-arguments, but acknowledging and subsequently providing reasons as to why the counter-arguments are weak can go a long way in strengthening your essay and improving your grade. It shows that you are able to think in a more far-sighted manner and that you are objective in treating the topic. Think of this step as placing a roof above your house to keep the wind and rain away. If you've addressed the counter-arguments, it's less likely that someone else can come along and say, "What about this aspect? Have you thought about that?"

In short, the funnel technique is as follows:

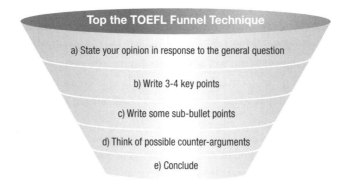

Top the TOEFL Funnel Technique

a) State your opinion in response to the general question

b) Write 3-4 key points

c) Write some sub-bullet points

d) Think of possible counter-arguments

e) Conclude

1. *State your opinion in response to the general question*

When you state your opinion, always remember that it is not about choosing the stance that you think is morally correct or the one that you feel you like the most. It is about choosing the stance that you can back up with solid logical reasoning.

We have met students who think that complex arguments will be able to impress the grader. As a result, they deliberately choose the stance that is harder to argue. However, here's the reality: you do not get points for making difficult arguments. You get points for making well-reasoned arguments.

Sample question:

Some people believe that children should not watch television. Do you agree or disagree? Use specific reasons and examples to support your answer.

Sample opinion:

I disagree with the statement that children should not watch television.

2. *Generate key points and sub-bullet points for each paragraph*

If you're not sure whether you can argue your stance well enough, this step will help you decide. List out each key point that you can make to support your stance. If you have only two or fewer points, then you have to reconsider changing your stance.

To check and see whether your points are strong, ask yourself the following questions:

- Is the point relevant to the question?
- Can I very confidently summarize the key message of the point?
- Have I repeated this point somewhere else within the essay?

Let's take a look at a sample of solid key points.

Key points outlining the benefits of television:

a) There are educational programs on television that can help a child's development:
   - Instead of shunning television, use it as a tool to educate children
   - Television is interactive and may be able to more effectively teach children about language, general knowledge etc.

b) Television can pique children's interest in other aspects such as literature
   - Watching a television show about Spongebob, for example, may encourage the child to read Spongebob books

3. *Think of possible counter-arguments*

After you have a few key points, think of counter-arguments that could poke holes in your reasoning. Then, modify your structure to anticipate these counter-arguments. You should at least acknowledge and if possible rebut these counter-arguments to make your argument more convincing.

Alternatively, if you run out of key supporting points, you can use rebuttals of counter-arguments to bolster your essay. The additions are below in bold:

a) There are educational programs on television that can help a child's development
   - Instead of shunning television, use it as a tool to educate children
   - Television is interactive and may be able to more effectively teach children about language, general knowledge etc.

b) Television can pique children's interest in other aspects such as literature
  • Watching a television show about Spongebob, for example, may encourage the child to read Spongebob books.

c) **Television is not harmful as long as it is allowed in controlled amounts of time**
  • **There is no hiding from the influence of the media, as the world has become very developed**
  • **Rather than trying to actively stop children from watching television, it is better to teach them how to exert self-discipline**
  • **As long as the child knows how to be disciplined, the ill effects of television such as inducing poor eyesight can be diminished**

In conclusion, the general framework of any essay is below. Once you have a general framework, you can use that as a guide when writing the TOEFL essays. Following the guide will make sure that you do not go off topic and also that your reasoning is clear, which is very much emphasized by the TOEFL graders.

Introduction	What is your stance? **Children should watch television**
	In general terms, how will you support your stance? **Television can bring benefits to children as long as you take advantage of it carefully**
Paragraph-Builder	Paragraph 1 There are educational programs on television that can help a child's development • Instead of shunning television, use it as a tool to educate children • Television is interactive and may be able to more effectively teach children about language, general knowledge etc.
	Paragraph 2 Television can pique children's interest in other aspects such as literature: • Watching a television show about Spongebob, for example, may encourage the child to read Spongebob books

	Television is not harmful as long as it is allowed in controlled amounts of time • There is no hiding from the influence of the media, as the world has become very developed • Rather than trying to actively stop children from watching television, it is better to teach them how to exert self-discipline • As long as the child knows how to be disciplined, the ill effects of television such as inducing poor eyesight can be diminished
Wrap-Up	Restate your stance **Television can be beneficial towards children if it is allowed in controlled amounts of time**

TOEFL Trainer

Write skeleton structures for each of the sample questions below.

1. Do you agree or disagree with the following statement? Giving students timed examinations is a better way to assess them than giving research-based assignments. Use specific reasons and examples to support your answer.

Step I: *State your opinion in response to the general question*

Step II: *Generate key points and sub-bullet points for each paragraph*

Step III: *Think of possible counter-arguments*

Introduction	What is your stance?
	In general terms, how will you support your stance?
Paragraph-Builder	Paragraph 1
	Paragraph 2
	Paragraph 3
	Paragraph 4
Wrap-Up	Restate your stance

2. Participating in extracurricular activities is a crucial element of every child's education. What is your opinion? Use specific reasons and examples to support your answer.

Step I: *State your opinion in response to the general question*

Step II: *Generate key points and sub-bullet points for each paragraph*

Step III: *Think of possible counter-arguments*

Introduction	What is your stance?
	In general terms, how will you support your stance?
Paragraph-Builder	Paragraph 1
	Paragraph 2
	Paragraph 3
	Paragraph 4
Wrap-Up	Restate your stance

3. What is the most effective way to learn English? Use specific reasons and examples to support your answer.

Step I: *State your opinion in response to the general question*

Step II: *Generate key points and sub-bullet points for each paragraph*

Step III: *Think of possible counter-arguments*

Introduction	What is your stance?
	In general terms, how will you support your stance?
Paragraph-Builder	Paragraph 1
	Paragraph 2
	Paragraph 3

	Paragraph 4
Wrap-Up	Restate your stance

4. Some people prefer living in the countryside whereas others prefer living in the cities. Which do you prefer? Use specific reasons and examples to support your answer.

Step I: *State your opinion in response to the general question*

Step II: *Generate key points and sub-bullet points for each paragraph*

Step III: *Think of possible counter-arguments*

Introduction	What is your stance?
	In general terms, how will you support your stance?

Paragraph-Builder	Paragraph 1
	Paragraph 2
	Paragraph 3
	Paragraph 4
Wrap-Up	Restate your stance

5. Many students work very hard to obtain internship positions during the summer vacations. Why do students do internships? Use specific reasons and examples to support your answer.

Step I: *State your opinion in response to the general question*

Step II: *Generate key points and sub-bullet points for each paragraph*

Step III: *Think of possible counter-arguments*

Introduction	What is your stance?
	In general terms, how will you support your stance?
Paragraph-Builder	Paragraph 1
	Paragraph 2
	Paragraph 3
	Paragraph 4
Wrap-Up	Restate your stance

Answers:

Note: These answers are provided for reference only. Students may choose to express any opinion for each essay topic.

1. Do you agree or disagree with the following statement? Giving students timed examinations is a better way to assess them than giving research-based assignments. Use specific reasons and examples to support your answer.

Step I: *State your opinion in response to the general question*

I disagree. Giving students research-based assignments is a better way to assess their abilities.

Step II: *Generate key points and sub-bullet points for each paragraph*

a) Research-based assignments tests the student's ability to gather and analyze information, which is what real life requires of them
   - On the other hand, timed examinations focus more on the student's ability to memorize and regurgitate facts. Being able to do so may not necessarily mean the student has understood the material

b) At the college level, students are expected to produce their own research work
   - Since students will have to eventually do extensive research assignments, assessing this aspect is a better indicator of their abilities

c) Research work will also test the student's ability to structure a question and find an answer in a creative yet logical manner
   - Furthermore, research work will be able to reveal whether the student is creative and logical in approaching questions

Step III: *Think of possible counter-arguments*

a) Research-based assignments tests the student's ability to gather and analyze information, which is what real life requires of them
   - On the other hand, timed examinations focus more on the student's ability to memorize and regurgitate facts. Being able to do so may not necessarily mean the student has understood the material

b) At the college level, students are expected to produce their own research work
   - Since students will have to eventually do extensive research assignments, assessing this aspect is a better indicator of their abilities

c) Research work will also test the student's ability to structure a question and find an answer in a creative yet logical manner
  - Furthermore, research work will be able to reveal whether the student is creative and logical in approaching questions

d) **Those who are in favor of timed examinations may argue that timed examinations test a student's ability to work under pressure**
  - **However, when given research assignments, students are also given certain deadlines**
  - **Timed examinations are more a test of a student's ability to memorize, which is not a good indicator of a student's ability**

Introduction	What is your stance? **Disagree**
	In general terms, how will you support your stance? Show that research assignments offer a more holistic assessment of a student's abilities as compared to timed examinations
Paragraph-Builder	Paragraph 1 **Research-based assignments tests the student's ability to gather and analyze information, which is what real life requires of them**
	Paragraph 2 **At the college level, students are expected to produce their own research work**
	Paragraph 3 **Research work will also test the student's ability to structure a question and find an answer in a creative yet logical manner**
	Paragraph 4 **Those who are in favor of timed examinations may argue that timed examinations test a student's ability to work under pressure**
Wrap-Up	Restate your stance **While timed examinations offer some benefits, they are too few in comparison to research-based assignments**

2. Participating in extracurricular activities is a crucial element of every child's education. What is your opinion? Use specific reasons and examples to support your answer.

Step I: *State your opinion in response to the general question*

I agree that extracurricular activities are a crucial element of every child's education.

Step II: *Generate key points and sub-bullet points for each paragraph*

a) Extracurricular activities are a way for children to discover their interests and strengths

- Academics are not everything. Discovering one's strengths and interests in other areas is also important because these will all contribute to the child's eventual skill set in the future
- This can also be an outlet for the child to release stress

b) Once they discover their interest and strengths, they can develop it through the activities

- Extracurricular activities are a platform for children to hone their skills. For example, if they are interested in chess, they can prepare for chess competitions through the club
- Winning awards at these competitions will also go a long way in building the child's confidence

c) Children will be able to make more friends and have a more wholesome education as they will also be able to learn how to cooperate in teams

- Through clubs, children will meet more friends and have opportunities to cooperate with each other on projects
- For example, if the child is part of a soccer team, he or she will learn how to cooperate with others

Step III: *Think of possible counter-arguments*

a) Extracurricular activities are a way for children to discover their interests and strengths

- Academics are not everything. Discovering one's strengths and interests in other areas is also important because these will all contribute to the child's eventual skill set in the future

- This can also be an outlet for the child to release stress

b) Once they discover their interest and strengths, they can develop it through the activities
    - Extracurricular activities are a platform for children to hone their skills. For example, if they are interested in chess, they can prepare for chess competitions through the club
    - Winning awards at these competitions will also go a long way in building the child's confidence

c) Children will be able to make more friends and have a more wholesome education as they will also be able to learn how to cooperate in teams
    - Through clubs, children will meet more friends and have opportunities to cooperate with each other on projects
    - For example, if the child is part of a soccer team, he or she will learn how to cooperate with others
    - **Children can also make friends in class, but cooperating on a project is much different from just knowing each other. It is important to start developing teamwork skills since young**

d) **Extracurricular activities may take up a lot of a child's time, but it is worthwhile and will not be detrimental as long as the child maintains a balance between academics and extracurricular activities**
    - **Sometimes, extracurricular activities can even support and complement academics. For example, if the child is part of a mathematics club, he or she can further explore the subject through the club**

Introduction	What is your stance? **Agree**
	In general terms, how will you support your stance? **Extracurricular activities offer many opportunities for a child to develop interests and other soft skills. It can even support and complement whatever the child is learning in the classroom**
Paragraph-Builder	Paragraph 1 **Extracurricular activities are a way for children to discover their interests and strengths**

	Paragraph 2 **Once they discover their interest and strengths, they can develop it through the activities**
	Paragraph 3 **Children will be able to make more friends and have a more wholesome education as they will also be able to learn how to cooperate in teams**
	Paragraph 4 **Extracurricular activities may take up a lot of a child's time, but it is worthwhile and will not be detrimental as long as the child maintains a balance between academics and extracurricular activities**
Wrap-Up	Restate your stance **Children should participate in extracurricular activities, as they offer many benefits that cannot be gained within the classroom**

3. What is the most effective way to learn English? Use specific reasons and examples to support your answer.

Step I: *State your opinion in response to the general question*

The most effective way to learn English is to keep practicing it often, whether it is in terms of reading, writing or speaking.

Step II: *Generate key points and sub-bullet points for each paragraph*

a) Since language is a tool for communication, the only way to keep improving is through constant practice

   - We should take time to write, speak and read English everyday

b) At the same time, we should practice with native English speakers and welcome their corrections should we make mistakes

   - We learn from mistakes but we will never know whether we have made a mistake if no one else tells us

   - Practicing with native English speakers and letting them know that they are welcome to provide corrections or suggestions is a good way to identify and improve on mistakes

c) If we have the chance, we should also immerse ourselves in an English-speaking country for some time
   - Being in an English-speaking environment will force us to think and communicate solely in English
   - We will also be able to learn the words that native speakers commonly use

Step III: *Think of possible counter-arguments*

a) Since language is a tool for communication, the only way to keep improving is through constant practice
   - We should take time to write, speak and read English everyday
   - **Although some of us are very busy, we can squeeze time out by downloading English books onto our smartphones and reading them on the subway, for example**

b) At the same time, we should practice with native English speakers and welcome their corrections should we make mistakes
   - We learn from mistakes but we will never know whether we have made a mistake if no one else tells us
   - Practicing with native English speakers and letting them know that they are welcome to provide corrections or suggestions is a good way to identify and improve on mistakes

c) If we have the chance, we should also immerse ourselves in an English-speaking country for some time
   - Being in and English-speaking environment will force us to think and communicate solely in English
   - We will also be able to learn the words that native speakers commonly use

Introduction	What is your stance?
	In general terms, how will you support your stance? **The most effective way to learn English is to keep practicing it often, whether it is in terms of reading, writing or speaking**
Paragraph-Builder	Paragraph 1 **Since language is a tool for communication, the only way to keep improving is through constant practice**

	Paragraph 2 **We should practice with native English speakers and welcome their corrections should we make mistakes**
	Paragraph 3 **If we have the chance, we should also immerse ourselves in an English-speaking country for some time**
	Paragraph 4
Wrap-Up	Restate your stance **Through constant practice, we can improve our English**

4. Some people prefer living in the countryside whereas others prefer living in the cities. Which do you prefer? Use specific reasons and examples to support your answer.

Step I: *State your opinion in response to the general question*

I prefer to live in the city.

Step II: *Generate key points and sub-bullet points for each paragraph*

a) Living in the city is more convenient because everything you need is just a short distance away
   - There may be situations whereby you need something urgently. For example, if you are very sick and you need to go to the hospital, it is only a short distance away. If you live in the countryside, it will take more time
   - There are also more amenities in the city such as cinemas, gyms and shopping malls

b) There are more job and educational opportunities in the city
   - If you prefer jobs in industries such as finance and technology, these are usually only available in the cities
   - Most schools and colleges are also located in the city, for example New York University and Boston University. If you stay in the countryside, you may lose out on such opportunities

c) There are more people to meet and make friends with in the city

- Having an active social life is important, and living in the city will provide more opportunities to meet and make friends with new people
- The larger population that can be found in cities also means that you can meet a greater variety of different people and that you will be more likely to find people with similar interests

Step III: *Think of possible counter-arguments*

a) Living in the city is more convenient because everything you need is just a short distance away

- There may be situations whereby you need something urgently. For example, if you are very sick and you need to go to the hospital, it is only a short distance away. If you live in the countryside, it will take more time
- There are also more amenities in the city such as cinemas, gyms and shopping malls

b) There are more job and educational opportunities in the city

- If you prefer jobs in industries such as finance and technology, these are usually only available in the cities
- Most schools and colleges are also located in the city, for example New York University and Boston University. If you stay in the countryside, you may lose out on such opportunities

c) There are more people to meet and make friends with in the city

- Having an active social life is important, and living in the city will provide more opportunities to meet and make friends with new people
- The larger population that can be found in cities also means that you can meet a greater variety of different people and that you will be more likely to find people with similar interests
- **Some may argue that you will have a tighter and more close-knit community in the countryside. But nothing stops you from also creating similar close-knit community in the city**

d) Cities may come with drawbacks such as pollution, noise and higher living costs
- Higher living costs will be offset by higher wages in the city
- There will be some noise and pollution, but as long as you find an appropriate place to stay, these effects should be minimized

Introduction	What is your stance? **I prefer cities**
	In general terms, how will you support your stance? **Cities offer more convenience and opportunities**
Paragraph-Builder	Paragraph 1 **Living in the city is more convenient because everything you need is just a short distance away**
	Paragraph 2 **There are more job and educational opportunities in the city**
	Paragraph 3 **There are more people to meet and make friends with in the city**
	Paragraph 4 **Cities may come with drawbacks such as pollution, noise and higher living costs**
Wrap-Up	Restate your stance **The benefits of living in a city far outweigh the benefits of living in the countryside**

5. Many students work very hard to obtain internship positions during the summer vacations. Why do students do internships? Use specific reasons and examples to support your answer.

Step I: *State your opinion in response to the general question*

Students do internships in order to gain more experience and to advance further in life.

Step II: *Generate key points and sub-bullet points for each paragraph*

a) By doing an internship, students can decide whether a particular industry or field is suitable for them
   - Many students do not know what they want to do until they try it out
   - It is nearly impossible to fully understand what a company or industry is about until you experience it
   - Therefore, an internship is extremely valuable in helping the student decide what career path suits them best

b) Students can get more experience within the field and learn things that cannot be learnt from textbooks alone
   - Some skills, such as soft skills, cannot be learnt from textbooks
   - For example, students can learn how to write professional emails, interact with clients and work with professional colleagues

c) Students will be able to meet more people through the internship and possibly gain valuable mentors
   - Many students keep in touch with their bosses after the conclusion of the internships
   - These former bosses serve as valuable mentors who can provide life advice to students even after the internship ends

Step III: *Think of possible counter-arguments*

a) By doing an internship, students can decide whether a particular industry or field is suitable for them
   - Many students do not know what they want to do until they try it out
   - It is nearly impossible to fully understand what a company or industry is about until you experience it
   - Therefore, an internship is extremely valuable in helping the student decide what career path suits them best

b) Students can get more experience within the field and learn things that cannot be learnt from textbooks alone
   - Some skills, such as soft skills, cannot be learnt from textbooks
   - For example, students can learn how to write professional emails, interact with clients and work with professional colleagues
   - **Technically, all these skills can be learnt through extra classes and sometimes even in school. Some schools do offer more practical work-related classes. However, nothing beats real experience as real life is unpredictable and cannot be fully covered by any class**

c) Students will be able to meet more people through the internship and possibly gain valuable mentors
- Many students keep in touch with their bosses after the conclusion of the internships
- These former bosses serve as valuable mentors who can provide life advice to students even after the internship ends
- **Not every student who does an internship will end up with a mentor. But, even if students do not have a good experience at their internship, it is a valuable experience nonetheless that can teach them about what the real working world is like**

Introduction	What is your stance? **Students do internships in order to gain more experience and to advance further in life**
	In general terms, how will you support your stance? **List out the different benefits that can be gained from internships**
Paragraph-Builder	Paragraph 1 **By doing an internship, students can decide whether a particular industry or field is suitable for them**
	Paragraph 2 **Students can get more experience within the field and learn things that cannot be learnt from textbooks alone**
	Paragraph 3 **Students will be able to meet more people through the internship and possibly gain valuable mentors**
	Paragraph 4
Wrap-Up	Restate your stance **It is no surprise that students want to do internships, because they have all to gain and nothing to lose**

Bridging Ideas

In this "Top Tip", we will show you how to easily and quickly combine, join and create more sophisticated sentences that will bring your writing up to the next level. The Multi-Word-Kit will be categorized clearly, so you will always know *when* and *how* to use *what*.

The Multi-Word-Kit essentially helps you form more complicated sentence structures. But from experience, when we have brought up the words "sentence structure" to students, there is immediately apprehensiveness because sentence structure tends to come with many complex grammar structures that are hard to comprehend.

But you need not worry about needlessly complex grammar. *Top the TOEFL* is here to help you get the top grade, and we will show you the shortcuts to the top. In the following pages, we break down sentence structures according to situation and need. This will make it a lot easier for you when you need to pull out these tricks in essay writing.

If you can memorize these words, and comfortably put them into use, you are already a few steps closer to *Top the TOEFL*.

Simple Steps

Note: These are not steps per se, but categories of bridging words that you can learn in order to help link sentences together.

1. Justification words.
2. Time-markers.
3. Making comparisons.
4. Stating conditions.
5. Highlighters.
6. Twists and Turns.
7. Warnings.
8. Doubt Dealers.
9. Opinion words.

Elaboration with Examples

1. *Justification words*

The following is a list of keywords that will be very useful when you need to justify something, meaning when you need to explain the reason why something occurs. The model will show how these words can transform into extra points for you.

Justification words are essential in helping you link events together, and to let your reader understand how one scene relates to the next. Without justification words, your essay might be choppy and not make much sense.

Since
Because
In order to
So
Owing to
Due to
As a result
The reason being
Thanks to
Consequently
On the grounds that
Therefore
Hence
Thus

Suppose the TOEFL asks you whether you believe that sports should be a compulsory part of every student's schedule. You will need to explain why, for example:

Sports should be a compulsory part of every student's schedule **because** physical health is just as important as academics.

Sports should be a compulsory part of every student's schedule **since** physical health is just as important as academics.

Sports should be a compulsory part of every student's schedule, **the reason being** that physical health is just as important as academics.

In order to ensure students have good physical health, sports should be a compulsory part of every student's schedule.

The justification words above can be used in a myriad of ways, covering just about every situation that you can think of. Memorize a few that you feel confident using, and make sure that you apply them in your essay.

2. *Time-markers*

Being able to give events a sense of time is also important in creating a convincing and believable argumentative essay. Without the ability to pinpoint when an event occurs, or to give a story the sense of pace and rhythm, it is very hard to keep the reader engaged. These time-markers are especially useful when you use analogies in your essay or tell short anecdotes as examples to support your argument.

Here are some handy words (or time-markers!) that you can use to help position different stages of your essay:

Fast Pace:
As soon as
Immediately
Promptly
Shortly thereafter
The moment

Regular Sequencing:
After
Soon
When
Once
While
Before
Then

Same Time:
Simultaneously
At the same time
Concurrently

Already Happened/Too Late:
By the time
Already

Let's see how this is put into practice. We will use different time-markers in order to show the different effects of each word-tool. The common situation that we will use is this:

Students should take music lessons in school.

Fast Pace:

As soon as students enter school, they should take music lessons.

The moment children enter school, they should take music lessons.

Children should take music lessons **immediately** after they enter school.

Note: The time-positioning words here lend a sense of the act being instantaneous and quick. It quickens the pace by implying that the action happens immediately.

Regular Sequencing:

Before students enter school, they may not have learned any music at all.

After entering school, students should be given a chance to learn music.

When students are in school, they should take music lessons.

Note: The time-positioning words have more of a sequencing effect, letting the reader know what happened first, what came later, and what came last.

Same Time:

Music lessons are important for every child's development and children should be encouraged to learn a musical instrument in school. But, **at the same time**, teachers should also spend a great deal of time developing other creative skills such as painting and drawing.

Note: In this instance, "at the same time" was used to freeze the moment and to give the other creative skills such as painting and drawing the same importance as music lessons.

In other examples, the same words may be used for sequencing purposes and to literally show that two events are equal or that they should happen at the same time.

Already Happened/Too Late:

> **By the time** students enter school, it may **already** be too late to teach them music.

Note: This has the "close shave" effect — showing that the student urgently needs to learn music as soon as possible.

3. *Making comparisons*

Being able to make comparisons in writing will not only help expand your essay, it will also help make your argument stronger. Why? One way of arguing that Item A is good is to argue that Item B is bad in comparison.

Here's an example. You would like to say that Milk A is tastier than Milk B. You could say, "Milk A tastes so good!"

But if you want to convince people to buy Milk A, you may have to make a comparison. You might say: "Milk A tastes much creamier than Milk B!" By doing this, you will immediately let everyone know what extra benefit they can expect should they select Milk A, and that is they will have creamier milk.

Here are some of the comparison words that you can memorize in order to help you get a better grade:

As though
As … as
Than
Like
Similar
Unlike
Just as
Compared to
While

Let's start with something simple. Let's describe something we all know very well, and which also happens to be the mascot of Princeton University — a tiger.

> Some say tigers are just **like** large cats. This is misleading. **Unlike cats**, tigers are instinctively much more aggressive and therefore much more dangerous.

Just as a lion hunts and devours its prey, a tiger follows its predator instincts and does the same. A tiger's teeth are **as** sharp **as** razor-sharp knives, and its body weight is heavier **than** three fully-grown men put together. In cartoons and storybooks, tigers have been portrayed **as though** they are cute and fluffy animals, such as Hobbes in "Calvin and Hobbes" and Tigger in "Winnie the Pooh." The truth is, tigers are **similar** to any other predator out there in the wild. If they have the chance to kill, they will.

Comparisons can also be used to strengthen an argument. It lets the reader know that you are aware of and concede certain points about the item you are arguing against. At the same time, you can highlight certain positive aspects about the item you are arguing for in order to show the vast difference between the two.

For example:

While taking the subway will take up more travelling time than driving a car, it is actually better because it reduces environmental pollution.

You can also use comparisons to make a more general point. This type of comparison is more abstract:

Giving someone a handmade gift is **like** giving someone your heart **compared to** buying just any gift from the store.

In the example above, what happened was that we used a separate image as a proxy or yardstick with which we can understand the value of a handmade gift. Instead of simply saying that a handmade gift is meaningful, we liken the handmade gift to "giving someone your heart."

If you are uncomfortable using general symbols, you can use popular images, representations, or figures that everyone can relate to. This is also effective. For example:

Going for extra tuition is just **like** attending more classes at school.

Motorcycles and bicycles are very **similar** except that bicycles do not require fuel and do not pollute the environment.

The ideas that one can get from brainstorming with friends are not **as good as** the ones that you obtain just by thinking on your own.

4. *Stating conditions*

In order to expand your essay and get more points, you may sometimes have to use words that state conditions for something else to occur:

Only if
Unless
Provided
As long as
Without
If
In order to ... need to

What does this mean? In simpler words, it means that X cannot happen without Y, or vice versa.

This is useful when you need to emphasize the importance of something, and also highlight what you need to do in order to obtain that something.

To make it clearer, we will <u>underline</u> the thing that is being emphasized as important.

The condition that needs to be fulfilled will be in *italics*.

I know that I can <u>get into a good university</u> **only if** I *work hard and score well in my exams.*

Unless I *set my alarm clock*, I will not be able to <u>wake up tomorrow morning</u>.

My mother will allow me to <u>watch a movie this weekend</u>, **provided that** I *complete my homework by Friday night.*

This method is useful in showing the step-by-step process in a plot. A needs to happen before B can occur. C needs to be done before you can move to D.

Let's recall what we learnt at the start of this sub-chapter, which is on justification words. Here, we can combine justification words to follow from the condition that we have stated. These justification words can use the stated conditions to explain a certain course of action. To use the sentences in the previous example:

I know that I can <u>get into a good university</u> **only if** I *work hard and score well in my exams.* **Therefore**, I have decided to make a timetable for myself and I promise to stick to it.

Unless I *set my alarm clock,* I will not be able to <u>wake up tomorrow morning</u>. **Thus**, can you please remind me to do so before I go to bed tonight?

My mother will allow me to <u>watch a movie this weekend</u>, **provided that** I *complete my homework by Friday night*. **Hence**, I really cannot spend too much time playing with you today.

Do you see how the essay grows with the use of these sentence structures? A single sentence can grow into a paragraph, and paragraphs make bodies of words. Pretty soon, you will have an entire essay!

The other way in which you can state conditions is to do so in hindsight. That means **after** something has occurred. This is often used upon reflection (so use the past tense), and usually to express gratitude. It could also be used to express relief that things could have gone badly, but did not.

For example:

Without my *teacher's help*, I would not have been able to turn over a new leaf and <u>get into university</u>.

If not for *my parents*, I would not be able to <u>speak Chinese</u> today.

If *you had not warned me*, I would have made a wrong turn and ended up in the traffic jam.

This second method is especially useful when it comes to thanking others, especially in speeches and letters. Essentially, you are saying that something good was not possible without them.

But, this can also be flipped around to assign blame to someone or something. Previously, we underlined what was seen as important, and italicized the condition that needs to be fulfilled.

In this case, the components are slightly different. The first part, which we will <u>underline</u> states the problem with the person or situation. This problem is the condition that the writer implicitly hopes will be rectified.

The second part, which we will italicize, indicates the outcome of possible improvement that may or may not have already occurred.

For example:

If you were not so <u>lazy</u>, you would have *graduated* by now! (Has not occurred)

If it were not <u>raining</u>, we could go and *fly a kite*! (Has not occurred)

Without the <u>noise in the classroom,</u> I could *concentrate a lot better*. (Has occurred)

Without a television to distract me, I *finished my homework a lot faster*. (Has occurred)

5. *Highlighters*

For some of you, highlighting while studying helps in making clear what the important points are. It saves you a lot of time when you go back to your textbooks for extra revision.

Similarly, while composing an essay, you will also need to highlight certain points. This is to signal to the reader that a particular point is important. Apart from that, "highlighters" (as we will call it) make your essay interesting. How is this possible?

Let's consider an example. A strong argumentative point must have an edge, or something that makes it unique. Part of what makes something unique is that it must be exceptional in a certain area. For example, if you want to argue that Coca-Cola is better than Pepsi, perhaps you want to highlight the fact that Coca-Cola delivers the same great taste with lower calories.

How do you highlight certain points? Just memorize the highlighters that we have compiled in the box below:

Especially
Particularly
Specifically
In particular
Primarily
Notably
Before all else
Of all the …
Markedly
Mainly
Chiefly
Not only … but also
Not just … but also

The usage of highlighters in a factual essay can be condensed into three basic steps:

- **State** a range of options or facts
- **Select** one of them with a highlighter
- Proceed to **elaborate** on the fact that you have highlighted

Remember: **State, Select,** and **Elaborate!**

For example:

> There are many different modes of transportation in Singapore. **Of all the** options available, MRT is one of the most popular, **especially** for students. This is because most students do not have driving licenses. They are therefore limited to the MRT, buses, and taxis.

> Former Prime Minister Lee Kuan Yew accomplished many things for Singapore, **most notably** in terms of economic growth. Because of Lee, Singapore has transformed from a resource-poor island into one of the strongest economies worldwide.

6. *Twists and Turns*

One thing you don't want is for your essay to be flat. Think about your favorite movies or books. Something always happens. The hero never remains all-powerful throughout the entire book, and neither is the villain always defeated. There are ups and downs, and this is all part of being a good writer.

So how do you incorporate twists and turns into your essay? It's very simple, as long as you know the right words. We've already summarized the important ones for you in the box below:

Turn the Tables:
However
Yet
Despite
But
Nonetheless
Still
Nevertheless
Although

Be that as it may be
In spite of
On the contrary
Though
Regardless
Even though
Even if
Instead

The Thrill Factor:
Suddenly
All of a sudden
All at once
Without warning
Straightaway
Instantly
Immediately
Fortunately/Unfortunately
Luckily/Unluckily
Miraculously
Happily/Sadly
By a stroke of luck/chance
In the nick of time

The first category, "Turning the Tables," consists of milder words. These words help signal to the reader that you are taking a different tack, and you will use these more often in TOEFL essays.

Alternatively, you can use these words to signal to the reader that you have acknowledged certain facts or points, but that you would like to present a different view. This is also important because readers will be more welcoming of your views if you first acknowledge and accept the opposing view. Otherwise, the reader may assume that you have not considered other views or thoughts when you completed your logical reasoning.

Here is an example of how you can apply this in your TOEFL essay:

> Students should learn as much as possible in their home country. **However,** after a certain age, students should explore other countries and cultures to broaden their horizons.

The second category, "The Thrill Factor," injects a bit of an action-movie flavor into your essay. You should only use this when you are about to introduce a sudden major event or action that will substantially change things. Examples include (but are of course not limited to) falling down, a car swerving, or the weather suddenly changing. These events must occur rapidly in general. Students normally use these words less often in the TOEFL examination.

To see how you can apply this in the TOEFL, please refer to the example below:

> Disciplining children is an important part of bringing them up well. Without proper discipline, a child may become overly spoilt and pampered. The purpose of punishment is to let the child know **immediately** after making a mistake that there are some things that cannot and should not be done.

7. *Warnings*

There may be situations where the examination question requires you to warn or share advice with another party. For example, in the TOEFL examination, part of your argument may include emphasizing why having traffic policemen is so important ("Without traffic policemen, traffic jams would not be able to disperse so easily.")

If this is the case, don't worry. All the tools that you need to do so are here.

Here are the four warning words:

Lest
Otherwise
Or else
If not

We have simplified the warning formula for you:

<u>Do this</u> + **Warning word** + *Consequence if you do not do this*

For example:

> Make sure you <u>print out your boarding pass</u> before you go to the airport, **or else** you may *not be able to get onto the plane.*

> <u>Go to bed</u> at a reasonable hour, **lest** you start *falling asleep in class.*

<u>Take Vitamin C</u> everyday, **otherwise** you might *fall sick.*

Always <u>listen more</u> than you speak. **If not,** *people might not like you.*

The format is simple enough, but just remember, of all these four words, "lest" is probably the most formal. To avoid the risk of losing points, try to use it only when you feel it is absolutely appropriate to do so. The substitutes are also acceptable otherwise.

8. *Doubt Dealers*

Not everything that you write must be happy, positive, and firm. Sometimes, you may need to express doubt, or to express that something is just a possibility — both in a positive and negative sense. This section is dedicated to helping you do that precisely, with the Doubt Dealers.

Study the following list of words carefully.

Possibility:
Maybe/may be
Perhaps
Likely
Possibly
Probably
Supposedly

Possibility + Description:
Apparently/Appeared
Seemingly/Seemed

The first category is straightforward. It is used to indicate possibility and some doubt to pretty much any sentence you can construct. As before, you can mix and match with other techniques in this chapter. This would help in improving sentence sophistication and therefore your grade.

For example:

Don't disturb her. She **may be** sleeping, as she was very tired yesterday.

Command + *Possibility* + *Justification*

The meeting is **likely** to be postponed due to the bad weather.

Possibility   +   Justification

That is easy enough. Now, if you want to name the source of your doubt, you may also do so, like this:

Source:	Possibility:
Based on	Maybe/may be
According to	Perhaps
From	Likely
Upon	Possibly
After	Probably
	Supposedly
	Possibility + Description:
	Apparently/Appeared
	Seemingly/Seemed

Hence, if we were to add a source to the sentences in the previous example, they would look something like this:

Don't disturb her. According to her mother, she **may be** sleeping, as she was very tired yesterday.

Command   +   Source   +   Possibility   +   Justification

Based on my instincts, the meeting is **likely** to be postponed due to the bad weather.

Source   +   Possibility   +   Justification

Note: It is perfectly fine for the source to be based upon your own instincts, gut feeling, or observations. **You are** *also a legitimate source.*

The last category of "Possibility + Description" is a little more than just expressing doubt. The doubt is more based on one's doubt in one's own perception, and one's own skepticism (sense of disbelief).

For example, compare the following two sentences:

She **seemed** fine to me.

She said that she was ill, **but** she **seemed** fine to me.

Both sentences emphasize that she seemed fine based on personal observation. The second is obviously more heavily coated in skepticism, as it places to different claims together.

The first claim is that the girl claimed to be ill. The second is that personal observation shows she seemed fine. Since only one of the two claims can be true, it casts a deeper layer of skepticism.

The formula for creating deeper doubt with a Doubt Dealer is:

Contradictory claim + Twist & Turn + Doubt Dealer + Observation

Let's look at a couple more examples:

Contradictory claim: The car salesman told me that the car was in good condition.

However, after test-driving it, I felt that it **appeared** to be faulty.
Twist & Turn + Source + Doubt Dealer + Observation

Contradictory claim: My friends told me that the mall was new.

But, after a quick glance, I thought that the mall **appeared** to be run-down.
Twist & Turn + Source + Doubt Dealer + Observation

As you can see, you can bridge sentences in a multitude of different ways. The key is learning how to use these tools to correctly express what you want to say. Flip to the **TOEFL Trainer** if you would like to put yourself to the test.

9. Opinion words

Everyone has an opinion. When you are in a supermarket trying to choose from a wide range of chocolates, you would have an opinion too. Similarly, in the TOEFL, you will have to express your opinion. If you have taken a look at the sample essay topics for the TOEFL, you would have noticed that all of them require you to state an opinion. The question is, how do you do so in an elegant and polished manner?

Here are some keywords to help you get your opinion across:

- I feel that
- I believe that
- I am of the opinion that/In my opinion
- It seems to me that

- It appears as though
- I think that
- It is clear to me that
- From my perspective
- In my view/from my viewpoint/in my point of view
- To me

How can you apply these words in the TOEFL? Let's take a look at a sample question:

> **Sample question:** Do you agree or disagree with the following statement? Drinking fruit juice is better than drinking soft drinks. Use specific reasons and examples to support your answer.

In order to state your opinion, first use any of the opinion words provided, followed by your own opinion. The formula is as follows:

Opinion words + *Your opinion*

From my perspective, *drinking fruit juice is indeed better than drinking soft drinks.*

Just like that, you have successfully used opinion words to state your viewpoint. Here's another example:

> **Sample question:** Do you agree or disagree with the following statement? Recycling should not be made compulsory for every household. Use specific reasons and examples to support your answer.

In my point of view, *recycling should be a choice and not something that is forced upon different households.*

Skip to the *TOEFL Trainer* if you would like to try it out on your own.

TOEFL Trainer

1. *Justification words*

It is your turn to try it out. Link up the sentences with the justification word provided in the box. You can use more than one sentence. You should aim to produce a more sophisticated sentence.

(1) Anna was thirsty. Anna bought two bottles of water from the canteen. [Since]

(2) Peter was expelled. Peter had been caught smoking in the school toilets. [On the grounds that]

(3) There was a 50 percent discount on all items in Armani Exchange. The Armani Exchange store was so packed that one could hardly breathe in it. [Owing to]

(4) It was Lisa's mother's 60th birthday. Lisa went out of her way to do something special. [Therefore]

(5) Joshua had not studied for the exam. Joshua obtained the lowest grade in the entire school. [Consequently]

(6) Kee Meng bought a bicycle. Kee Meng no longer needs to walk to school. [So]

(7) Siti is not good with directions. Siti got lost on the way to the new shopping mall. [Because]

(8) There was a massive traffic jam this morning. Lionel was late to work. [Owing to]

(9) Sheila cancelled all of her appointments. Sheila spent time with her uncle. [In order to]

(10) Anand refused to go to the hospital. Anand has a fear of doctors. [The reason being]

Answers:

(1) **Since** Anna was thirsty, she bought two bottles of water from the canteen.

(2) Peter was expelled **on the grounds** that he had been caught smoking in the school toilets.

(3) **Owing to** the 50 percent discount on all items in Armani Exchange, the store was so packed that one could hardly breathe in it.

(4) It was Lisa's mother's 60th birthday. **Therefore**, she went out of her way to do something special.

(5) Joshua had not studied for the exam, and **consequently** obtained the lowest grade in the entire school.

(6) Kee Meng bought a bicycle, **so** he no longer needs to walk to school.

(7) **Because** Siti is not good with directions, she got lost on the way to the new shopping mall.

(8) **Owing to** the massive traffic jam this morning, Lionel was late to work.

(9) Sheila cancelled all of her appointments **in order to** spend time with her uncle.

(10) Anand refused to go to the hospital, **the reason being** that he has a fear of doctors.

2. *Time-marker*

Let's practice placing time-markers in a situation that we are familiar with — waking up and brushing one's teeth. Link up the separate sentences below, and do this by using the time-markers in the boxes provided. Feel free to shift the sentences around.

(1) I wake up. The alarm clock rings at 7 am. [Once]
(2) But I hit the snooze button five or six times. I wake up properly. [After]
(3) I drag myself to the bathroom. My brother also wakes up at 7 am. He uses another bathroom so he can brush his teeth. [Simultaneously]
(4) My brother and I get ready. My mother prepares breakfast. [While]
(5) We go downstairs. Two bowls of cereal on the table and some hot toast. [By the time]
(6) I finish my food. I have to rush to the bus stop because I am always late. [As soon as]
(7) The bus leaves at 8 am. If I do not rush, I will miss it. [Promptly]
(8) I get on the bus. I can relax. [Once]
(9) I pack my bag. I go to school. [Immediately after]
(10) The school will punish the student. You make a complaint. [As soon as]

Answers:

(1) **Once** the alarm clock rings at 7 am, I wake up.
(2) But, I only wake up properly **after** hitting the snooze button five or six times.
(3) I drag myself to the bathroom. My brother also wakes up at 7 am. He uses another bathroom so that we can both brush our teeth **simultaneously.**
(4) **While** my brother and I get ready, my mother prepares breakfast.
(5) **By the time** we go downstairs, there are already two bowls of cereal on the table and some hot toast.
(6) **As soon as** I finish my food, I have to rush to the bus stop because I am always late.

(7) The bus leaves **promptly** at 8 am. If I do not rush, I will miss it.

(8) **Once** I get on the bus, I can relax.

(9) I go to school **immediately after** I pack my bag.

(10) The school will punish the student **as soon as** you make a complaint.

3. *Making comparisons*

Practice making comparisons to strengthen your arguments. Link up the separate sentences below, and do this by using the comparison words in the boxes provided.

(1) Without light, we will not be able to see. But, without electricity, we will not be able to have light. [More important than]

(2) Children should be allowed to have pets. This can teach them how to be more responsible. [Like a responsibility]

(3) The United States has four seasons. The United Kingdom also has four seasons. [Similar]

(4) Chocolate tastes better and may have nutrition benefits. Candy is just made from pure sugar. [Compared to]

(5) Mock examinations are designed very carefully. They should be like real examinations. [As though]

(6) Young people are dependent on smartphones. Old people are not dependent on smartphones. [Unlike]

Answers:

(1) Electricity is **more important than** light, because we will not be able to have light without electricity.

(2) Children should be allowed to have pets because having a pet is **like a responsibility.**

(3) The United States is **similar** to the United Kingdom in the sense that both have four seasons.

(4) Chocolate is better **compared to** candy because it tastes better and may have nutrition benefits.

(5) Mock examinations are designed carefully, **as though** they are real examinations.

(6) **Unlike** young people, old people are not dependent on smartphones.

4. Stating conditions

4.1. Stating conditions (I)

In this section, we will provide you with two items: (1) The important goal and (2) What you need to achieve that goal. Your job is to link up the two with the new words that you have learnt. Try to use each word instead of relying on just one. As a refresher, here they are again:

Only if

Unless

Provided

As long as

Without

If

In order to... need to

---

(1) Goal: To climb Mount Everest
     What you need to achieve: Exercise regularly

(2) Goal: To learn how to cook
     What you need to achieve: Start watching cooking shows and buy some cookbooks

(3) Goal: To visit Paris one day
     What you need to achieve: Save up money for a flight ticket

(4) Goal: To become fluent in Spanish
     What you need to achieve: Have more frequent conversations with native Spanish-speakers

(5) Goal: To visit Myanmar
     What you need to achieve: Apply for a visa

(6) Goal: To be a good skier
     What you need to achieve: Learn the basic skills and practice hard

(7) Goal: To improve your grades
     What you need to achieve: Study harder and to seek guidance from teachers

(8) Goal: To prepare a birthday surprise for your father
     What you need to achieve: Plan carefully with your siblings

Answers:

(1) **In order to** climb Mount Everest, **I need to** exercise more regularly.

(2) **If** I start watching cooking shows and buy some cook books, I can learn how to cook.

(3) I can visit Paris one day **only if** I save up money for a flight ticket.

(4) **Unless** I have more frequent conversations with native Spanish-speakers, I cannot become fluent in Spanish.
(Note: This is a tricky one! If you are using "unless," you need to negate the goal. "Unless" is more like a threat or warning. It implies that something will not happen **unless** X happens. Think carefully before you use this.)

(5) You can visit Myanmar **provided** you have already applied for a visa.

(6) **As long as** you learn the basic skills and practice hard, you can become a good skier.

(7) You can improve your grades **only if** you study harder and seek guidance from your teachers.

(8) **In order to** prepare a birthday surprise for my father, **I need to** plan carefully with my siblings.

4.2. Stating Conditions (II)

In this section, we will focus on stating the condition in order to express gratitude or to assign blame. We will provide two pieces of information: (A) What the other party did for you and (B) What would have happened if they had not done that.

The two keywords that you should use in this section to link up the two pieces of information are:

- Without
- If

Example:

What they did: The dog had been properly trained
What would have happened: It would not have dug up the entire garden
[Assign blame]

Ideal answer: **If** the dog had been properly trained, it would not have dug up the entire garden.

(1) What they did: Your mother paid for violin lessons

     What would have happened: You would not have discovered your passion for playing the violin

[Express gratitude]

(2) What they did: Yolanda had not lost the map

     What would have happened: We would have gotten to the hotel an hour ago

[Assign blame]

(3) What they did: Your friend, Bala, reminded you about the extra homework

     What would have happened: You would have been punished in front of the whole class

[Express gratitude]

(4) What they did: The receptionist called for a taxi in advance

     What would have happened: You would not have made it to the airport on time

[Express gratitude]

(5) What they did: The doctor diagnosed your cousin, Jeremy, correctly

     What would have happened: Jeremy would have been hospitalized

[Express gratitude]

(6) What they did: Your teacher is very dedicated

     What would have happened: You would have failed Geography

[Express gratitude]

(7) What they did: The contractor had been honest

     What would have happened: The house would be in a better shape.

[Assign blame]

(8) What they did: The security guard had been more alert

     What would have happened: He would have caught the burglars

[Assign blame]

Answers:

(1) **If** my mother had not paid for violin lessons, I would not have discovered my passion for playing the violin.

(2) **If** Yolanda had not lost the map, we would have gotten to the hotel an hour ago.

(3) **If** Bala had not reminded me about the extra homework, I would have been punished in front of the entire class.

(4) **If** the receptionist had not called for a taxi in advance, I would have not made it to the airport on time.

(5) **Without** the doctor's correct diagnosis, my cousin Jeremy would have been hospitalized.

(6) **Without** my teacher's dedication, I would have failed Geography.

(7) **If** the contractor had been honest, the house would have been in better shape.

(8) **If** the security guard had been more alert, he would have caught the burglars.

5. *Highlighters*

Study the highlighters in the box below. Use the State, Select, and Elaborate three-step process to link up the basic information given in each question.

Especially
Particularly
Specifically
In particular
Primarily
Notably
Before all else
Of all the…
Markedly
Mainly
Chiefly
Not only… but also
Not just… but also

(1) State: Sangeeta has many pets in her house (list at least three)
    Select: Which is her favorite?
    Elaborate: Write one line about her favorite pet.

(2) State: Muthu loves playing sports (list at least three)
    Select: Which sport did Muthu start learning first?
    Elaborate: Write one line about how Muthu came to learn about that sport.

(3) State: Kelly has visited many countries with her family (list at least three)

   Select: Which is her favorite?

   Elaborate: Write one line about why that country is her favorite.

(4) State: Robert learns about many different subjects at school (list at least three)

   Select: Of these subjects, which one is Robert doing the best in?

   Elaborate: Does Robert want to pursue a career related to that subject? Explain

(5) State: Jacob has many uncles (list at least three)

   Select: Which uncle is Jacob closest to?

   Elaborate: What do Jacob and his uncle often do together?

(6) State: Han Wei loves eating (list at least three dishes)

   Select: Which is his favorite?

   Elaborate: How often does Han Wei eat that particular dish?

(7) State: Tim has many different hobbies (list at least three)

   Select: Which is his favorite?

   Elaborate: How did Tim start getting into this particular hobby?

(8) State: Preetha has many dresses in different colors (list at least three)

   Select: Which color is her favorite?

   Elaborate: Write one line about why that color is her favorite.

Note: At the end of this exercise, you should be comfortable with the system of State, Select, and Elaborate. This will already automatically give you three sentences that you can use. Just add one or two more sentences, and it becomes a paragraph!

Answers:

(1) At home, Sangeeta has a dog, a cat, as well as a tank full of fish. **Of all** these pets, Sangeeta loves her dog, Bobo, the most. She had rescued Bobo from a drain when Bobo was just a few months old, and nursed him back to health.

(2) Muthu loves playing any kind of sports, including squash, tennis, and football. But, **above all else**, he **especially** likes playing football. His father had begun teaching him football techniques since he was five years old, and even sent him to football training camps.

(3) Kelly has visited many countries with her family, **mainly** countries in Europe such as France, England, and Germany. Kelly **particularly** liked France. She was simply enthralled by the beautiful buildings, as well as the wonderful pastries in the French bakeries.

(4) Robert takes many subjects at school, including Biology, Physics, and Literature. His best subject by far is Physics. He intends to pursue a career related to Physics, or more **specifically** as an engineer.

(5) Jacob has many uncles from both his father and mother's side. **Of all** these uncles, Jacob is closest to Uncle Shen. They do **not just** spend time chatting with each other at family reunions, **but also** make it a point to catch a meal together now and then.

(6) Han Wei loves eating anything and everything from pork buns, to chicken rice, to lasagna. His absolute favorite **above all else** is chicken rice. Once, he ate chicken rice every single day for an entire month!

(7) Tim likes running, watching television, as well as reading in his spare time. **Of all these** hobbies, Tim enjoys reading the most. He began reading when his mother gave him his first book — Harry Potter.

(8) Preetha has many dresses in a variety of colors — black, red, and blue — you name it, she's probably got it. **Of all these** colors, her favorite is red because it goes well against her light brown skin.

6. *Twists and Turns*

Connect the information together using the Twists and Turns in the boxes provided. Feel free to adapt the sentences as you wish.

(1) Poor. Difficult. Parents sacrifice for children. [Regardless]

(2) Fought in the past. Now best of friends. [But]

(3) Raining. Remembered an umbrella. [Fortunately]

(4) Rushed all the way to school for exam. It was the wrong day. [Unfortunately]

(5) Thought you had forgotten to bring a textbook. Your mother packed it for you. [By a stroke of luck]

(6) It was a very hot day. Thunderstorm. [All of a sudden]

(7) You are not angry with your parents for making you work hard. You appreciate it. [On the contrary]

(8) Car on highway. Swerve to the right. [Without warning]

(9) 30-hour plane ride. Willing to see cousin. [Even though]

(10) Car coming at high speed. Pulled sister away. [In the nick of time]

Answers:

(1) Regardless of how poor or how difficult life may be, parents will always be willing to sacrifice everything for their children.

(2) They used to fight in the past, but now they are best of friends.

(3) It started raining this afternoon, but fortunately I remembered to bring an umbrella.

(4) I rushed all the way to school for an exam yesterday, but unfortunately I had misread my schedule and it was the wrong day.

(5) I thought that I had forgotten to bring my textbook. However, by a stroke of luck, my mother had packed it for me!

(6) It was a very hot day. All of a sudden, the skies opened up and a thunderstorm struck!

(7) I am not angry with my parents for making me work hard. On the contrary, I appreciate it a lot.

(8) The car that was on the highway swerved to the right without warning!

(9) Even though there is a 30-hour plane ride separating us, I am always willing to visit my cousin.

(10) The car was coming at us at high speed, but luckily I managed to pull my sister away in the nick of time.

7. Warnings

We will provide the three components to the Warning formula (<u>Do this</u> + **Warning word** + *Consequence if you do not do this). Write out the warning sentence in full.*

(1) Do: Brush your teeth twice a day
    Warning: Otherwise
    Consequence: Cavities

(2) Do: Listen in class
    Warning: If not
    Consequence: Struggle when exams come

(3) Do: Count your blessings
    Warning: Otherwise
    Consequence: Cannot appreciate what you have

(4) Do: Eat something before you leave
    Warning: Lest
    Consequence: Get very hungry

(5) Do: Abide by the traffic rules
     Warning: Or else
     Consequence: Summons

(6) Do: Travel as much as possible when you are young
     Warning: Otherwise
     Consequence: Might not be able to do so when you are old

(7) Do: Get enough sleep
     Warning: Lest
     Consequence: Fall sick

(8) Do: Be kind to others
     Warning: Otherwise
     Consequence: Others won't be kind to you

(9) Do: Calculate your change
     Warning: Lest
     Consequence: Shortchanged you

(10) Do: Bargain at the market
     Warning: Otherwise
     Consequence: Get cheated

Answers:

(1) Brush your teeth twice a day, **otherwise** you may get cavities.

(2) Do listen in class. **If not**, you will struggle when exams come.

(3) Count your blessings every day. **Otherwise**, you cannot appreciate what you have.

(4) Make sure to eat something before you leave, **lest** you get very hungry later on.

(5) Please abide by the traffic rules, **or else** you risk getting a summons.

(6) Seize the opportunity to travel as much as possible when you are young. **Otherwise,** you might not be able to do so when you are old.

(7) Do get enough sleep, **lest** you fall sick later.

(8) Be kind to others, **otherwise** others won't be kind to you.

(9) Calculate the change carefully **lest** the shopkeeper shortchanged you.

(10) Do bargain at the market, **otherwise** you risk getting cheated.

8. *Doubt Dealers*

Link up the sentences with the words provided in the boxes. As soon as you get used to breaking down sentences into different components, and then getting comfortable with reconstructing them again, you are well on your way to the top grade!

(1) Contradictory claim: The class teacher said that grades would be out today.

Source: Rumor from classmate [According to]

Twist & Turn: [However/But]

Observation: It was nearly the end of the day, still no sight of exam papers. [Appeared]

(2) Contradictory claim: Uncle Louis loves animals.

Source: Your cousin, Kenny. [Based on]

Twist &Turn: [However/But]

Observation: Uncle Louis never had pets. [Supposedly]

(3) Contradictory claim: Mother seems to be in a bad mood.

Source: Your sister, Cindy [From]

Twist & Turn: [Nonetheless]

Observation: Heard mother singing in the kitchen. [Seem]

(4) Contradictory claim: Blue House would win the school sports competition.

Source: Personal calculations [Based on]

Twist & Turn: [However/But]

Observation: Red House stood a chance, started winning many races at the last minute. [Seemed]

(5) Contradictory claim: You had done badly in an English exam.

Source: Own experience [Based on]

Twist & Turn: [On the contrary]

Observation: English teacher was very happy and congratulated you after class. [Seemed]

(6) Contradictory claim: The cleaner had done her job.

Source: The schedule [According to]

Twist & Turn: [Despite]

Observation: Saw dirty dishes piled high in the sink. [Appeared]

(7) Contradictory claim: The students at Olympia High are well behaved.

     Source: Rumor from friend [According to]

     Twist & Turn: [However/But]

     Observation: Noticed lots of graffiti on the school grounds. [Appeared]

(8) Contradictory claim: Your friend, Katie, is very positive and upbeat.

     Source: Katie's email [According to]

     Twist & Turn: [Though]

     Observation: Katie says many negative things in person [Seemed]

Answers:

(1) According to my classmate, the class teacher had said that the grades would be out today. But it was nearly the end of the day, and there still appeared to be no sight of the exam papers.

(2) Based on what Kenny told me, Uncle Louis loves animals. But Uncle Louis supposedly has never had any pets!

(3) From what Cindy told me, mum was in a bad mood this morning. Nonetheless, I seem to have heard her singing in the kitchen.

(4) Based on my personal calculations, it was clear that Blue House would win the school sports competition. However, Red House started winning many races at the last minute and it seemed like Red House stood a chance.

(5) Based on what I felt, I had done very badly in the English exam. On the contrary, my English teacher seemed very happy with me and even congratulated me after class today.

(6) According to the schedule, the cleaner had done her job. Despite the fact that the cleaner was supposed to have already been in, there appeared to be many dirty dishes piled high in the sink.

(7) According to a friend, the students at Olympia High are very well behaved. However, there appeared to be a lot of graffiti on the school grounds.

(8) According to Katie's email, she sounded very positive and upbeat. Though she used many encouraging words in the email, she seemed very negative in person, as she said many discouraging things.

9. *Opinion words*

For each of the essay topics below, state your opinion by using any of the opinion words listed below.

- I feel that
- I believe that
- I am of the opinion that/In my opinion
- It seems to me that
- It appears as though
- I think that
- It is clear to me that
- From my perspective
- In my view/from my viewpoint/in my point of view
- To me

(1) Do you agree or disagree with the following statement? Making friends on the Internet is just as good as making friends in person. Use specific reasons and examples to support your answer.

(2) Some high schools require all students to take both arts and science subjects. Other high schools allow students to select the subjects that they like, even if these subjects are arts-only subjects or science-only subjects. Which of these two school policies do you think is better? Use specific reasons and examples to support your answer.

(3) Do you agree or disagree with the following statement? Shopping online is more convenient than shopping in malls. Use specific reasons and examples to support your answer.

(4) Do you agree or disagree with the following statement? Children should be made to learn more than one language since a young age. Use specific reasons and examples to support your answer.

(5) Imagine that you were given a chance to meet any famous person or celebrity of your choice. Who would you want to meet? Use specific details and examples to support your answer.

(6) Do you agree or disagree with the following statement? All students should participate in some form of volunteer activity at least once in their lifetimes. Use specific reasons and examples to support your answer.

(7) Imagine that you were walking on the street and that you came across a beggar. Would you donate some money to the beggar? Use specific reasons and examples to support your answer.

(8) Do you agree or disagree with the following statement? Smartphones have become a necessity, and they are no longer a luxury. Use specific reasons and examples to support your answer.

(9) You have a choice to either go for a jog outdoors or to exercise in a gym. Which would you prefer? Use specific reasons and examples to support your answer.

(10) Do you agree or disagree with the following statement? Learning about other cultures should be made compulsory. Use specific reasons and examples to support your answer.

Answers:

(1) **I believe that** making friends in person is better than making friends on the Internet.

(2) **From my perspective**, requiring all students to take both arts and science subjects is better than giving students a choice to choose only the subjects that they like.

(3) **I feel that** shopping online is certainly more convenient than shopping in malls.

(4) **From my viewpoint**, children should indeed be made to learn more than one language since a young age.

(5) **To me**, it would be a dream come true to meet Steve Jobs in person.

(6) **I am of the opinion** that students should participate in some form of volunteer activity at least once in their lifetimes.

(7) **From my point of view**, I would donate some money to the beggar.

(8) **It appears as though** smartphones have indeed become a necessity, and they are no longer a luxury.

(9) **From my perspective**, exercising in a gym is always better than jogging outside.

(10) **I think that** learning about other cultures should be made compulsory.

Introductions Made Easy

Many students have trouble starting their essay. They spend ages worrying over how they should begin, and as a result have little time for the rest of the essay. In actual fact, introductory paragraphs are very easy to write and there's a secret formula to writing the "perfect introduction."

Simple Steps

1. Restate the question.
2. State your opinion.
3. Briefly outline the key points that you will make to support your opinion.

Elaboration with Examples

To explain how introductions can be written very easily, let's refer to one of the essay structures that we build in a previous chapter:

Sample Topic: Do you agree or disagree with the following statement? Giving students timed examinations is a better way to assess them than giving research-based assignments. Use specific reasons and examples to support your answer.

Introduction	What is your stance? **Disagree**
	In general terms, how will you support your stance? **Show that research assignments offer a more holistic assessment of a student's abilities as compared to timed examinations**
Paragraph-Builder	Paragraph 1 **Research-based assignments tests the student's ability to gather and analyze information, which is what real life requires of them**
	Paragraph 2 **At the college level, students are expected to produce their own research work**

	Paragraph 3 **Research work will also test the student's ability to structure a question and find an answer in a creative yet logical manner**
	Paragraph 4 **Those who are in favor of timed examinations may argue that timed examinations test a student's ability to work under pressure**
Wrap-Up	Restate your stance **While timed examinations offer some benefits, they are too few in comparison to research-based assignments.**

Step I: *Restate the question*

There has been a great deal of debate as to whether timed examinations or research-based assignments are better ways of assessing a student's ability.

Step II: *State your opinion*

While more traditional people may think that timed examinations are still the best, I believe that research-based assignments provide a better assessment of students' abilities.

Step III: *Briefly outline the key points that you will make to support your opinion*

This is because research-based assignments test students' abilities from many aspects, whereas timed examinations mainly focuses on the student's ability to memorize and regurgitate facts in a short amount of time.

By following these three simple steps, you have constructed a solid introduction:

There has been a great deal of debate as to whether timed examinations or research-based assignments are better ways of assessing a student's ability. While more traditional people may think that timed examinations are still the best, I believe that research-based assignments provide a better assessment of students' abilities. This is because research-based assignments test students' abilities from many aspects, whereas timed examinations mainly focuses on the student's ability to memorize and regurgitate facts in a short amount of time.

TOEFL Trainer

Use the Simple Steps to create introductory paragraphs for each sample essay topic.

1. Participating in extracurricular activities is a crucial element of every child's education. What is your opinion? Use specific reasons and examples to support your answer.

Introduction	What is your stance? **Agree**
	In general terms, how will you support your stance? **Extracurricular activities offer many opportunities for a child to develop interests and other soft skills. It can even support and complement whatever the child is learning in the classroom**
Paragraph-Builder	Paragraph 1 **Extracurricular activities are a way for children to discover their interests and strengths**
	Paragraph 2 **Once they discover their interest and strengths, they can develop it through the activities**
	Paragraph 3 **Children will be able to make more friends and have a more wholesome education as they will also be able to learn how to cooperate in teams**
	Paragraph 4 **Extracurricular activities may take up a lot of a child's time, but it is worthwhile and will not be detrimental as long as the child maintains a balance between academics and extracurricular activities**
Wrap-Up	Restate your stance **Children should participate in extracurricular activities, as they offer many benefits that cannot be gained within the classroom**

Step I: *Restate the question*

Step II: *State your opinion*

Step III: *Briefly outline the key points that you will make to support your opinion*

2. What is the most effective way to learn English? Use specific reasons and examples to support your answer.

Introduction	What is your stance?
	In general terms, how will you support your stance? **The most effective way to learn English is to keep practicing it often, whether it is in terms of reading, writing or speaking.**
Paragraph-Builder	Paragraph 1 **Since language is a tool for communication, the only way to keep improving is through constant practice**
	Paragraph 2 **We should practice with native English speakers and welcome their corrections should we make mistakes**
	Paragraph 3 **If we have the chance, we should also immerse ourselves in an English-speaking country for some time**
	Paragraph 4
Wrap-Up	Restate your stance **Through constant practice, we can improve our English**

Step I: *Restate the question*

Step II: *State your opinion*

Step III: *Briefly outline the key points that you will make to support your opinion*

3. Some people prefer living in the countryside whereas others prefer living in the cities. Which do you prefer? Use specific reasons and examples to support your answer.

Introduction	What is your stance? **I prefer cities**
	In general terms, how will you support your stance? **Cities offer more convenience and** opportunities
Paragraph-Builder	Paragraph 1 **Living in the city is more convenient because everything you need is just a short distance away**
	Paragraph 2 **There are more job and educational opportunities in the city**
	Paragraph 3 **There are more people to meet and make friends with in the city**
	Paragraph 4 **Cities may come with drawbacks such as pollution, noise and higher living costs**
Wrap-Up	Restate your stance **The benefits of living in a city far outweigh the benefits of living in the countryside**

Step I: *Restate the question*

Step II: *State your opinion*

Step III: *Briefly outline the key points that you will make to support your opinion*

4. Many students work very hard to obtain internship positions during the summer vacations. Why do students do internships? Use specific reasons and examples to support your answer.

Introduction	What is your stance? **Students do internships in order to gain more experience and to advance further in life**
	In general terms, how will you support your stance? **List out the different benefits that can be gained from internships**
Paragraph-Builder	Paragraph 1 **By doing an internship, students can decide whether a particular industry or field is suitable for them**
	Paragraph 2 **Students can get more experience within the field and learn things that cannot be learnt from textbooks alone**
	Paragraph 3 **Students will be able to meet more people through the internship and possibly gain valuable mentors**

	Paragraph 4
Wrap-Up	Restate your stance **It is no surprise that students want to do internships, because they have all to gain and nothing to lose**

Step I: *Restate the question*

Step II: *State your opinion*

Step III: *Briefly outline the key points that you will make to support your opinion*

Answers:

1.

Step I: *Restate the question*

Nowadays, most students participate in some form of extracurricular activity.

Step II: *State your opinion*

In my opinion, these extracurricular activities are crucial for each child's educational development and can bring my benefits.

Step III: *Briefly outline the key points that you will make to support your opinion*

This is largely because extracurricular activities offer many opportunities for a child to develop interests and other soft skills, and can also support as well as complement whatever the child is learning in the classroom.

2.

Step I: *Restate the question*

Many people have tried various ways to master the English language in the most efficient way possible.

Step II: *State your opinion*

In my opinion, the best way to learn English is to keep practicing it often, whether it is in terms of reading, writing or speaking.

Step III: *Briefly outline the key points that you will make to support your opinion.*

Since language is a tool for communication, the only way to keep improving is through practice, especially with native English speakers or through immersion in an English-speaking country.

3.

Step I: *Restate the question*

Today, most people have a choice between living in the countryside and living in the city.

Step II: *State your opinion*

For me at least, living in the city is much more preferable.

Step III: *Briefly outline the key points that you will make to support your opinion*

This is mainly because cities offer more convenience and opportunities.

4.

Step I: *Restate the question*

It is very common to see students doing internships during summer or even winter vacations these days.

Step II: *State your opinion*

I believe that students do this in order to gain more experience that will help them advance further in life.

Step III: *Briefly outline the key points that you will make to support your opinion*

These experiences and benefits are items that they cannot obtain from the classroom, and can only be obtained through internships.

Topic Sentences

Up till now, you have learnt how to structure your essay. You've written introductory paragraphs. You've also learnt how to get the tone right. Now, what do you do? Should you jump into writing an essay straightaway?

If you want to get the top grade in the TOEFL, then that's not all you need to learn how to do. You may have heard that apart from structure and tone, a good essay must also "flow." Well, what does it mean to flow? What is this vague concept of an essay that just "clicks"? We're here to tell you the secret, and that is to make sure you write good topic sentences.

A topic sentence refers to the first sentence of every paragraph. To give an example, when you read an advertisement, you always start with the first sentence. If the first sentence is not gripping or exciting enough, you probably won't continue. And that is why the first sentence of each paragraph is the most important.

Simple Steps

You only need to follow these three simple steps in order to write good topic sentences

1. Introduce the main point of the paragraph.
2. Link to the idea in the previous paragraph.
3. Be concise and brief.

Elaboration with Examples

Let's continue building on some of the examples that we completed under "Top Tip 9: Skeletons to Success." In "Top Tip 9," we built the structures for some of the practice essay topics. Now, let's see how we can create topic sentences for each paragraph.

Sample Topic: Do you agree or disagree with the following statement? Giving students timed examinations is a better way to assess them than giving research-based assignments. Use specific reasons and examples to support your answer.

Introduction	What is your stance? **Disagree**
	In general terms, how will you support your stance? **Show that research assignments offer a more holistic assessment of a student's abilities as compared to timed examinations**
Paragraph-Builder	Paragraph 1 **Research-based assignments tests the student's ability to gather and analyze information, which is what real life requires of them**
	Paragraph 2 **At the college level, students are expected to produce their own research work**
	Paragraph 3 **Research work will also test the student's ability to structure a question and find an answer in a creative yet logical manner**
	Paragraph 4 **Those who are in favor of timed examinations may argue that timed examinations test a student's ability to work under pressure**
Wrap-Up	Restate your stance **While timed examinations offer some benefits, they are too few in comparison to research-based assignments**

Paragraph 1

Step I: *Introduce the main point of the paragraph*

This key point must be within the topic sentence.

Main Point: Research-based assignments test the student's ability to gather and analyze information, which is what real life requires of them.

Step II: *Link to the idea in the previous paragraph*

Next, the topic sentence must also at least make a reference to the previous paragraph's key point.

Previous Paragraph: Research assignments offer **a more holistic assessment** of a student's abilities as compared to timed examinations.

Analyze the main point in the previous paragraph and you will note that it emphasizes a "more holistic assessment" of the student's abilities.

Step III: *Be concise and brief*

Among the many aspects that research-based assignments are able to test but that timed examinations cannot is the student's ability to gather and analyze information, which is crucial in preparing them for what lies ahead in life.

Paragraph 2

Step I: *Introduce the main point of the paragraph*

Main Point: At the college level, students are expected to produce their own research work.

This paragraph states that research work is central to what needs to be done at the college level, implying therefore that the ability to complete research-based assignments is more valuable than the ability to score in timed examinations.

Step II: *Link to the idea in the previous paragraph*

As demonstrated in the previous example, do link the paragraph's main point with the previous paragraph.

Previous Paragraph: Among the many aspects that research-based assignments are able to test but that timed examinations cannot is the student's ability to gather and analyze information, which is crucial in preparing them for what lies ahead in life.

Step III: *Be concise and brief*

Furthermore, being able to produce good research work will be indispensable to students, especially when they reach the college level where students are expected to produce their own research.

Paragraph 3

Step I: Introduce the main point of the paragraph

Main Point: Research work will also test the student's ability to structure a question and find an answer in a creative yet logical manner.

Step II: *Link to the idea in the previous paragraph*

Previous Paragraph: Furthermore, being able to produce good research work will be indispensable to students, especially when they reach the college level where students are expected to produce their own research.

Step III: *Be concise and brief*

In addition, research work will test various other aspects that timed examinations cannot cover, such as the student's ability to structure a question and find an answer in a creative yet logical manner.

Paragraph 4

Step I: *Introduce the main point of the paragraph*

Main Point: Those who are in favor of timed examinations may argue that timed examinations test a student's ability to work under pressure.

Here, the key point that you can infer is that research-based assignments can also test a student's ability to work under pressure, just like timed examinations.

Step II: *Link to the idea in the previous paragraph*

Previous Paragraph: In addition, research work will test various other aspects that timed examinations cannot cover, such as the student's ability to structure a question and find an answer in a creative yet logical manner.

Step III: *Be concise and brief*

Many of the aspects tested by timed examinations are also tested by research-based assignments, such as the student's ability to work under pressure.

TOEFL Trainer

Create topic sentences for each paragraph.

1. Participating in extracurricular activities is a crucial element of every child's education. What is your opinion? Use specific reasons and examples to support your answer.

Introduction	What is your stance? **Agree**
	In general terms, how will you support your stance? **Extracurricular activities offer many opportunities for a child to develop interests and other soft skills. It can even support and complement whatever the child is learning in the classroom**
Paragraph-Builder	Paragraph 1 **Extracurricular activities are a way for children to discover their interests and strengths**
	Paragraph 2 **Once they discover their interest and strengths, they can develop it through the activities**
	Paragraph 3 **Children will be able to make more friends and have a more wholesome education as they will also be able to learn how to cooperate in teams**
	Paragraph 4 **Extracurricular activities may take up a lot of a child's time, but it is worthwhile and will not be detrimental as long as the child maintains a balance between academics and extracurricular activities**
Wrap-Up	Restate your stance **Children should participate in extracurricular activities, as they offer many benefits that cannot be gained within the classroom**

Paragraph 1

Step I: *Introduce the main point of the paragraph*

Step II: *Link to the idea in the previous paragraph*

Step III: *Be concise and brief*

Paragraph 2

Step I: *Introduce the main point of the paragraph*

Step II: *Link to the idea in the previous paragraph*

Step III: *Be concise and brief*

Paragraph 3

Step I: *Introduce the main point of the paragraph*

Step II: *Link to the idea in the previous paragraph*

Step III: *Be concise and brief*

Paragraph 4

Step I: *Introduce the main point of the paragraph*

Step II: *Link to the idea in the previous paragraph*

Step III: *Be concise and brief*

2. What is the most effective way to learn English? Use specific reasons and examples to support your answer.

Introduction	What is your stance?
	In general terms, how will you support your stance? **The most effective way to learn English is to keep practicing it often, whether it is in terms or reading, writing or speaking**
Paragraph-Builder	Paragraph 1 **Since language is a tool for communication, the only way to keep improving is through constant practice**
	Paragraph 2 **We should practice with native English speakers and welcome their corrections should we make mistakes**
	Paragraph 3 **If we have the chance, we should also immerse ourselves in an English-speaking country for some time**
	Paragraph 4
Wrap-Up	Restate your stance **Through constant practice, we can improve our English**

Paragraph 1

Step I: *Introduce the main point of the paragraph*

Step II: *Link to the idea in the previous paragraph*

Step III: *Be concise and brief*

Paragraph 2

Step I: *Introduce the main point of the paragraph*

Step II: *Link to the idea in the previous paragraph*

Step III: *Be concise and brief*

Paragraph 3

Step I: *Introduce the main point of the paragraph*

Step II: *Link to the idea in the previous paragraph*

Step III: *Be concise and brief*

Paragraph 4

Step I: *Introduce the main point of the paragraph*

Step II: *Link to the idea in the previous paragraph*

Step III: *Be concise and brief*

3. Some people prefer living in the countryside whereas others prefer living in the cities. Which do you prefer? Use specific reasons and examples to support your answer.

Introduction	What is your stance? **I prefer cities**
	In general terms, how will you support your stance? **Cities offer more convenience and opportunities**
Paragraph-Builder	Paragraph 1 **Living in the city is more convenient because everything you need is just a short distance away**
	Paragraph 2 **There are more job and educational opportunities in the city**
	Paragraph 3 **There are more people to meet and make friends with in the city**
	Paragraph 4 **Cities may come with drawbacks such as pollution, noise and higher living costs**
Wrap-Up	Restate your stance **The benefits of living in a city far outweigh the benefits of living in the countryside**

Paragraph 1

Step I: *Introduce the main point of the paragraph*

Step II: *Link to the idea in the previous paragraph*

Step III: *Be concise and brief*

Paragraph 2

Step I: *Introduce the main point of the paragraph*

Step II: *Link to the idea in the previous paragraph*

Step III: *Be concise and brief*

Paragraph 3

Step I: *Introduce the main point of the paragraph*

Step II: *Link to the idea in the previous paragraph*

Step III: *Be concise and brief*

Paragraph 4

Step I: *Introduce the main point of the paragraph*

Step II: *Link to the idea in the previous paragraph*

Step III: *Be concise and brief*

4. Many students work very hard to obtain internship positions during the summer vacations. Why do students do internships? Use specific reasons and examples to support your answer.

Introduction	What is your stance? **Students do internships in order to gain more experience and to advance further in life**
	In general terms, how will you support your stance? **List out the different benefits that can be gained from internships**
Paragraph-Builder	Paragraph 1 **By doing an internship, students can decide whether a particular industry or field is suitable for them**
	Paragraph 2 **Students can get more experience within the field and learn things that cannot be learnt from textbooks alone**
	Paragraph 3 **Students will be able to meet more people through the internship and possibly gain valuable mentors**

	Paragraph 4
Wrap-Up	Restate your stance **It is no surprise that students want to do internships, because they have all to gain and nothing to lose**

Paragraph 1

Step I: *Introduce the main point of the paragraph*

Step II: *Link to the idea in the previous paragraph*

Step III: *Be concise and brief*

Paragraph 2

Step I: *Introduce the main point of the paragraph*

Step II: *Link to the idea in the previous paragraph*

Step III: *Be concise and brief*

Paragraph 3

Step I: *Introduce the main point of the paragraph*

Step II: *Link to the idea in the previous paragraph*

Step III: *Be concise and brief*

Paragraph 4

Step I: *Introduce the main point of the paragraph*

Step II: *Link to the idea in the previous paragraph*

Step III: *Be concise and brief*

Answers:

1. Suggested Answer to Exercise 1

Paragraph 1

Step I: *Introduce the main point of the paragraph*

Main Point: Extracurricular activities are a way for children to discover their interests and strengths.

Step II: *Link to the idea in the previous paragraph*

Previous Paragraph: Extracurricular activities offer many opportunities for a child to develop interests and other soft skills. It can even support and complement whatever the child is learning in the classroom.

Step III: *Be concise and brief*

Among the many opportunities offered by extracurricular activities is the chance for children to discover their interests and strengths.

Paragraph 2

Step I: *Introduce the main point of the paragraph*

Main Point: Once they discover their interest and strengths, they can develop it through the activities.

Step II: *Link to the idea in the previous paragraph*

Previous Paragraph: Among the many opportunities offered by extracurricular activities is the chance for children to discover their interests and strengths.

Step III: *Be concise and brief*

After the children discover their interest and strengths, they can further develop these through extracurricular activities.

Paragraph 3

Step I: *Introduce the main point of the paragraph*

Main Point: Children will be able to make more friends and have a more wholesome education as they will also be able to learn how to cooperate in teams.

Step II: *Link to the idea in the previous paragraph*

Previous Paragraph: After the children discover their interest and strengths, they can further develop these through extracurricular activities.

Step III: *Be concise and brief*

Apart from developing interests and strengths, children can also make more friends and have a more wholesome education, as they will be able to learn how to cooperate in teams.

Paragraph 4

Step I: *Introduce the main point of the paragraph*

Main Point: Extracurricular activities may take up a lot of a child's time, but it is worthwhile and will not be detrimental as long as the child maintains a balance between academics and extracurricular activities.

Step II: *Link to the idea in the previous paragraph*

Previous Paragraph: Apart from developing interests and strengths, children can also make more friends and have a more wholesome education, as they will be able to learn how to cooperate in teams.

Step III: *Be concise and brief*

Although extracurricular activities may take up a lot of a child's time, it is worthwhile and will not be detrimental as long as the child maintains a balance between academics and extracurricular activities.

2. Suggested Answer to Exercise 2

Paragraph 1

Step I: *Introduce the main point of the paragraph*

Main Point: Since language is a tool for communication, the only way to keep improving is through constant practice.

Step II: *Link to the idea in the previous paragraph*

Previous Paragraph: The most effective way to learn English is to keep practicing it often, whether it is in terms of reading, writing or speaking.

Step III: *Be concise and brief*

The first and most fundamental way to improve English is to keep improving through constant practice, especially since language is a tool for communication.

Paragraph 2

Step I: *Introduce the main point of the paragraph*

Main Point: We should practice with native English speakers and welcome their corrections should we make mistakes.

Step II: *Link to the idea in the previous paragraph*

Previous Paragraph: The first and most fundamental way to improve English is to keep improving through constant practice, especially since language is a tool for communication.

Step III: *Be concise and brief*

At the same time, we should practice with native English speakers and welcome their corrections should we make mistakes.

Paragraph 3

Step I: *Introduce the main point of the paragraph*

Main Point: If we have the chance, we should also immerse ourselves in an English-speaking country for some time.

Step II: *Link to the idea in the previous paragraph*

Previous Paragraph: At the same time, we should practice with native English speakers and welcome their corrections should we make mistakes.

Step III: *Be concise and brief*

Apart from practicing with native speakers, we should also immerse ourselves in an English-speaking country for some time if we have the chance.

Paragraph 4

Step I: *Introduce the main point of the paragraph*

Not applicable

Step II: *Link to the idea in the previous paragraph*

Not applicable

Step III: *Be concise and brief*

Not applicable

3. Suggested Answer to Exercise 3

Paragraph 1

Step I: *Introduce the main point of the paragraph*

Main Point: Living in the city is more convenient because everything you need is just a short distance away.

Step II: *Link to the idea in the previous paragraph*

Previous Paragraph: Cities offer more convenience and opportunities.

Step III: *Be concise and brief*

To begin with, cities are exceptionally convenient because everything you need is just a short distance away.

Paragraph 2

Step I: *Introduce the main point of the paragraph*

Main Point: There are more job and educational opportunities in the city.

Step II: *Link to the idea in the previous paragraph*

Previous Paragraph: To begin with, cities are exceptionally convenient because everything you need is just a short distance away.

Step III: *Be concise and brief*

Furthermore, there are more job and educational opportunities in the city.

Paragraph 3

Step I: *Introduce the main point of the paragraph*

Main Point: There are more people to meet and make friends with in the city.

Step II: *Link to the idea in the previous paragraph*

Previous Paragraph: Furthermore, there are more job and educational opportunities in the city.

Step III: *Be concise and brief*

Moreover, there are more people to meet and to make friends with in the city.

Paragraph 4

Step I: *Introduce the main point of the paragraph*

Main Point: Cities may come with drawbacks such as pollution, noise and higher living costs

Step II: *Link to the idea in the previous paragraph*

Previous Paragraph: Moreover, there are more people to meet and to make friends with in the city.

Step III: *Be concise and brief*

Although cities may come with drawbacks such as pollution, noise and higher living costs, the benefits still outweigh the costs.

4. Suggested Answer to Exercise 4

Paragraph 1

Step I: *Introduce the main point of the paragraph*

Main Point: By doing an internship, students can decide whether a particular industry or field is suitable for them.

Step II: *Link to the idea in the previous paragraph*

Previous Paragraph: Students do internships in order to gain more experience and to advance further in life. List out the different benefits that can be gained from internships.

Step III: *Be concise and brief*

There are numerous reasons why students decide to do internships, and one of them is to decide whether a particular industry or field is suitable for them.

Paragraph 2

Step I: *Introduce the main point of the paragraph*

Main Point: Students can get more experience within the field and learn things that cannot be learnt from textbooks alone

Step II: *Link to the idea in the previous paragraph*

Previous Paragraph: There are numerous reasons why students decide to do internships, and one of them is to decide whether a particular industry or field is suitable for them.

Step III: *Be concise and brief*

Furthermore, students can get more experience within the field and learn things that cannot be learnt from textbooks alone.

Paragraph 3

Step I: *Introduce the main point of the paragraph*

Main Point: Students will be able to meet more people through the internship and possibly gain valuable mentors.

Step II: *Link to the idea in the previous paragraph*

Previous Paragraph: Furthermore, students can get more experience within the field and learn things that cannot be learnt from textbooks alone.

Step III: *Be concise and brief*

Apart from gaining experience during the internship, students may also continue learning from valuable mentors that they have met.

Paragraph 4

Step I: *Introduce the main point of the paragraph*

Not applicable

Step II: *Link to the idea in the previous paragraph*

Not applicable

Step III: *Be concise and brief*

Not applicable

Stitching the Essay Together

You have structure, tone, an introductory paragraph as well as topic sentences for each key point you want to make. Now, it's time to finally stitch the essay together.

In this final section, we will teach you some useful words that you can apply in your essay to make it better. There is no dictionary or guide in the world that will put these useful words and phrases together for you.

No.	Word/Phrase	Usage	Example
1	Arduous	A synonym for "challenging," "difficult," etc.	The road to recovery was an arduous one.
2	Arguable	When you want to state that an argument is not so clear-cut	It is arguable that smartphones are good for children.
3	At stake	To describe something that is at risk	He began to feel nervous because he realized that there was a lot at stake.
4	Benefits outweigh the costs	The item has some downsides, but the positives are far more than the negatives	After thinking for some time, I decided to go for it, as the benefits outweigh the costs.
5	Consequences	A synonym for "results" of an action. It may sometimes mean something negative	As the global economy is interlinked, one country may have to suffer negative consequences if it is too reliant on another country's economy.
6	Crux	A synonym for "center" or "core"	The crux of the matter is that there was a lack of communication between all parties.
7	Delved deeper	To go more intensely into something	The students could not understand the professor once he delved deeper into the topic.
8	Detrimental	A synonym for "negative," "adverse"	The collapse of this industry may have a detrimental effect on the rest of the economy.

9	Discrepancies	To describe inconsistencies or items that are not quite accurate	He began to feel very suspicious because there were many discrepancies between his uncle's account and his sister's account.
10	Drastically	Used to emphasize that something has had very serious consequences	The crisis drastically reduced his belief in himself.
11	Dubbed	Also known as	The 1980s is dubbed the "lost decade" of Latin American growth.
12	Emerged	A synonym for "surfaced" or "came about"	As time passed, more problems emerged.
13	Ensure	To make sure	To ensure that students adhere to the rule, a public notice was pasted in every dormitory.
14	Essentially	A synonym for "in a nutshell," "most importantly," "most notably" etc.	Essentially, the concept of the regime was based on simple ideology.
15	Exacerbate	Become worse; a synonym for "deteriorate"	International factors did exacerbate the depths of the crisis.
16	Explicitly	To describe something that is stated very obviously and out in the open	The policeman explicitly mentioned that there was no real danger.
17	Hands were tied	Being stuck in a situation where you can do nothing	The government wanted to help, but its hands were tied.
18	Imperative	A synonym for "very important," "necessary"	It is imperative that central banks attempt to nullify the incidence of crises.
19	Implement	A better word for "put into action"; a synonym for "execute," "undertake" etc.	The government implemented numerous policies to curb the spread of the disease.
20	In a bid	Synonymous to "in an attempt to"	He tried to meet the judge in a bid to plead his case.

21	In contrast to	Used to compare two different items	In contrast to the previous decade, this decade has seen rapid economic growth.
22	Incorporate	Synonym for "integrate," or "join together"	Central banks incorporate all factors into the determination of monetary policy.
23	Indeed	Used to emphasize your statement	The people were indeed happy when the government declared more subsidies.
24	Insight	To describe a very special and meaningful realization or piece of knowledge	Through research, we can gain a more comprehensive and profound insight into a country's culture.
25	Integral	To describe something that is very important	The managing director is an integral part of any company.
26	Led to	A synonym for "caused"	Poor hygiene led to poor health.
27	Notion	A synonym for "idea" or "thought"	A more interesting notion in which to examine is the aspect of circulation.
28	Plausible	Used to describe something that is logical and possible; a synonym for "valid"	It is plausible that the Prime Minister could have made this choice upon advice from the Minister of Finance.
29	Played a role	To state that something was among the factors involved in causing something else	A good diet certainly plays a role in determining your health.
30	Potential	A synonym for "possible"	The losses could potentially go up to billions of dollars.
31	Substantial	A synonym for "significant"	The hurricane dealt substantial damage to the city.
32	These factors served to …	"Served" can be used to describe the role played by certain factors or elements	These factors served to exacerbate the economic problems of the nation.
33	This raises the question	To introduce some doubt	This raises the question of whether restricting the amount of fast food children eat is fine.

34	Ultimately	A better word for "finally" or "at last"	The crisis was ultimately resolved.
35	Unquestionable	Used to state a forceful argument	It is unquestionable that the conditions were very harsh on developing countries.

TOEFL Trainer

Use the words in the brackets to rewrite the sentences.

1. The earthquake had a very large impact on the villagers. [Drastically]
2. The Industrial Revolution is one of the reasons why we are able to enjoy cheap mass-produced items today. [Played a role]
3. Ding is a nasty and ill-mannered little boy. [Indeed]
4. Athena is a very important member of the company's sales team. [Integral]
5. It is possible that the suspect is not the one who murdered Mr. Richards. [Plausible]
6. At the heart of the matter is the fact that he has too big an ego to admit that he had made a mistake. [Crux]
7. She jumped into the ocean in an attempt to save her drowning brother. [In a bid to]
8. The government wanted to do something to save its people, but in its weak state, it could do nothing. [Hands were tied]
9. It is not rational for someone to do something that would negatively affect his or her own interests. [Detrimental]
10. In a nutshell, this war is being fought over the scarcity of oil in the region. [Essentially]
11. There are many possible outcomes, depending on which course of action the company chooses to take. [Potential]
12. It took over a decade of investigation, but the truth came out in the end. [Emerged]

Answers:

1. The earthquake impacted the villagers drastically.
2. The Industrial Revolution played a role in ensuring that we are able to enjoy cheap mass-produced items today.

3. Ding is a nasty and ill-mannered little boy indeed. Or, Ding is indeed a nasty and ill-mannered little boy.

4. Athena is an integral member of the company's sales team.

5. It is plausible that the suspect is not the one who murdered Mr. Richards.

6. At the crux of the matter is the fact that he has too big an ego to admit that he had made a mistake.

7. She jumped into the ocean in a bid to save her drowning brother.

8. The government wanted to do something to save its people, but in its weak state, its hands were tied.

9. It is not rational for someone to do something that is detrimental towards his or her own interests.

10. Essentially, this war is being fought over the scarcity of oil in the region.

11. There are many potential outcomes, depending on which course of action the company chooses to take.

12. It took over a decade of investigation, but the truth emerged in the end.

Model Essays

Last but not least, this section contains model essays for the different types of topics that you may encounter in the TOEFL. They have been categorized into the four broad types of questions that you will receive in the TOEFL:

a) Agree or Disagree
b) Explanation/Description
c) Preference
d) Compare and contrast
e) What If

Agree or Disagree

Model Answer 1

Do you agree or disagree with the following statement? Giving students timed examinations is a better way to assess them than giving research-based assignments. Use specific reasons and examples to support your answer.

There has been a great deal of debate as to whether timed examinations or research-based assignments are better ways of assessing a student's ability. While more traditional people may think that timed examinations are still the best, I believe that research-based assignments provide a better assessment of students' abilities. This is because research-based assignments test students' abilities from many aspects, whereas timed examinations mainly focuses on the student's ability to memorize and regurgitate facts in a short amount of time.

Among the many aspects that research-based assignments are able to test but that timed examinations cannot is the student's ability to gather and analyze information, which is crucial in preparing them for what lies ahead in life. Because the students have to find and also interpret the information themselves, they must truly understand the material. Timed examinations, on the other hand, test the student's ability to memorize and regurgitate facts, which a student can do without truly understanding the material.

Furthermore, being able to produce good research work will be indispensable to students, especially when they reach the college level where students are expected to produce their own research. There is little point in assessing students from an aspect that is not a relevant factor in determining their future trajectory. Thus, assessing the student's ability to research is a better indicator of their present and future abilities.

In addition, research work will test various other aspects that timed examinations cannot cover, such as the student's ability to structure a question and find an answer in a creative yet logical manner. These qualities are also very important in assessing a student's abilities. Essentially, research-based assignments should not be overlooked because they consider various dimensions, whereas timed examinations focus solely on memorization skills.

Many of the aspects tested by timed examinations are also tested by research-based assignments, such as the student's ability to work under pressure. Some may argue that timed examinations give a better sense of whether the student can withstand pressure, since the time restriction is much stricter. However, it is unquestionable that research-based assignments also test the student's ability to work under pressure as well. When given research assignments, students also have to complete the work within certain deadlines. In some circumstances, the pressure can be even greater than a timed examination because the students have to discipline themselves over an extended period of time.

While both methods of testing have their pros and cons, research-based assignments are able to provide a more holistic assessment of students.

Model Answer 2

Do you agree or disagree with the following statement? Reading non-fiction such as true stories or history is better than reading fiction. Use specific reasons and examples to support your answer.

Books, which are sometimes also called "soul food," are of great importance. People read books to gain knowledge, cultivate thought or simply just for fun. However, some argue that reading non-fiction such as true stories or history is better than reading fiction. In my opinion, I believe this viewpoint is ill founded because fiction also has its benefits.

Fiction plays an undoubtedly important role as a literary genre due to its ability to appeal to a wide range of audiences. Reading fiction can cultivate an interest in reading, even in children as young as four or five. To young children, non-fiction may be too dry to absorb and understand. Fiction, on the other hand, is meant to be light-hearted and fun. As a result, children will spend more time reading, which can prepare them for reading more complex works in the future.

In addition, fiction helps to stretch the imagination and promotes creativity. We often marvel at the wonders technological advancement has brought us, but it is easy to forget that creativity is the spark that lies at the heart of innovation. We should not write off fiction simply because it is not true. Rather, we should appreciate it for its role in encouraging creative thought.

Those who believe that non-fiction is much more useful argue that people can acquire more knowledge through history. However, this is questionable because history itself is a debatable topic. Different writers have varying views on the same event in history, and there is no single truth. Therefore, to propagate reading non-fiction solely because it is "true" is flawed.

To conclude, reading itself should be encouraged and we should not favor one genre over another. After all, to each his own — as long as you enjoy what you read, that should be sufficient.

Model Answer 3

Student should be allowed to change their major even after they have entered college. What is your opinion? Use specific reasons and examples to support your answer.

For some, students should be allowed to alter their major even after they have enrolled in college. In my opinion, I believe that such a policy change will be beneficial overall in letting students have more flexibility in finding out and deciding what they truly want to do in life.

In China, where I come from, students will choose their major before they sit for the College Entrance Examination. It is possible that they may make a decision that they will regret, because they only have basic understanding of the subjects and careers involved. Students need to spend some time in college understanding each major and what this decision means for a future career.

Not allowing students to change their major can have a negative emotional impact on students. On one level, students who do not feel interested in their major may stop putting in effort, and this can lead to diminishing student morale as well as academic performance. On a more serious level, being stuck with a major that they do not like can cause emotional stress amongst students that can eventually lead to depression.

I concede that changing majors can cause numerous problems such as a potentially disordered education system in college. Indeed, some students may keep changing their minds, causing a waste of education resources. Having said this, however, colleges can impose rules and restrictions on changing majors. For instance, perhaps students can only have one chance to change their major before their second year in college. Or, perhaps only the top 10 percent in college can have the opportunity to transfer to another department.

Having considered all the arguments above, I believe that students should have the right to choose the major they like. Colleges should do their utmost best to facilitate this process of self-discovery, even if it means allowing students to change their major after entering college.

Model Answer 4

Participating in extracurricular activities is a crucial element of every child's education. What is your opinion? Use specific reasons and examples to support your answer.

Nowadays, most students participate in some form of extracurricular activity. In my opinion, these extracurricular activities are crucial for each child's educational development and can bring many benefits. This is largely because extracurricular activities offer many opportunities for a child to develop interests and other soft skills, and can also support as well as complement whatever the child is learning in the classroom.

Among the many opportunities offered by extracurricular activities is the chance for children to discover their interests and strengths. Academic grades alone do not determine the child's success in life, and discovering one's passion and talents is also important because these will all contribute to the child's eventual skill set. At the same time, extracurricular activities can also play a role in being a stress outlet for children. If faced with purely academics day in and day out, the child may become over-stressed.

After the children discover their interest and strengths, they can further develop these through extracurricular activities. This can be done with more guidance from teachers as well as support from schoolmates. For example, if they are interested in chess, they can prepare for chess competitions through the club. Winning awards at these competitions will also go a long way in building the child's confidence.

Apart from developing interests and strengths, children can also make more friends and have a more wholesome education, as they will be able to learn how to cooperate in teams. For instance, if the child is part of a soccer team, he or she will learn how to work together in order to win matches. Over time, the child will know how to be a "team player," which is a quality that is much desired no matter where you go. While children can also make friends in class, this cannot even begin to compare with the experience gained from working in a team. It is not just about getting to know each other, but also knowing how to deal with conflict as well as understanding the value of sacrifice.

Although extracurricular activities may take up a lot of a child's time, it is worthwhile and will not be detrimental as long as the child maintains a balance between academics and extracurricular activities. Sometimes, extracurricular activities can even support and complement academics. For example, if the child is part of a mathematics club, he or she can further explore the subject through the club.

Explanation/Description

Model Answer 1

What is the most effective way to learn English? Use specific reasons and examples to support your answer.

Many people have tried various ways to master the English language in the most efficient way possible. In my opinion, the best way to learn English is to keep practicing it often, whether it is in terms of reading, writing or speaking. Since language is a tool for communication, the only way to keep improving is through practice, especially with native English speakers or through immersion in an English-speaking country.

The first and most fundamental way to improve English is to keep improving through constant practice, especially since language is a tool for communication. We should take time to write, speak as well as read English every day. Although most of us have very busy schedules, we can find creative ways to squeeze time out. For example, we can download English books onto our smartphones and read them on the subway.

At the same time, we should practice with native English speakers and explicitly welcome their corrections should we make mistakes. This is because others may not point out our mistakes otherwise, as it may come across as rude to do so. Without understanding our mistakes, we can never improve and thus we should take every comment seriously.

Apart from practicing with native speakers, we should also immerse ourselves in an English-speaking country for some time if we have the chance. Being in an English-speaking environment will force us to think and communicate solely in English. Furthermore, we will be able to learn the words that native speakers commonly use. This is an integral part of language learning, as there are often many synonymous words. Knowing which word is the most appropriate for each context requires us to delve much deeper into how native speakers use the language in reality.

There are many ways to improve English, but central to all of them is the willingness to work hard and the desire to succeed. It is only through constant practice and hard work that we can improve our English.

Model Answer 2

Many students work very hard to obtain internship positions during the summer vacations. Why do students do internships? Use specific reasons and examples to support your answer.

It is very common to see students doing internships during summer or even winter vacations these days. I believe that students do this in order to gain more experience that will help them advance further in life. These experiences and benefits are items that they cannot obtain from the classroom, and can only be obtained through internships.

There are numerous reasons why students decide to do internships, and one of them is to decide whether a particular industry or field is suitable for them. It is nearly impossible to fully understand what a company or industry is about until you experience it. Therefore, an internship is extremely valuable in helping the student decide what career path suits them best because it allows them to have a small taste of what the company is like without making any long-term commitments.

Furthermore, students can get more experience within the field and learn things that cannot be learnt from textbooks alone. There are many skills and lessons that cannot be learnt from textbooks alone. For example, students cannot learn how to write professional emails, interact with clients and work with professional colleagues just by staying in school. While some educational providers do offer to teach students such soft skills through extra classes, nothing can beat real experience, as real life is unpredictable and cannot be fully covered by any class.

Apart from gaining experience during the internship, students may also continue learning from valuable mentors that they have met. Many students do keep in touch with their former bosses after the conclusion of internships, and these former bosses serve as mentors who can provide continuous life advice to students. Such mentorship cannot be bought, and can only be obtained through experience. Thus, in effect, the student does not only learn from the brief one or two months spent interning but has the opportunity to continue learning.

It is easy to see why students want to do internships during their free time. They have all to gain and very little to lose. Even if the experience is a poor one, that in itself is a valuable lesson about what the real working world is like.

Model Answer 3

Some schools and colleges make it compulsory for students to have roommates during their course of study. Why do you think this policy was set in place? Use specific reasons and examples to support your answer.

Having roommates in college is something that nearly everyone goes through in life. Some elect to have roommates out of choice, but in some cases, the college dictates that having roommates is mandatory. I believe that such a policy was set in place due to practical reasons, as well as the benefits that having a roommate can have for a student's personal development.

From a practical viewpoint, since many colleges have restrictions in terms of space and dormitories available, making it compulsory for students to have roommates may be the only way the college is able to accommodate so many students. This translates into higher space-efficiency, and will also reduce wastage in terms of resources.

From an educational standpoint, however, there are also many benefits that come along with having a roommate. First, many students who enter college may have had a private room all their life. Living with another person forces you to be more considerate and to learn how to get along with another person in a confined space. This is indirectly an education in soft skills, which is important for any student.

Moreover, colleges that impose this rule may be looking to ensure that students have some form of "social safety net" in the form of friends. There have been cases in the past where students have entered college, only to find it extremely difficult to make friends. Some of these students end up depressed and there have also been a few suicide cases. Making roommates mandatory ensures that even shy students are able to make at least one friend, and ensures that they have someone looking out for them all the time.

There will always be ups and downs when it comes to having a roommate. After all, most people quarrel with their siblings, what more with a roommate? Ultimately, however, having a roommate has a positive effect on one's wellbeing and development, which is likely to be at the core of why colleges instate such a policy.

Preference

Model Answer 1

Some people prefer living in the countryside whereas others prefer living in the cities. Which do you prefer? Use specific reasons and examples to support your answer.

Today, most people have a choice between living in the countryside and living in the city. For me at least, living in the city is much more preferable. This is mainly because cities offer more convenience and opportunities.

To begin with, cities are exceptionally convenient because everything you need is just a short distance away. This is especially important because there may be situations whereby you need something very urgently. For example, if you are very sick and you need to go to the hospital, at least it is only a short distance away if you live in the city. On the contrary, if you live in the countryside, it will take more time and it may even be too late by the time you reach the hospital. Even for non-urgent situations, living in the city can be very convenient. There are more amenities nearby, such as cinemas, gyms and shopping malls.

Furthermore, there are more job and educational opportunities in the city. If you prefer jobs in industries such as finance and technology, for example, these are usually only available in the cities. This is also an important consideration for students. Many schools and colleges are located in cities, for example New York University and Boston University. If you stay in the countryside, you may lose out on the opportunity to study at such institutions.

Moreover, there are more people to meet and to make friends with in the city. Humans are naturally social creatures and having a support network of friends is very important. Living in the city will provide more opportunities to meet and make friends with new people. This is especially the case because the larger population that can be found in cities also means that you can meet a larger variety of different people, and that you will be more likely to find people with similar interests. While some may argue you can find tighter and more close-knit communities in the countryside, nothing stops you from also creating or finding similar close-knit communities within the city.

Although cities may come with drawbacks such as pollution, noise and higher living costs, the benefits still outweigh the costs. The higher living costs would be offset by higher wages that one can attain by working in the city.

Regarding pollution and noise, these can be minimized by finding appropriate places to stay.

While the choice of a place to live is ultimately up to one's personal preferences, I personally believe that living in the city is the better choice because of the convenience and opportunities it offers.

Model Answer 2

Some people prefer environmentally friendly hybrid or electric vehicles, while others believe conventional vehicles are still the best. Which kind of vehicle would you prefer to drive, and why? Use specific reasons and examples to support your answer.

Today, the automobile industry is a significant contributor to environmental pollution and the question of using environmentally friendly vehicles or conventional vehicles has aroused many people's concern. Some people hold the view that hybrid or electric vehicles are better for their high technology and environmental protection. Personally, I believe that we should begin to embrace more environmentally friendly vehicles.

Regardless of whether you consider this from the standpoint of the business or the consumer, environmentally friendly vehicles are still the best choice. This is largely due to favorable government policies. For example, many governments reduce or even waive tax for the production of such vehicles, and give bonuses to consumers who purchase these vehicles.

Furthermore, environmentally friendly vehicles can also help reduce your daily expenses. The amount of petrol consumed by these vehicles will certainly be much lower than conventional vehicles. With the rising cost of fuel, this will translate into significant savings in the long run.

Admittedly, compared with conventional vehicles, environmentally friendly vehicles may have a limited driving range or limited power. However, these shortcomings will only be temporary. Governments are investing more into facilities for this new industry, whereas automobile companies are similarly pouring investment into research and design to improve environmentally friendly vehicles.

In conclusion, buying environmentally friendly hybrid or electric vehicles will not only reduce pollution, but is also beneficial for the consumer. Businesses will also benefit as long as favorable government policies are in place.

Model Answer 3

Some people prefer drinking tea, while others prefer coffee. Which beverage do you prefer, and why? Use specific reasons and examples to support your answer.

Tea and coffee are among the most traditional beverages available today. If I had to choose between them, I would choose tea.

Both drinks are similar in the sense that they contain caffeine, which is a drug that can boost energy levels. However, one of the main reasons I prefer tea is due to the health benefits. There are various kinds of tea, ranging from medicinal tea to herbal tea. Some of these teas are reported to have significant health benefits. For example, green tea is said to be rich in antioxidants, while Chinese "pu-erh" tea is said to be good for the kidneys.

Coffee, on the other hand, does not come with clear health benefits. On the contrary, coffee can have a negative impact on the body. The most obvious side effect is that it may stain your teeth, causing it to have a yellowish hue. This is due to natural dyes found in coffee itself. Coffee also contains a higher amount of caffeine than tea. If you drink too much coffee, you will be at the risk of overdosing on caffeine.

Moreover, good coffee is expensive and hard to make. You need all sorts of expensive equipment to replicate the coffee that is made at places like Starbucks. For example, you need a milk steamer, coffee bean grinder and coffee machine. Tea, on the other hand, requires very little. As long as you have a good tea bag, all you need to do is to add some hot water and you can enjoy a steaming cup of tea.

To conclude, I prefer tea because of the health benefits that it offers and the convenience.

Compare and Contrast

Model Answer 1

In the past, people only had the choice of living in landed houses. Nowadays, living in high-rise condominiums and apartments is very common. Compare and contrast these two ways of living. Which would you prefer? Use specific reasons and details to support your answer.

In this day and age, as the population increases, modern high-rise ondominiums and apartments continue to sprout up across various cities. These high-rise buildings are soon replacing traditional landed properties, but different people have varying views as to which type of home is better. In my opinion, I prefer high-rise condominiums.

To begin with, high-rise buildings are much more space-efficient, because the buildings can accommodate a great number of people. This translates into more room for other public facilities and amenities in the area such as shopping malls, parks and transport hubs.

Moreover, the concept of high-rises includes numerous shared facilities. Most buildings will have 24-hour security guards and CCTVs to ensure safety. In addition, you will also enjoy other shared facilities such as gyms, swimming pools and recreational areas. If you lived in a landed property, you may be able to have a park nearby but security guards and gyms would be out of the question unless you are willing to pay extra.

I concede that landed properties do have extra benefits. For example, they have more space and there is the option of having your own private garden. The area is also usually more private and less noisy. However, to me, recreational facilities provided by a high-rise condominium would be sufficient, and I would enjoy the benefit of getting to know more of my neighbors.

In conclusion, both high-rise apartments and landed houses have advantages and disadvantages. Personally, I prefer the former mainly due to the convenience it offers.

Model Answer 2

Some people prefer to eat at home, while others eat out most of the time. Compare and contrast eating at home with eating outside. Which do you think is better? Use specific reasons and details to support your answer.

Many people often face a dilemma when it comes to cooking at home, or eating out. Some feel that cooking at home is much healthier, while others prefer eating out due to the convenience it offers. In my opinion, I believe that cooking at home is the better option.

One of the main considerations when choosing between cooking and eating out is cost. In this aspect, cooking at home is certainly the better option. There is no need to pay an extra service charge or tax, and you can be sure that your food is cheaper than a restaurant. This is because restaurants have to mark up prices and make a profit in order to survive.

In addition, home-cooked food is healthier, as it is free of additives such as monosodium glutamate (MSG). You can also ensure that you use only the freshest ingredients in your cooking. On the contrary, if you were to eat out, there is no way of telling whether or not the ingredients are clean and fresh, or whether additives were used. For this reason, there is always the risk of getting food poisoning when eating out.

Those who prefer eating out may argue that it is more convenient. There is no need to waste time chopping and cooking. The time saved could be used on other activities. Though this may be the case, it is entirely possible for someone to prepare home-cooked food in minutes. What many people often do is cook in bulk, and then freeze small quantities into separate containers. Whenever it is time to eat, all you have to do is microwave the food.

Last but not least, cooking can be an avenue for stress release and can be an enjoyable hobby. This is especially true if you have a family, as nothing can convey love quite as well as a lovingly delicious homemade meal.

What If

Model Answer 1

If you had a million dollars to spend on anything you like, what would you choose and why? Use specific reasons and details to support your answer.

A million dollars is a large sum of money. If I had this amount, I would divide it between the following: money for my parents, investment and personal expenses. In my opinion, the precise breakdown is not as important as the principles that should govern the money. To me, the funds should be focused on saving for and protecting my loved ones.

As filial piety is an important pillar of my culture, I would immediately set aside at least $500,000 for my parents. This is only the right thing to do, as they are the most important people in my life and the ones who have unconditionally taken care of me all this while. The money would enable them to enjoy life after retirement and to ensure that they have a source of emergency funds in case illness or a disaster strikes.

Next, I would set aside another $400,000 for investment purposes and to ensure that there is a steady stream of income for my family. This would include setting aside money in unit trusts or even property so that I can further my studies in the future. If any of my siblings were to want to further their studies as well, the money could come from this pot of funds. It is not just a monetary investment, but also an investment in our future.

The last thing I would do is to set aside $100,000 for personal expenses. This covers insurance expenses that will provide some form a protection should I fall sick or meet with an accident. It would also cover daily expenses, such as paying the bills and servicing loans.

Model Answer 2

If you had to convince someone to visit your country for a holiday, what would you tell them? Use specific reasons and details to support your answer.

When you think of holidays, you probably want the following: culture, shopping and scenery. In this regard, my home country, China, fulfills all your needs and requirements.

Without a doubt, China has one of the richest cultures and histories in the world that stretches back thousands of years. We are home to numerous ethnic cultures and minorities, as well as UNESCO heritage sites. Some of the more well-known tourist attractions include the Great Wall of China, the Terracotta Warriors of Xi'an and the Forbidden City. You could venture through China for months without even discovering a tenth of its history.

Moreover, China today is incredibly developed. It boasts some of the most advanced public transportation systems worldwide, which include the Maglev train in Shanghai — a train that literally floats and is suspended by magnets. With such development also come sophisticated shopping malls for everyone's needs. Regardless of whether you want to find high-end goods or budget items, there will be a shopping mall that suits your needs.

Furthermore, China is endowed with unparalleled natural beauty. Head out to Yunnan in the west or even just to the province of Hangzhou, and you will be able to witness breathtaking scenery. For example, in Hangzhou, you will be able to visit the famous tea farms and sample fresh green tea. If you feel more adventurous, you can also pay a visit to the Rainbow Mountains in the Gansu province. These beautiful mountains are made out of layers of multicolored sandstone and minerals, giving it a "rainbow" effect.

Whatever it is that you desire to see during your vacation, China will not disappoint. An added bonus is that travelling in China is still relatively cheap, especially once you factor in the foreign currency exchange. It is best to seize the opportunity now, before the main attractions are overwhelmed by tourists.

Model Answer 3

Imagine a situation whereby you were asked to determine the criteria for selecting a model student in your country. What criteria would you come up with, and why? Use specific reasons and details to support your answer.

Depending on how you view the world, what constitutes a "model student" may differ. In my view, if I had to determine such a criteria, I would incorporate the following aspects: character, academics, special achievements and experience.

The most important aspect would be the student's character. Essentially, this refers to the student's personality and demeanor. A model student should be kind, respectful and grateful at all times. Most of all, he or she should be a person of integrity — not easily swayed to perform misdeeds for the sake of mere money or the promise of rewards.

The second criterion would be academics. While academics do not determine everything in life, a model student should demonstrate exceptional ability and aptitude in academic studies. This is a test of willpower, discipline and determination, as hard work can surmount any obstacle. At the very least, the student should be able to demonstrate academic excellence in his or her major.

In addition, a model student should have a special achievement of some sort. On top of being a good person and having excellent academic grades, the student must have done something special to set himself or herself apart from the rest. This can include winning an international sports championship, creating a company or writing a book. Owing to the fact that many students would be able to fulfill the first and second criteria, an additional assessment of the student's exceptional achievements is also required.

Last but not least, it is important to consider the student's work experience as well. Ambitious and driven students would have secured some form of work experience even prior to graduation. Since working life is very different from college life, those who have had some work experience tend to adapt better to a professional working environment upon graduation.

Topping the Integrated Writing Section

Introduction

This last section focuses on the Integrated Writing task, which is integrated in the sense that it contains a reading, writing as well as listening component. It differs from the Independent Writing task in the following ways:

	Independent Writing	Integrated Writing
Main Purpose	Tests ability to generate points to support an independent opinion	Tests ability to understand arguments and rephrase them in writing
Components Involved	Reading an essay prompt, and generating a response to the prompt	Reading an essay that articulates one viewpoint Listening to a lecture that articulates the opposing viewpoint Writing an essay that explains both viewpoints
Skills Required	Critical thinking Writing	Reading comprehension Listening comprehension Writing

As you can see from the above, you will still need writing skills in the integrated writing task, much of which has been covered in the Independent Writing section. The key difference is that the Integrated Writing task focuses more on your ability to comprehend arguments that are delivered via text and lecture, as well as your ability to articulate those arguments in writing.

As such, this section focuses on two key additional skills that you need for the Integrated Writing task. The first, which is "Top Tip 14: Effective Note-Taking," teaches you the skills needed to quickly understand the two different viewpoints that will be given in the TOEFL. Subsequently, "Top Tip 15: Framing Arguments" will teach you how to articulate the viewpoints. You will need to use some of the transition words learnt in the Independent Writing section, but you will also have to pick up some new transition phrases that are tailored towards the Integrated Writing task.

Top Tip 14: Effective Note-Taking
Top Tip 15: Framing Arguments

Effective Note-Taking

The Integrated Writing tasks tests your ability to take notes in a swift and accurate manner. This chapter teaches you a framework that you can use to organize your thoughts. It also introduces you to the general structure of the written passage and the lecture that you will be given in the TOEFL. Mentally prepare yourself and make sure you know what's to come — that will ensure you are better prepared to take good notes.

After you have mastered the skill of note-taking, you will learn how to write a summary incorporating both arguments in the next "Top Tip".

Simple Steps

1. Draw a framework to organize your notes.
2. Understand the main question and viewpoint of the written passage/lecture.
3. Identify and underline the three key supporting points.

Elaboration with Examples

1. Draw a framework to organize your notes

It's absolutely essential to draw a framework because this leads to better organization especially when you're under time pressure. It will also provide better guidance for when you begin writing your essay.

Your best bet is to memorize the framework below and to recreate it during the examination. It is designed in the following manner for the following reasons:

a) You need to spend an even amount of time on both the written passage and lecture. This is an "integrated" writing test, so if you only demonstrate a good command of interpreting the written passage without including points from the lecture, then you will lose points because you have not demonstrated that you have integrated skills.

b) The views of the written passage and lecture will always be in opposition to each other, and will usually be supported by three points. Having this framework helps condition your mind into thinking the right way and looking out for the correct points.

c) When we get to the next "Top Tip," which is about preparing the written essay for this task, you will rely on the framework below. Essentially, this involves one paragraph for a brief introduction that is based on the main question and the viewpoints discussed. Subsequently, there should be three body paragraphs that discuss each supporting point that was raised.

Main Question:	
Passage:	Lecture:
Supporting Point 1:	Supporting Point 1:
Supporting Point 2:	Supporting Point 2:
Supporting Point 3:	Supporting Point 3:

2. *Understand the main viewpoint of the passage/lecture*

Let's begin by looking at a sample written passage:

Gordon Moore, the founder of Intel, famously predicted that the number of transistors in a dense integrated circuit would double approximately every two years. So far, his prediction has held true. Just think about the large number of people who are able to own high-powered smartphones today as compared to a decade ago. Technological advancement is a good sign for mankind, which has benefited greatly from technological advancement. Such technology has enabled the world to become a much smaller place — all of a sudden, you can contact anyone halfway across the world with just the click of a button. We no longer have to wait weeks or even months for a letter to reach our loved ones. This has also led to a significant decrease in costs. For example, calls can now be made via the Internet, reducing the need for high expenses on traditional long-distance telephone calls.

With technology, companies can also provide better services and products. A popular success story is that of Uber, the taxi-hailing mobile application that allows people to obtain taxis more conveniently. Doctors can also save more patients, even those with very serious diseases. All in all, technological advancement should be supported, as it brings numerous benefits for everyone.

While reading the written passage, ask yourself what the passage is trying to answer. Imagine needing to set a question for this particular passage. Such a question would normally have a "yes or no" answer, for example: Should we introduce sports to children at a young age?

Once you have done this, if the written passage supports the main question, just write "good" to indicate so. Else, write "bad." Whatever viewpoint the written passage takes, you can be sure that the lecture will take the opposing view. This is just a simple way of focusing your thoughts and to mentally prepare yourself for what the lecture will cover. For example, based on this exercise, you know that the written passage supports technological advancement. Therefore, you also know that the lecture will *oppose* technological advancement.

Main Question: Is technological advancement good for mankind?	
Passage: Good	Lecture: Bad
Supporting Point 1:	Supporting Point 1:
Supporting Point 2:	Supporting Point 2:
Supporting Point 3:	Supporting Point 3:

3. *Identify and underline the three key supporting points*

When reading the passage, <u>underline</u> the supporting points as you go along. This will help you when you fill in the framework below:

Gordon Moore, the founder of Intel, famously predicted that the number of transistors in a dense integrated circuit would double approximately every two years. So far, his prediction has held true. Just think about the large number of people who are able to own high-powered smartphones today as compared to a decade ago. Technological advancement is a good sign for mankind, which has benefited greatly from technological advancement. <u>Such technology has enabled the world to become a much smaller place</u> — all of a sudden, you can contact anyone halfway across the world with just the click of a button. We no longer have to wait weeks or even months for a letter to reach our loved ones. <u>This has also led to a significant decrease in costs.</u> For example, calls can now be made via the Internet, reducing the need for high expenses on traditional long-distance telephone calls.

<u>With technology, companies can also provide better services and products</u>. A popular success story is that of Uber, the taxi-hailing mobile application that allows people to obtain taxis more conveniently. Doctors can also save more patients, even those with very serious diseases. All in all, technological advancement should be supported, as it brings numerous benefits for everyone.

When you listen to the lecture, you won't have the chance to underline words. But what you can do is to mentally prepare yourself for what is to come — three points arguing that technological advancement is **bad** for mankind. As soon as you hear anything that claims technological advancement is bad, jot it down immediately in one of the three boxes below.

Here's a sample transcript of what you might hear from a lecture:

There are so many movies, books and television shows about the dangers of technology that we tend to not take them seriously. But the fact is, we should. Recently, even the most high-profile scientists, innovators and inventors of our time such as Stephen Hawking, Bill Gates and Elon Musk have come out to stress the dangers of technology.

For one, there's always the risk that <u>artificial intelligence may one day become too intelligent for us to control.</u> We can't imagine such a scenario right now, because our devices just don't seem "smart" enough yet. But just imagine what could happen a few decades down the road when machines are able to see, move and think independently — it is possible that they could one day overtake the human race.

Those who are strong supporters of technological advancement often do not consider other immediate negative effects that this rapid development has brought. For example, technology has managed to decrease expenses but this comes at the cost of <u>getting rid of many jobs and rendering many unemployed</u>. If machines take up all the jobs, how will humans survive? Another aspect that people often overlook is how <u>technology has become such a distraction</u> to the point where people focus more on their smartphones or tablets instead of having a proper face-to-face conversation.

Main Question: Is technological advancement good for mankind?	
Passage: Good	**Lecture:** Bad
Supporting Point 1: Communication made easier	**Supporting Point 1:** Distraction
Supporting Point 2: Lower costs	**Supporting Point 2:** Higher unemployment
Supporting Point 3: Better services and products	**Supporting Point 3:** Machines could take over humans

You'll learn how to make use of this framework in the next chapter. For now, hone your note-taking skills and make sure you train your mind to think in the three-point structure of the passage as well as lecture.

TOEFL Trainer

Fill in the framework based on the written passages below. For the lecture, please refer to the "Companion Media Pack" instructions.

1.

Written passage:

Having a pet can bring a large amount of joy to your life, and is certainly something that everyone should consider. This can include anything from dogs, cats and even fish.

One of the main benefits of having a pet is the company that they provide. Even though pets are just animals, they are still living beings and can interact with you. This is especially the case when it comes to more sociable pets such as cats and dogs. There's a reason, after all, why dogs are called "man's best friend." In fact, there have even been cases where pets have saved their owners from danger.

Pets can also help inculcate a sense of responsibility, which is important especially for young children. Being tasked to take care of a pet helps young ones understand the importance of being responsible. For example, they will learn that feeding pets the wrong types of food may lead to sickness. They will also get used to doing routine chores such as cleaning out the fish tank.

Pets may also be more effective than going to the gym and can be beneficial for your physical health. A dog, for example, needs to be walked several times a day. Having this duty will ensure that you get physical exercise daily.

Main Question:	
Passage:	Lecture:
Supporting Point 1:	Supporting Point 1:
Supporting Point 2:	Supporting Point 2:

Supporting Point 3:	Supporting Point 3:

2.

Written passage:

Vegetarianism is becoming more and more common today, as people become aware of the benefits that adopting a plant-based diet has to offer. However, it may still seem strange to some people as to why anyone would give up meat products. One strong reason for becoming vegetarian is the health benefits that come along with this diet. A vegetarian diet tends to be low in fat and cholesterol, and can prevent numerous life-threatening diseases such as heart attacks. This can also help one reduce weight, which can fend off obesity-related diseases.

Those who are concerned about the environment may also opt to become a vegetarian. The meat industry causes a significant amount of pollution, which is generated by animal and chemical waste from factories and farms. Breeding billions of animals for human consumption also causes much more pollution than basic agricultural farming of vegetables. Of course, this is not to mention the possible animal cruelty involved. To produce meat on a mass scale, numerous animals are packed into confined spaces and live only to be slaughtered. If both of the reasons above are not enough, consider the financial benefits of adopting a plant-based diet. Your food costs would reduce dramatically, as vegetables tend to be much cheaper than meat. When you take into account the cost savings on a per-year basis, this can work out to a significant sum.

Main Question:	
Passage:	Lecture:
Supporting Point 1:	Supporting Point 1:
Supporting Point 2:	Supporting Point 2:
Supporting Point 3:	Supporting Point 3:

3.

Written passage:

Homeschooling is a relatively new educational phenomenon. Instead of sending children to traditional schools, some parents opt for their children to be schooled in a less formal "home" environment. The teaching is usually done by a parent or a tutor, and class sizes tend to be very small.

Homeschooling has a positive impact on the child's development, as it allows parents to become more involved in the child's learning. If the child were to attend a formal school, the only way parents could be involved would be through parent–teacher's night. This seems ironic, given that the parents are the ones who know the child best. Therefore, allowing parents to play a greater and more direct role in the child's education can only be beneficial for the child.

The smaller class sizes also allow the child to receive more direct and personalized attention. Parents no longer need to worry about their children falling behind in class simply because the teacher has no time to spend on a child who is particularly weak at a certain subject. With homeschooling, children can develop at their own pace and need not feel unnecessarily pressured. At the same time, homeschooling provides safe environment that is free from the potentially negative influence of misbehaving peers. Parents also need not worry about their child getting bullied at school, or having poor teaching instructions.

Main Question:	
Passage:	Lecture:
Supporting Point 1:	Supporting Point 1:
Supporting Point 2:	Supporting Point 2:
Supporting Point 3:	Supporting Point 3:

4.

Written passage:

Graffiti art has always been a subject of controversy because it involves spray-painting public areas. Some people view graffiti as an act of vandalism, while others see it as a work of art. Should graffiti truly be viewed in such negative light and should we stop graffiti artists from propagating their work?

We have to give graffiti artists credit for introducing art to the public, especially to those who would not otherwise visit art museums or galleries. Because graffiti art can be seen everywhere, this helps stimulate interest as well as creativity amongst the public. When the art is done well, it can also help brighten up the area and give otherwise soulless walls some personality. The works of some graffiti artists, such as the well-known British artist Banksy, have even become tourist attractions.

Last but not least, graffiti art is a valuable form of public self-expression for the artists. It is different from painting in private, as graffiti art can send out a strong public and sometimes even political message. To encourage the freedom of self-expression, we should therefore not dismiss graffiti art as an important channel of free speech.

Main Question:	
Passage:	Lecture:
Supporting Point 1:	Supporting Point 1:
Supporting Point 2:	Supporting Point 2:
Supporting Point 3:	Supporting Point 3:

5.

Written passage:

These days, people are becoming increasingly concerned about health. This is reflected in the growing sales of health-related products such as pedometers, health supplements and organic food products. An important component of good health is exercise, and it is encouraging to see that an increasing number of people are taking up gym memberships. It is better for people to exercise indoors rather than outdoors, for a variety of reasons.

First, many underestimate the injury risks that exercising outdoors can bring. Running on a tarred road, for example, can wear out your knees and cause problems for you in the future. In the gym, you need not worry. You can use machines such as the elliptical machine that ensures you get vigorous exercise without damaging your joints.

Exercise also requires a significant amount of personal willpower, and here is where gyms can help. You can enlist a personal trainer who will help push you beyond your physical limits, and who will keep you disciplined during each workout session. This ensures that you do more during each exercise session.

Another benefit of exercising indoors is that you can always exercise regardless of the weather. Many who are on an exercise routine often end up with schedule disruptions due to poor weather. This can have a detrimental effect on your exercise plans, especially if you have trouble instilling discipline in yourself. With a gym membership, there are no excuses — rain or shine, the workout session will continue.

Main Question:	
Passage:	Lecture:
Supporting Point 1:	Supporting Point 1:
Supporting Point 2:	Supporting Point 2:
Supporting Point 3:	Supporting Point 3:

Answers:

1.

Main Question: Are pets good or bad?	
Passage: Good	**Lecture:** Bad
Supporting Point 1: Provide company	**Supporting Point 1:** May be allergic to fur, attract pests such as ticks
Supporting Point 2: Sense of responsibility	**Supporting Point 2:** Costly and expensive to take care of
Supporting Point 3: Physical exercise	**Supporting Point 3:** Burden, would not be able to go on holidays without finding someone to take care of pet

2.

Main Question: Should we become vegetarian?	
Passage: Good	**Lecture:** Bad
Supporting Point 1: Health benefits	**Supporting Point 1:** Vegetarians may lack protein. Also, one can be a vegetarian and eat unhealthily
Supporting Point 2: Environment	**Supporting Point 2:** Certain vegetarian foods can be environmentally unfriendly
Supporting Point 3: Reduce costs	**Supporting Point 3:** Limited meal choices; eating out can be a challenge

3.

Main Question: Is homeschooling good?	
Passage: Good	**Lecture:** Bad
Supporting Point 1: Parents more involved	**Supporting Point 1:** Parents may not have expertise in every subject
Supporting Point 2: More attention	**Supporting Point 2:** Become too dependent on personalized attention, not ready for the real world
Supporting Point 3: Safe learning environment	**Supporting Point 3:** Not able to learn how to socialize and make friends

4.

Main Question: Is graffiti art good?	
Passage: Good	**Lecture:** Bad
Supporting Point 1: Introduce art to the public	**Supporting Point 1:** Disrespectful to those who dislike graffiti as a form of art
Supporting Point 2: Brighten up area	**Supporting Point 2:** Most graffiti is an eyesore
Supporting Point 3: Form of self-expression	**Supporting Point 3:** Costly to remove; there are other avenues for self-expression

5.

Main Question: Is an indoor gym membership better than exercising outdoors?	
Passage: Yes	**Lecture:** No
Supporting Point 1: Safer, fewer injuries	**Supporting Point 1:** Fresh air and sunlight are good for health
Supporting Point 2: Personal trainer to help with discipline	**Supporting Point 2:** Personal trainers are expensive, whereas outdoor exercise is free
Supporting Point 3: Will not be disrupted by poor weather	**Supporting Point 3:** Saves time, no need to travel to gym

Framing Arguments

In the Integrated Writing section, you will see the following instructions appear:

> You have 20 minutes to plan and write your response. Your response will be judged on the basis of the quality of your writing and on how well your response presents the points in the lecture and their relationship to the reading passage. Typically, an effective response will be 150 to 225 words.
>
> Summarize the points made in the lecture you just heard, explaining how they cast doubt on points made in the reading.

Make sure you understand that you are not expected to provide your own opinion. Draw only from the lecture and written passage provided. More emphasis is placed on whether you understood the passage and lecture. Thus, in this "Top Tip," we will guide you through a standard format that you can apply when writing your response. This allows you to focus more of your energy on comprehending the materials provided in order to get the best grade possible.

Simple Steps

1. Write an introduction that summarizes both viewpoints.
2. Allocate one body paragraph for each point that is debated.
3. Memorize and apply transitional phrases/words when summarizing the debate on each point.

Elaboration with Examples

1. *Write an introduction that summarizes both viewpoints*

The introduction should be kept short and simple. Here's a formula that you can use when writing your introductions. All you have to do is to fill in the blanks during the examination:

> The article and lecture discuss (a) _____. The article believes that (b) _____. However, the lecture disagrees and says that (c) _____.

All you have to do is to fill in the blanks. Here's where the framework you built in the previous "Top Tip" will come in handy. Let's revisit the framework:

Main Question: Is technological advancement good for mankind?	
Passage: Good	**Lecture:** Bad
Supporting Point 1:	**Supporting Point 1:**
Communication made easier	Distraction
Supporting Point 2:	**Supporting Point 2:**
Lower costs	Higher unemployment
Supporting Point 3:	**Supporting Point 3:**
Better services and products	Machines could take over humans

Here's how you can use the framework above as a guide to fill in the blanks:

Blank	Framework Reference	Sentence
(a)	Main Question	The article and lecture discuss **whether technological advancement is good for mankind.**
(b)	Passage	The article believes **that technological advancement can bring numerous benefits.**
(c)	Lecture	However, the lecture disagrees and says that **technological advancement comes with risks that could wipe out humanity.**

Note: Refer to "Top Tip 5: Perfect Paraphrasing" if you continue to have trouble filling in the blanks.

By using this simple formula and the framework as a reference, you already have a decent introduction on your hands:

> The article and lecture discuss whether technological advancement is good for mankind. The article believes that technological advancement can bring numerous benefits. However, the lecture disagrees and says that technological advancement comes with risks that could wipe out humanity.

2. *Allocate one body paragraph for each point that is debated*

To keep the structure as straightforward as possible, make sure that each paragraph only focuses on a single point that both sides disagree upon. This has already indirectly been done through the framework created during the note-taking process:

Supporting Point 1:	**Supporting Point 1:**
Communication made easier	Distraction
Supporting Point 2:	**Supporting Point 2:**
Lower costs	Higher unemployment
Supporting Point 3:	**Supporting Point 3:**
Better services and products	Machines could take over humans

Based on the framework above, the body paragraphs would be structured as follows:

Paragraph 1 — Passage says that communication has been made easier, but the lecture says that it is a distraction.
Paragraph 2 — Passage says that costs are lower, but lecture states that there is now higher unemployment.
Paragraph 3 — Passage says that there are better services and products, but lecture states that machines could take over humans.

To add more content to the paragraphs, you can do the following:

State the passage/lecture's view + Paraphrase elaboration on the view

Most people will find it easier to do this for the passage's view, since you will be able to refer to the passage again after you listen to the lecture. Here's an example of how the above can be done:

Original Passage:

Technological advancement is a good sign for mankind, which has benefited greatly from technological advancement. Such technology has enabled the world to become a much smaller place — all of a sudden, you can contact anyone halfway across the world with just the click of a button. We no longer have to wait weeks or even months for a letter to reach our loved ones.

Restated and Paraphrased:

First, the passage is of the view that technological advancement is beneficial, since it has made communication much more convenient. For example, we can now contact anyone in the world with just the click of a button as compared to the past when we had to wait weeks or even months for a letter to reach our loved ones.

3. *Memorize and apply transitional phrases/words when summarizing the debate on each point*

To keep it simple, you can start each paragraph with "first," "second" and "third." However, you're not going to state each side's view by just repetitively writing "he said this," and "she said that."

You need to memorize two types of transitional phrases. The first type will help you introduce the passage's view while the second will help you introduce the lecture's countering viewpoint. You may also need a *third* type of transitional phrase, and that is to introduce sentences where you paraphrase sentences that elaborated on a point.

Because you only have three body paragraphs, don't waste time memorizing too many transitional phrases. Four or five good phrases will be enough to ensure that you are able to write an articulate essay.

Type 1: Introducing the Passage's Viewpoint

No.	Transitional Phrase	Example
1	Is of the view that ... is good because	The passage is **of the view that** technological advancement **is good because** ...
2	Supports ... because	The passage **supports** technological advancement **because** ...
3	Advocates for ... because	The passage **advocates for** technological advancement **because** ...
4	Is a proponent of ... because	The passage **is a proponent of** technological advancement **because** ...
5	Believes that ... is good because	The passage **believes that** technological advancement **is good because** ...

Note: If interested, refer to "Top Tip 10: Bridging Ideas" for more justification words that can replace "because."

Type 2: Introducing the Lecture's Countering Viewpoint

No.	Transitional Phrase	Example
1	Contests ... by highlighting	The lecture **contests** this point, **by highlighting** how we have become so distracted by smartphones and gadgets that face-to-face communication has in fact reduced.
2	Objects ... by reminding	The lecture **objects** this point, **by reminding** us of how we have become so distracted by smartphones and gadgets that face-to-face communication has in fact reduced.
3	Rejects ... suggests instead	The lecture **rejects** this point, and **suggests instead** that we have become so distracted by smartphones and gadgets that face-to-face communication has in fact reduced.
4	On the contrary ... believes that ... because	**On the contrary**, the lecture **believes that** technological advancement is bad **because** we have become so distracted by smartphones and gadgets that face-to-face communication has in fact reduced.
5	Casts doubt on ... by suggesting that ... instead	The lecture **casts doubt on** the reading **by suggesting that** we have **instead** become so distracted by smartphones and gadgets that face-to-face communication has in fact reduced.
6	Questions ... by raising the fact that ...	The lecture **questions** this **by raising the fact that** we have become so distracted by smartphones and gadgets that face-to-face communication has in fact reduced.

Other words for "point":

View
Argument
Claim
Line of thought
Perspective
Standpoint

Type 3: Introducing Paraphrased Elaboration

No.	Transitional Phrase	Example
1	In other words	**In other words**, we can now contact anyone in the world with just the click of a button as compared to the past when we had to wait weeks or even months for a letter to reach our loved ones.
2	To elaborate	**To elaborate**, we can now contact anyone in the world with just the click of a button as compared to the past when we had to wait weeks or even months for a letter to reach our loved ones.
3	For example/For instance	**For example**, we can now contact anyone in the world with just the click of a button as compared to the past when we had to wait weeks or even months for a letter to reach our loved ones.
4	That is to say	**That is to say**, we can now contact anyone in the world with just the click of a button as compared to the past when we had to wait weeks or even months for a letter to reach our loved ones.
5	Put differently	**Put differently**, we can now contact anyone in the world with just the click of a button as compared to the past when we had to wait weeks or even months for a letter to reach our loved ones.

TOEFL Trainer

Use the frameworks you have designed in the previous chapter. Reread and listen to the lecture again if you have to. Then, apply the transitional phrases in your response.

1.

Written passage:

Having a pet can bring a large amount of joy to your life, and is certainly something that everyone should consider. This can include anything from dogs, cats and even fish.

One of the main benefits of having a pet is the company that they provide. Even though pets are just animals, they are still living beings and can interact with you. This is especially the case when it comes to more sociable pets such as cats and dogs. There's a reason, after all, why dogs are called "man's best friend." In fact, there have even been cases where pets have saved their owners from danger.

Pets can also help inculcate a sense of responsibility, which is important especially for young children. Being tasked to take care of a pet helps young ones understand the importance of being responsible. For example, they will learn that feeding pets the wrong types of food may lead to sickness. They will also get used to doing routine chores such as cleaning out the fish tank.

Pets may also be more effective than going to the gym and can be beneficial for your physical health. A dog, for example, needs to be walked several times a day. Having this duty will ensure that you get physical exercise daily.

Main Question: Are pets good or bad?	
Passage: Good	**Lecture:** Bad
Supporting Point 1: Provide company	**Supporting Point 1:** May be allergic to fur, attract pests such as ticks
Supporting Point 2: Sense of responsibility	**Supporting Point 2:** Costly and expensive to take care of
Supporting Point 3: Physical exercise	**Supporting Point 3:** Burden, would not be able to go on holidays without finding someone to take care of pet

2.

Written passage:

Vegetarianism is becoming more and more common today, as people become aware of the benefits that adopting a plant-based diet has to offer. However, it may still seem strange to some people as to why anyone would give up meat products. One strong reason for becoming vegetarian is the health benefits that come along with this diet. A vegetarian diet tends to be low in fat and cholesterol, and can prevent numerous life-threatening diseases such as heart attacks. This can also help one reduce weight, which can fend off obesity-related diseases.

Those who are concerned about the environment may also opt to become a vegetarian. The meat industry causes a significant amount of pollution, which is generated by animal and chemical waste from factories and farms. Breeding billions of animals for human consumption also causes much more pollution than basic agricultural farming of vegetables. Of course, this is not to mention the possible animal cruelty involved. To produce meat on a mass scale, numerous animals are packed into confined spaces and live only to be slaughtered. If both of the reasons above are not enough, consider the financial benefits of adopting a plant-based diet. Your food costs would reduce dramatically, as vegetables tend to be much cheaper than meat. When you take into account the cost savings on a per-year basis, this can work out to a significant sum.

Main Question: Should we become vegetarian?	
Passage: Yes	**Lecture:** No
Supporting Point 1: Health benefits	**Supporting Point 1:** Vegetarians may lack protein. Also, one can be a vegetarian and eat unhealthily
Supporting Point 2: Environment	**Supporting Point 2:** Certain vegetarian foods can be environmentally unfriendly
Supporting Point 3: Reduce costs	**Supporting Point 3:** Limited meal choices, eating out can be a challenge

3.

Written passage:

Homeschooling is a relatively new educational phenomenon. Instead of sending children to traditional schools, some parents opt for their children to be schooled in a less formal "home" environment. The teaching is usually done by a parent or a tutor, and class sizes tend to be very small.

Homeschooling has a positive impact on the child's development, as it allows parents to become more involved in the child's learning. If the child were to attend a formal school, the only way parents could be involved would be through parent-teacher's night. This seems ironic, given that the parents are the ones who know the child best. Therefore, allowing parents to play a greater and more direct role in the child's education can only be beneficial for the child.

The smaller class sizes also allow the child to receive more direct and personalized attention. Parents no longer need to worry about their children falling behind in class simply because the teacher has no time to spend on a child who is particularly weak at a certain subject. With homeschooling, children can develop at their own pace and need not feel unnecessarily pressured. At the same time, homeschooling provides safe environment that is free from the potentially negative influence of misbehaving peers. Parents also need not worry about their child getting bullied at school, or having poor teaching instructions.

Main Question: Is homeschooling good?	
Passage: Good	**Lecture:** Bad
Supporting Point 1:	**Supporting Point 1:**
Parents more involved	Parents may not have expertise in every subject
Supporting Point 2:	**Supporting Point 2:**
More attention	Become too dependent on personalized attention, not ready for the real world
Supporting Point 3:	**Supporting Point 3:**
Safe learning environment	Not able to learn how to socialize and make friends

4.

Written passage:

Graffiti art has always been a subject of controversy because it involves spray-painting public areas. Some people view graffiti as an act of vandalism, while others see it as a work of art. Should graffiti truly be viewed in such negative light and should we stop graffiti artists from propagating their work?

We have to give graffiti artists credit for introducing art to the public, especially to those who would not otherwise visit art museums or galleries. Because graffiti art can be seen everywhere, this helps stimulate interest as well as creativity amongst the public. When the art is done well, it can also help brighten up the area and give otherwise soulless walls some personality. The works of some graffiti artists, such as the well-known British artist Banksy, have even become tourist attractions.

Last but not least, graffiti art is a valuable form of public self-expression for the artists. It is different from painting in private, as graffiti art can send out a strong public and sometimes even political message. To encourage the freedom of self-expression, we should therefore not dismiss graffiti art as an important channel of free speech.

Main Question: Is graffiti art good?	
Passage: Good	**Lecture:** Bad
Supporting Point 1:	**Supporting Point 1:**
Introduce art to the public	Disrespectful to those who dislike graffiti as a form of art
Supporting Point 2:	**Supporting Point 2:**
Brighten up area	Most graffiti is an eyesore
Supporting Point 3:	**Supporting Point 3:**
Form of self-expression	Costly to remove, there are other avenues for self-expression

5.

Written passage:

These days, people are becoming increasingly concerned about health. This is reflected in the growing sales of health-related products such as pedometers, health supplements and organic food products. An important component of good health is exercise, and it is encouraging to see that an increasing number of people are taking up gym memberships. It is better for people to exercise indoors rather than outdoors, for a variety of reasons.

First, many underestimate the injury risks that exercising outdoors can bring. Running on a tarred road, for example, can wear out your knees and cause problems for you in the future. In the gym, you need not worry. You can use machines such as the elliptical machine that ensures you get vigorous exercise without damaging your joints.

Exercise also requires a significant amount of personal willpower, and here is where gyms can help. You can enlist a personal trainer who will help push you beyond your physical limits, and who will keep you disciplined during each workout session. This ensures that you do more during each exercise session.

Another benefit of exercising indoors is that you can always exercise regardless of the weather. Many who are on an exercise routine often end up with schedule disruptions due to poor weather. This can have a detrimental effect on your exercise plans, especially if you have trouble instilling discipline in yourself. With a gym membership, there are no excuses — rain or shine, the workout session will continue.

Main Question: Is an indoor gym membership better than exercising outdoors?	
Passage: Yes	**Lecture:** No
Supporting Point 1: Safer, fewer injuries	**Supporting Point 1:** Fresh air and sunlight are good for health
Supporting Point 2: Personal trainer to help with discipline	**Supporting Point 2:** Personal trainers are expensive, whereas outdoor exercise is free
Supporting Point 3: Will not be disrupted by poor weather	**Supporting Point 3:** Saves time, no need to travel to gym

Model Answers

1. **Main Question:** Are pets good or bad?

The article and lecture discuss whether pets are good or bad. The article believes that pets can bring many benefits. However, the lecture disagrees and says that pets are more trouble than they are worth.

First, the article states that pets provide valuable company and can become loyal friends. For example, there have even been cases where pets have saved their owners from danger. However, the lecture casts doubts on the article by reminding us that pets may trigger allergies. Furthermore, they may attract pests such as ticks. Their company may therefore be more trouble than it is worth.

Second, while the article claims that pets can inculcate a sense of responsibility, especially in young children, the lecture opposes this point by highlighting that pets are very expensive to take care of. Imagine having to pay for pet food, healthcare and grooming every day. While instilling a sense of responsibility is important, there are other less expensive ways to do so.

Third, the article argues that having pets can encourage physical exercise. For example, a dog needs to be walked several times a day and this can ensure that you will get physical exercise daily. However, the lecture objects to this point by highlighting this could be more of a burden than a benefit. When you go on a holiday for instance, you would have to find a replacement who can take your pet on these walks.

2. **Main Question:** Should we become vegetarian?

The article and lecture discuss whether we should become vegetarian. The article believes that vegetarianism can bring many benefits. However, the lecture disagrees and says that vegetarianism has more disadvantages than advantages.

First, the article states that adopting a plant-based diet can bring many health benefits because such a diet is normally low in fat. That is to say, by becoming a vegetarian, we can reduce our chances of getting life-threatening diseases such as heart attacks and can also lose weight. However, the lecture casts doubt on this claim by highlighting that vegetarians tend to lack protein, which is not commonly found in vegetables. Furthermore, the lecture also states that one can be a vegetarian and still eat unhealthy food such as potato chips, pizza and chocolate.

Second, the article claims that being a vegetarian is good for the environment, because the meat industry generates a significant amount of pollution and also involves animal cruelty. The lecture opposes this point by stating that vegetarian food can also be unhealthy. For example, importing vegetables from halfway around the world can also cause pollution in the form of greenhouse gases.

Third, the article argues that becoming a vegetarian can help you reduce food costs, as vegetables tend to be much cheaper than meat. However, the lecture questions this by raising this fact that there are other unseen costs involved. For instance, when eating out, you will have limited meal choices. This can also affect your social life, as eating with friends can be a challenge due to your dietary constraints.

3. Main Question: Is homeschooling good?

The article and lecture discuss whether homeschooling is good. The article believes that homeschooling can bring many benefits. However, the lecture disagrees and says that homeschooling has more disadvantages than advantages.

First, the article states that homeschooling allows the parent to become more involved in the child's development. This is beneficial for the child, as the parents are the ones who know the child best. However, the lecture questions this claim by raising the fact that parents may not have expertise in every subject. Furthermore, they may not even be experts on education. If they are left with the sole responsibility of educating their child, the child may not receive a wholesome education.

Second, the article claims that homeschooling allows the child to receive a greater amount of attention than in a formal school. This is because the class sizes are much smaller. As a result, children can develop at their own pace and need not feel unnecessarily pressured. The lecture opposes this view and suggests instead that this may be detrimental for the child in the long run, as he or she may become too dependent on personalized attention. In the end, the child may not be ready to face the real world.

Third, the article argues that homeschooling provides a safe learning environment for the child, one that is free from the potentially negative influence of misbehaving peers and bullying. The lecture contests this view by highlighting that being overly protective of the child may prevent the child from learning how to socialize and overcome challenges at school. These are all part of necessary character building for each child.

4. Main Question: Is graffiti art good?

The article and lecture discuss whether graffiti art is good. The article believes that graffiti art has its benefits. However, the lecture disagrees and says that graffiti art has more disadvantages than advantages.

First, the article states that graffiti art plays an important role in introducing art to the public, particularly to those who would not otherwise appreciate art.

This can have the effect of stimulating interest and creativity. However, the lecture questions this claim by raising the fact that there are many forms of art, and not all graffiti art is of high enough quality to be considered pleasing to the eye. As such, supporting graffiti art is disrespectful to those who dislike this form of art.

Second, the article claims that graffiti art helps brighten up and give personality to otherwise soulless neighborhoods. For example, some graffiti art have become so famous that they have even turned into tourist attractions. The lecture opposes this view and reminds us that most graffiti is an eyesore. At times, graffiti art can even be vulgar and offensive. True artists like Banksy are very rare.

Third, the article argues that graffiti art is a valuable form of public self-expression and an important channel of free speech. The lecture contests this view by highlighting that not everyone may share the views of the graffiti artists. The fact that graffiti art is done in public areas is therefore unfair to those who find the art offensive. Furthermore, graffiti art is costly to remove and will use up valuable public funds. There are other avenues for public self-expression that graffiti artists can use, and this should not be an excuse to vandalize public property.

5. Main Question: Is an indoor gym membership better than exercising outdoors?

The article and lecture discuss whether exercising indoors is better than exercising outdoors. The article believes that exercising indoors is better. However, the lecture disagrees and says that exercising outdoors should be the preferred choice.

First, the article states that exercising indoors is better because it is safer and the risk of injury is therefore lower. In comparison for example, running outdoors may wear out your knees and cause health problems in the future. However, the lecture questions this claim by raising the fact that exercising outdoors also has its health benefits. Fresh air and natural sunlight are important. For example, exposing your skin to sunlight is a natural way of obtaining vitamin D.

Second, the article supports exercising indoors, because personal trainers are available to help push you beyond your physical limits and to assist in keeping you disciplined. In other words, you will gain more out of each workout session. The lecture opposes this view and reminds us that personal trainers are expensive while exercising outdoors is free. The physical challenge of natural terrain such as hills are also difficult to replicate in an indoor setting.

Third, the article argues that exercising indoors ensures that your workout routine will never be disrupted by poor weather. The lecture contests this view by highlighting that while poor weather may occasionally affect workout plans, exercising indoors is ultimately more troublesome. Each time, you have to battle through traffic congestion and fight for parking space before you can exercise in a gym. Exercising outdoors, on the other hand, can happen at any time you wish and will save you time in the long run.

Appendix — References for Sample Reading Passages

Books and Journals

Aeras (2014). Tuberculosis Vaccine Candidates. http://www.aeras.org/candidates (accessed May 3, 2014).

Alexandersen, A, Zhang, Z, Donaldson, AI, Garland, AJM (2003). Review: The Pathogenesis and Diagnosis of Foot-and-Mouth Disease. *Journal of Comparative Pathology* 129: 1–36.

Allison, Graham and Philip Zelikow (1999). *Essence of Decision: Explaining the Cuban Missile Crisis*. New York: Longman.

Asakawa, Kanichi (1904). *The Russo-Japanese Conflict: Its Causes and Issues*. Boston: Houghton Mifflin.

Ash, Timothy Garton (1993). *In Europe's Name: Germany and the Divided Continent*. New York: Random House.

Body, G, Ferte, H, Gaillard, J, Delorme, D, Klein, F, and Gilot-Fromont, E (2011). Population Density and Phenotypic Attributes Influence the Level of Nematode Parasitism in Roe Deer. *Oecologia*, 167: 635–646.

Bowker, Mike, and Phil Williams (1988). *Superpower Detente: A Reappraisal*. London: Royal Institute of International Affairs.

Bozo, Frédéric (2001). *Two Strategies for Europe: De Gaulle, the United States, and the Atlantic Alliance*. Lanham, MD: Rowman & Littlefield.

Cameron, Christina and Rossler, Mechtild (2011). Voices of the Pioneers: UNESCO's World Heritage Convention 1972–2000. *Journal of Cultural Heritage Management and Sustainable Development* 1(1): 43.

Christensen, Thomas J (2011). *Worse than a Monolith: Alliance Politics and Problems of Coercive Diplomacy in Asia*. Princeton, NJ: Princeton University Press.

Christian, David (1997). *Imperial and Soviet Russia*. New York: Macmillan Press.

Coombs, H. C (1989). *Land of Promises: Aborigines and Development in the East Kimberley*. Canberra: Centre for Resource and Environmental Studies, Australian National University.

Daly, HE (1990). Toward Some Operational Principles of Sustainable Development. *Ecological Economics* 2(1): 1–6.

De Roode, JC and Altizer, S (2009). Host-Parasite Genetic Interactions and Virulence-Transmission Relationships in Natural Populations of Monarch Butterflies. *Evolution* 64(2): 502–514.

Dingli, D, Traulsen, A, and Michor, F (2007). (A)Symmetric Stem Cell Replication and Cancer. *PLoS Computational Biology* 3:3: e53. doi:10.1371/journal.pcbi.0030053.

Du Bois, WEB (1965). The Souls of Black Folk. In *Three Negro Classics*, 239. New York: Avon.

Dunbabin, JPD (2008). *The Cold War: The Great Powers and Their Allies*. Harlow, England: Pearson Education.

Emmons, Terence (1970). *Emancipation of the Russian Serfs*. New York: Holt, Rinehart and Winston.

Evans, David and Jenkins, Jane (2004). *Years of Weimar and the Third Reich*. London: Hodder and Stoughton.

Finlay, A, Lancaster, J, Holz, T, Weyer, K, Miranda, A, and Walt, M (2012). Patient- and Provider-Level Risk Factors Associated with Default from Tuberculosis Treatment, South Africa, 2002: A Case-Control Study. *BMC Public Health* 12(56).

Gaddis, John Lewis (1992). *The United States and the End of the Cold War: Implications, Reconsiderations, Provocations*. New York: Oxford University Press.

Gaddis, John Lewis (1987). *The Long Peace: Inquiries into the History of the Cold War*. New York: Oxford University Press.

Garthoff, Raymond L (1985). *Détente and Confrontation: American-Soviet Relations from Nixon to Reagan*. Washington, D.C.: Brookings Institution.

Hines, AM, Ezenwa, VO, Cross, P, Rogerson, JD (2007). Effects of Supplemental Feeding on Gastrointestinal Parasite Infection in Elk (Cervus Elaphus): Preliminary Observations. *Veterinary Parasitology* 148: 350–355.

Hobbes, Thomas and Gaskin, JCA. (1998). *Leviathan*. Oxford: Oxford University Press.

Hokey, D and Ginsberg, A (2013). The Current State of Tuberculosis Vaccines. *Human Vaccines & Immunotherapeutics* 9(10): 2142–2146.

Homewood, K, Lambin, EF, Coast, E, Kariuki, A, Kiveliai, J, Said, M, Serneels, S, and Thompson, M (2001). Long-term Changes in Serengeti-Mara Wildebeest and Land Cover: Pastoralism, Population, or Policies?. *Proceedings of the National Academy of Sciences* 98(22): 12544–12549.

Jervis, Robert (1989). *The Meaning of the Nuclear Revolution: Statecraft and the Prospect of Armageddon*. Ithaca: Cornell University Press.

Jones, Do-While (2011). In A Whale of Trouble. Ridgecrest, California — Your Community Portal. http://www.ridgecrest.ca.us/~do_while/sage/v3i11f.htm (accessed April 4, 2011).

Ko, J, Gendron-Fitzpatrick, A, Ficht, TA, and Splitter, GA (2002). Virulence Criteria for *Brucella abortus* Strains as Determined by Interferon Regulatory Factor 1-Deficient Mice. *Infection and Immunity* 70(12): 7004–7012.

Kolko, Gabriel (1985). *Anatomy of a War: Vietnam, the United States, and the Modern Historical Experience*. New York: Pantheon.

Kowalski, Alexandra (2011). When Cultural Capitalization Became Global Practice. In Nina Bandelj and Frederick F. Wherry, eds., *The Cultural Wealth of Nations*. Stanford: Stanford University Press, 73–89.

Kuropatkin, Aleksey (1990). *The Russian Army and the Japanese War*. New York: E. P. Dutton and Company, 1909.

Langfield, Michelle, Logan, William and Máiréad, Nic Craith (eds.) (2011). *Cultural Diversity, Heritage, and Human Rights: Intersections in Theory and Practice*. London: Routledge.

Lebow, Richard Ned, and Janice Gross Stein (1994). *We All Lost the Cold War*. Princeton, NJ: Princeton University Press.

Mavrodes, George (1975). Conventions and the Morality of War, *Philosophy & Public Affairs* 4 (1975): 122.

Mduma, A, Sinclair, A, Hilbron, R (1999). Food Regulates the Serengeti Wildebeest: A 40-year Record. *Journal of Animal Ecology* 68: 1101–1122.

Molnar, Andrea Katalin (2010). *Timor Leste: Politics, History, and Culture*. London: Routledge.

Morris, Terry, and Derrick Murphy (2000). *Europe 1870–1991*. UK: Harper Collins.

Mosse, Werner Eugen (1992). *Alexander II and the Modernisation of Russia*. London: Tauris.

Neta, AVC, Mol, JPS, Xavier, MN, Paixao, T, Lage, AP, and Santos, RL (2010). Review: Pathogenesis of Bovine Brucellosis. *The Veterinary Journal* 184: 146–155.

Nish, Ian (1977). *Japanese Foreign Policy 1869–1942: Kasumigaseki to Miyakezaka*. London, Henley and Boston: Routledge & Kegan Paul.

Nye, Joseph S (2000). *Understanding International Conflicts: An Introduction to Theory and History (3rd edition)*. New York: Longman Publishing.

Osofsky, SA, Cleaveland, S, Karesh, WB, Kock, MD, Nyhus, PJ, Starr, L, and Yang, A (eds.) (2005). *Conservation and Development Interventions at the Wildlife/Livestock Interface: Implications for Wildlife, Livestock and Human Health*. IUCN, Gland, Switzerland and Cambridge, UK.

Ottenhof, T, and Kaufmann, S (2012). Vaccines against Tuberculosis: Where Are We and Where do We Need to Go? *PLoS Pathogens* 8(5): e1002607. doi:10.1371/ journal.ppat.1002607.

Pepper, JW, Sprouffske, K, and Maley, CC (2007). Animal Cell Differentiation Patterns Suppress Somatic Evolution. *PLoS Computational Biology* 12 (2007): e250.

Piatek, A, Van Cleef, M, Alexander, H, Coggin, W, Rehr, M, Van Kampen, S, Shinnick, T, and YaDiul, M (2013). GeneXpert for TB Diagnosis: Planned and Purposeful Implementation. *Global Health Science Practice* 1(1): 18–23.

Pollard, RA (1945). US Economic Diplomacy in East Asia: The Fall of China and the Reconstruction of Japan, 1945–50. *Economic Security and the Origins of the Cold War*, 50.

Reed, Adolph L Jr (1997). *W.E.B. Du Bois and American Political Thought: Fabianism and the Color Line*. Cary, North Carolina: Oxford University Press.

Report of the Special Rapporteur, Mr. P. Kooijmans, pursuant to Commission on Human Rights resolution 1991/38. http://daccess-dds-ny.un.org/doc/ UNDOC/GEN/G92/100/61/PDF/G9210061.pdf?OpenElement (accessed February 2, 2011).

Rossi, Aldo (1999). *The Architecture of the City*. Cambridge, Massachusetts: Opposition Books.

Serneels, S and Lambin, EF (2001). Impact of Land-use Changes on the Wildebeest Migration in the Northern Part of the Serengeti-Mara Ecosystem. *Journal of Biogeography* 28(3): 391–407.

Sinclair, ARE (1995). *Serengeti 2*. Chicago: University of Chicago Press.

Sonia Altizer, Rebecca Bartel, Barbara A. Han. (2011). Animal Migration and Infectious Disease Risk. *Science*, 331: 296–302.

Stuckler, D, Basu, S, McKee, M, Lurie, M. (2011). Mining and Risk of Tuberculosis in Sub-Saharan Africa. *American Journal of Public Health* 101(3): 524–530.

Tambling, CJ and Du Toit, JT (2005). Modelling Wildebeest Population Dynamics: Implications of Predation and Harvesting in a Closed System. *Journal of Applied Ecology* 42(3): 431–441.

The McGraw-Hill Companies, Inc. (2011). Whale Evolution. http://www-personal. umich.edu/~gingeric/PDFfiles/PDG413_Whaleevol.pdf (accessed April 4, 2011).

Thewissen, JGM. Whale Origins. Northeastern Ohio Universities Colleges of Medicine and Pharmacy. http://www.neoucom.edu/DEPTS/ANAT/ Thewissen/whale_origins/index.html (accessed April 04, 2011).

Thuy Tram, Dang (2007). *Last Night I Dreamed of Peace: The Diary of Dang Thuy Tram.* New York: Random House.

U.S. Energy Information Administration (2012). Annual Energy Review 2011. http://www.eia.doe.gov/totalenergy/data/annual/pdf/aer.pdf (accessed March 18, 2013).

UCMP — University of California Museum of Paleontology (2011). Cetaceans. http://www.ucmp.berkeley.edu/mammal/cetacea/cetacean.html (accessed April 04, 2011).

Ulfstrand, S (2002). *Savannah Lives: Animal Life and Human Evolution in Africa.* Oxford: Oxford University Press.

UNESCO (2013). UNESCO Constitution. http://portal.unesco.org/en/ev.php-URL_ID=15244&URL_DO=DO_TOPIC&URL_SECTION=201.html (accessed April 2, 2013).

West, Cornel (1989). *The American Evasion of Philosophy: A Genealogy of Pragmatism.* Madison, Wisconsin: University of Wisconsin Press.

WHO (2008). *Anthrax in Humans and Animals (4ᵗʰ edition).* Geneva: WHO Press.

WHO (2014). Tuberculosis Financing Tool — South Africa's Profile. https://extranet.who.int/sree/Reports?op=Replet&name=%2FWHO_HQ_Reports%2FG2%2FPROD%2FEXT%2FTBFinancingCountryProfile&ISO2=ZA&outtype=html (accessed May 3, 2014).

Wolfson, Robert and Laver, John (2007). *Years of Change, European History 1890–1990.* London: Hodder and Stoughton.

Woolf, Virginia (1985). A Sketch of the Past. In *Moments of Being.* Orlando: Houghton Mifflin Harcourt, 1985. 61–160.

Zachmann, Urs Matthias (2007). "Guarding the Gates of Our East Asia: Japanese Reactions to the Far Eastern Crisis (1897–98) as a Prelude to the War." In Rotem Kowner, ed., *Rethinking the Russo-Japanese War, 1904–05.* Folkestone, UK: Global Oriental, 11–30.

Webpages

http://science.nationalgeographic.com/science/prehistoric-world/dinosaur-extinction/?rptregcta=reg_free_np&rptregcampaign=2015012_invitation_ro_all#
http://www.dermnetnz.org/acne/acne-psychological-effects.html
http://www.mayoclinic.org/diseases-conditions/acne/expert-answers/adult-acne/FAQ-20058129
http://www.nhs.uk/Conditions/Acne/Pages/Causes.aspx
http://www.ucmp.berkeley.edu/diapsids/extincthypo.html

https://answersingenesis.org/dinosaurs/extinction/the-extinction-of-the-dinosaurs/

http://en.wikipedia.org/wiki/Fields_Medal.

http://en.wikipedia.org/wiki/Nassau_Hall.

http://en.wikipedia.org/wiki/National_Advisory_Committee_for_Aeronautics.

http://en.wikipedia.org/wiki/National_Park_Service.

http://theindustrial-revoultion9s1.wikispaces.com/Key+People+Of+The+Industrial+Revolution+-+Henry+Ford.

http://www.historylearningsite.co.uk/cotton_industrial_revolution.htm.

http://www.independent.co.uk/news/science/first-female-fields-medal-winner-maryam-mirzakhani-hopes-she-will-encourage-young-female-mathematicians-and-scientists-9666898.html.

http://www.mathunion.org/general/prizes/fields/details/.

http://www.nasa.gov/ames/kepler/nasas-kepler-mission-announces-a-planet-bonanza/.

http://www.princeton.edu/~achaney/tmve/wiki100k/docs/Industrial_Revolution.html.

(All the above webpages were accessed February 2, 2015)